Judaism, Christianity, and Islam

ALSO AVAILABLE FROM BLOOMSBURY

Judaism, Christianity, and Islam

An Introduction to Monotheism

**AMANULLAH DE SONDY,
MICHELLE A. GONZALEZ, AND
WILLIAM S. GREEN**

BLOOMSBURY ACADEMIC
LONDON • NEW YORK • OXFORD • NEW DELHI • SYDNEY

BLOOMSBURY ACADEMIC
Bloomsbury Publishing Plc
50 Bedford Square, London, WC1B 3DP, UK
1385 Broadway, New York, NY 10018, USA

BLOOMSBURY, BLOOMSBURY ACADEMIC and the Diana logo are trademarks
of Bloomsbury Publishing Plc

First published in Great Britain 2021

Cover design: Terry Woodley

Cover image © James Brunker / Alamy Stock Photo

A catalogue record for this book is available from the British Library.

Library of Congress Cataloging-in-Publication Data
Names: De Sondy, Amanullah, author. | Gonzalez, Michelle A., author. | Green, William Scott, author.
Title: Judaism, Christianity, and Islam : an introduction to monotheism / Amanullah De Sondy,
Michelle Gonzalez Maldonado, and William S. Green.
Description: First published in Great Britain 2020 | London ; New York ; Oxford ; New Dehli ; Sydney :
Bloomsbury Academic, 2020. | Includes bibliographical references and index.
Identifiers: LCCN 2020027236 | ISBN 9781474257244 (paperback) |
ISBN 9781474257251 (hardcover) | ISBN 9781474257268 (pdf) | ISBN 9781474257275 (epub) |
ISBN 9781474257282
Subjects: LCSH: Monotheism–Comparative studies. | Judaism. | Christianity. | Islam.
Classification: LCC BL221 .D47 2020 + | DDC 201/.4—dc23
LC record available at https://lccn.loc.gov/2020027236

ISBN: HB: 978-1-4742-5725-1
       PB: 978-1-4742-5724-4
       ePDF: 978-1-4742-5726-8
       eBook: 978-1-4742-5727-5

Typeset by RefineCatch Limited, Bungay, Suffolk

To find out more about our authors and books visit www.bloomsbury.com
and sign up for our newsletters

Contents

Image List

Acknowledgments

I would like to thank Dr. Katie Van Heest and Dr. Lloyd Ridgeon, University of Glasgow, for their help with the Islam sections of this book and Dr. Moya Carey from the Chester Beatty Library in Dublin for all her help with images from the Islamic collections.—Amanullah De Sondy

I would like to thank the students in my REL 101 class at the University of Miami for their insights on the Christianity sections of this monograph.—Michelle A. Gonzalez

I would like to thank Professors Alan Avery-Peck, Haim Shaked, Gary G. Porton, Ira Sheskin, Dexter Callender, David Graf, Michael McCullough and Richard Sosis; Cantor Israel Maya and Rabbi Lyle Rothman; and students Ronen Dar Pink, Ezra Remer, Daria J. Pietropaolo, Mark Mansfield, and Megan Lipsky for their help with the Introduction and Judaism sections of this book.—WS Green

Permissions

The global map of the three religions was created by Chris Hanson, Department of Geography, GIS and Spatial Statistics Lab, University of Miami.

The translation of the Grace After Meals by Rabbi Jonathan Klein is reprinted by permission.

The translation of the *Kiddush* prayer by Rabbi Jessica Minnen is reprinted by permission of OneTable.

"Vidui" from *Mishkan HaNefesh: Machzor for the Days of Awe, Yom Kippur* copyright © 2015, by Central Conference of American Rabbis, and are under copyright protection of the Central Conference of American Rabbis and reprinted for use by permission of the CCAR. All rights reserved.

The translation of *'Adon HaSlichot* by William Green and Alan Avery-Peck is reprinted by permission.

Jacob Neusner, trans., *Mekhilta According to Rabbi Ishmael: An Analytical Translation*, Volume 2, Bahodesh, VII:17, p. 81 (Scholars Press, 1988) is adapted and reprinted by permission.

Jacob Neusner, trans., *The Talmud of Babylonia: An American Translation. XVII. Tractate Sotah* (Scholars Press, 1984), pp. 101–102, is adapted and reprinted by permission.

Material from the Israeli Proclamation of Independence is reprinted through Creative Commons.

Scripture quotations from the Holy Bible, New International Version®, NIV® Copyright ©1973, 1978, 1984, 2011 by Biblica, Inc.® Used by permission. All rights reserved worldwide.

Pronunciation Guide for Judaism

Like other Semitic languages, Hebrew contains guttural consonants. These letters sound something like letters *ch* in the Scottish word "lo*ch*." There are three different ways transliterations of Hebrew represent this sound. One is with the letters *ch*, as in the words *Ch*abad or Sim*cha*. Another is with the letters *kh,* as in hala*kh*ah. In some transliterations, just the letter *h* signals a guttural sound, as in *H*asidism, *H*aredi, or *H*anukkah. This book uses the most conventional transliterations of Hebrew terms, so readers will encounter all three variations.

Preface

This book has been years in the making. It all began when three colleagues, teaching at the University of Miami, decided to team-teach a course entitled One God. Our desire to design and teach this course emerged from a strong sense that the three traditions in which we were specialists, Judaism, Christianity, and Islam, shared a common heritage that is too often ignored in academic circles and among everyday practitioners. We taught the course together, sitting in all of our lectures, having trialogue days when we would each discuss a shared theme from our traditions, trying to model for our students the academic life of discussion, critical debate, and respect.

The first time we taught the course we did not use a textbook. Instead we drew from an assortment of book chapters, articles, websites, and current events. This model proved challenging for a 100-level college course and for students, some of whom had never studied religion. In the course's next incarnation we attempted to use a textbook. While there are many fine monographs and textbooks that explore all three traditions, none shared our approach. They all treated each tradition distinctively, emphasizing difference and deconstructing each religion. Our emphasis was the opposite. We wanted to show the underlying structure that unites the three, while respecting their distinctiveness, internal diversity, and complicated histories. And so the idea for this book was born.

In addition to the academic, this book also emerges out of collegiality and friendship. The three of us have challenged each other, learned from each other, and taught each other. We are three very different types of scholars with different approaches to the study of religion. This will be noticeable as you move through this work. However, we felt it important to respect the particularity of our voices. Far from trying to confuse the reader, our goal is to demonstrate that there is more than one way to teach and write about religion.

We live in a world that constantly vacillates between highlighting what is exclusively negative and destructive about religion and offering eulogies for religion in our contemporary world. This book represents a rejection of both viewpoints. Instead, this book, like the religions within it, is optimistic and hopeful. Perhaps nothing shows us more promise than the students we encounter in our classrooms, in many ways the reason why we wrote this book. At the beginning of each academic semester, students choosing to study religion and asking those fundamental questions that academics have been exploring for centuries give us, dare we say, faith in the future of our field. We therefore dedicate this book to our students, not just those in One God, but all of our students, who continue to challenge and inspire us. This book is for you.

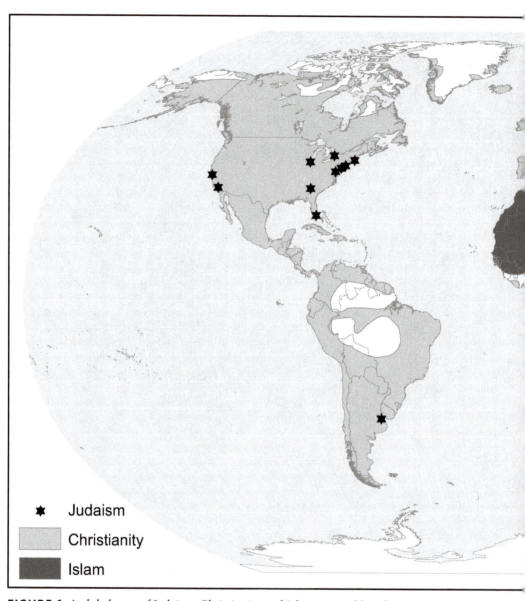

FIGURE 1 *A global map of Judaism, Christianity, and Islam, created by Chris Hanson, Department o*

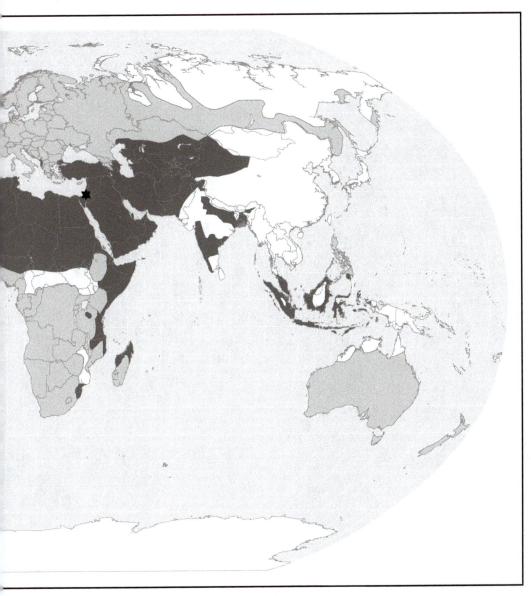

Geography, GIS and Spatial Statistics Lab, University of Miami.

1

Introduction

The idea that there is only one deity in the universe is a basic concept of Western civilization (often associated with, but not limited to, European culture). The primary expression of this One God is the monotheistic heritage that underlies Judaism, Christianity, and Islam. These three religions claim to know, understand, and follow the One God, who, they affirm, created the universe and humanity and revealed to their foundational figures (i.e. Abraham, Moses, Jesus, Muhammad) the terms of humans' proper relationship to God and one another. Many ideas and values we take for granted as secular—such as justice, equality before the law, care for the poor, respect for parents, the elderly and disabled, the dignity of life, to name a few—draw on this monotheistic legacy.

The monotheistic heritage contains a set of essential beliefs, practices, and institutions that shape these religions' conceptions of themselves and one another and inform their interactions, whether competitive or collaborative. Judaism, Christianity, and Islam acknowledge the Hebrew Bible as its source. This book attempts to describe the biblical monotheistic legacy—which the religions assume but often do not spell out—and to examine how it can help explain the commonalities and disagreements among them and between and among their significant denominations.

Numerous reports from the Pew Research Center project the continued impact of these religions and thus of the heritage that undergirds and generates them. Over half of the global population is either Jewish, Christian, or Muslim, with Christianity and Islam continuing to grow in parts of the globe. These projections must be contextualized, however, by the increasing number of individuals who identify as unaffiliated with any religion, whose numbers continue to increase in the United States and parts of Western Europe.

The growth of these religions will not be evenly distributed across the globe. Much of it will take place in sub-Saharan Africa. This means that by 2060, the religious heritage represented by Judaism, Christianity, and Islam will affect—in diverse ways, to be sure—the lives of nearly two-thirds of the people on earth.

Today Judaism, Christianity, and Islam interact in unprecedented ways. There are hostile interreligious encounters in the realms of global and national politics. There are constructive relationships in the religiously pluralist life of the world's great cities and within multi-religious families. At the same time, these religions also are experiencing increased scrutiny—and skepticism—particularly in Western industrialized societies. Among other factors, the global clergy sex abuse scandals in the Roman Catholic Church, increasing public acceptance of same-sex marriage and reproductive rights, the events of 9/11 and their aftermath, the rise of ISIS, and the ongoing conflict in the Middle East have coincided with a drop in religious participation and increasingly sharp divisions between secularists and religious people, particularly in the United States and Europe.

These considerations set the context for this book. To forge a global future, it is important for us to understand how the ideas, values, and behaviors of these longstanding religions may influence the political, social, and personal choices of the majority of the earth's population—particularly if we are part of a society and culture in which people increasingly do not subscribe to or share those ideas, values, and behaviors. While the internet enables people to know more about more religions than ever before, contemporary news and social media often foreground the most extreme or highly visible expressions of religion, so that much of what we think we know about religion may be either biased, incomplete, or wrong. This book aims to provide resources for understanding that can help us make sense both of what is familiar about religion in the West and what is not.

Understanding Religion

Before turning to the particulars of the monotheistic tradition, it will help to have a preliminary understanding of religion. The aim of this book is to develop a framework of analysis that can help us discern the shape and interrelationships, the similarities and differences, among the three monotheistic heritages in their diverse contexts. The academic study of religion developed overwhelmingly in Western Europe and the United States, and as a result is extremely influenced by a Christian framework. In other words, because the study of religion focused initially either on Christianity or Christianity's encounter with other religions through colonialism, many of our definitions of religion are created to mirror the structure of Christianity. While recognizing the limitations of any definition that claims to describe all religions in their diversity, we offer some initial insights to provide a shared framework for the three traditions discussed in this book. The work of anthropologist Roy Rappaport and sociologist Robert Bellah can help us with that exercise.

Rappaport observes that humanity is "a species that lives, and can only live, in terms of meanings it must construct in a world devoid of intrinsic meaning but subject to physical law." We humans live less by instinct than do other animals. We devise the purpose and significance of human life—our values, ethics, and community structures, for instance—rather than inherit them genetically as givens.

Bellah argues that we do this by creating what the philosopher George Santayana called "another world to live in." The "world of daily life"—the "ordinary reality all humans experience"—Bellah suggests, is the world of necessity, work, striving, and adapting, and "no one can stand to live" in that world all the time. We transcend the "world of daily life" through distinctly human activities, such as art, poetry, science, and religion. Creating these other worlds is part of human nature.

Rappaport notes that our unique capacity for language enables us to "transcend the concrete" and articulate and imagine alternative realities. When we say "will be, might be, could be, ought to be, was, could have been, should have been," etc., our very language lets us conceive and articulate possible worlds that differ from the empirical one we inhabit. Through language and imagination, we humans have the capacity to create structures of meaning that go beyond and do not entirely depend on the constraints of routine everyday life.

How does what we call "religion" fit into this picture? What makes religion's "non-ordinary reality" distinctive? Two traits help answer these questions.

First, these religions contain supernatural agents, figures who have the capacity to affect humans in ways that humans cannot affect them in return. The nature of these agents and the ways people are supposed to interact with them are culturally specific. Different cultures and societies envision supernatural agents and people's relationship to them in different ways.

Typically, religions claim that their supernatural agents revealed—and more often constructed—a cosmic order, which humans cannot alter. A religion explains to its adherents what they should do to live in accord with, and thus experience, the created order. It also asserts that people cannot acquire knowledge of cosmic reality by accident or on their own. They have to learn it, and the religion is their guide. Religion takes people out of the mundane and enables them to see and imagine things differently, to conceive that life is or might be otherwise. It tells people—no matter what is happening to them—who they *really* are by orienting them in a cosmic structure. It is important to note that by definition these religions understand themselves as self-contained systems whose teachings and practices do not lead to another religion; however, at times the way practitioners embody these religions can be more fluid.

Second, religion is all-encompassing. Unlike literature, music, athletics, politics, or philosophy, religion addresses and has addressed most, if not all, aspects of human experience: our communal and individual identities, what we eat, how we dress, how and with whom we have sex, how we raise children, how and whom we marry, how—and often with whom—we do business, how we die. Religion has come to expression in every mode of human creativity: architecture, art, music, clothing, dance, sculpture, film, and literature—to name the most obvious. And, historically, it has been both a primary legitimator of political structures and military action, and a source of resistance against political and military power. Because religion proposes a cosmic order, it reaches back before the present and forward after death. It tells people where they come from and where they are going. In a nutshell, religion enables human beings to live in accord with the conditions of the cosmos—once upon a time, now, and for eternity.

Rappaport observes that religions are grounded in what he calls "Ultimate Sacred Postulates," claims about reality that are "typically absolutely unfalsifiable and objectively unverifiable but are nonetheless taken to be unquestionable." Postulates are affirmations that people learn. People's experience, rather than logical argumentation or scientific experimentation and proof, validates them.

The idea of an Ultimate Sacred Postulate may sound technical and academic, but it represents a distinctly human activity that is more familiar than we may think. For instance, we conduct substantial portions of our individual lives according to what we might call "personal postulates," ideas or conceptions about ourselves that come from our experience and guide our attitudes and behaviors. These "personal postulates" assert what we feel about ourselves, and they resist falsification because the feelings are authentic. It is difficult to persuade people that they are not who they think and feel—who they "know"—that they are. When we assume, for instance, that we are not attractive enough to date someone ("I'm not handsome enough to ask her/him out"), or cannot do a certain kind of academic work ("I'm not a math person"), or cannot succeed at a particular activity ("I'm not smart/strong enough to do that"), or are immune to failure ("I'm a person who doesn't make mistakes"), or can triumph over disappointment ("I am not a quitter"), we are living parts of our lives in individual worlds of meaning shaped by these "personal postulates". However we may appear to others, to ourselves we are who our "personal postulates" tell us we are, and we negotiate the present and even may plan our futures in terms of them. To be sure, different experiences may disconfirm a "personal postulate" and replace it with another. The same thing can happen in religion, which helps explain why people abandon or change their religion.

In the religions we will explore in this book, Ultimate Sacred Postulates include, for instance, Judaism's *Shema'* declaration,

Hear, O Israel: the Lord is our God, the Lord is One,

or the Christian Gospel of John 3.16,

For God so loved the world that he gave his one and only Son, that whoever believes in him shall not perish but have eternal life,

or Islam's *Shahadah*,

There is no god but Allah. Muhammad is the messenger of God.

The singularity of the God of Israel, Jesus' role as savior, and Muhammad's mission as God's Prophet are unquestionable convictions that ground, shape, and generate particular beliefs, attitudes, and behaviors that make them real. Unlike "personal postulates," "Ultimate Sacred Postulates" are formalized and collective and constitute the basis for communal and social life and individual, group, or national identity. Non-empirical and unfalsifiable, they are about truths rather than facts. They are legitimated, reinforced, and validated by the authorities who teach them, by public reference to and recitation of them, and by being enacted in ritual, prayer, ethical behavior, and family and social life. Because Ultimate Sacred Postulates are abstract, different sectors of a religion can affirm them even if they may disagree about particular concrete teachings and practices.

By creating a "non-ordinary" reality grounded in Ultimate Sacred Postulates about supernatural agents and cosmic order, religion enables people to see through and beyond the concrete realities of everyday life, to find more than operational purpose in ordinary activities, and to envision and even plan for a future that is different and better, than the present. By opening possibilities that everyday life forecloses, religion creates the foundation of two other distinctly human traits: hope and faith.

To witness this dynamic at work, let us consider three pivotal moments in the monotheistic heritage: the destruction of two Temples in Jerusalem, the crucifixion of Jesus of Nazareth, and the death of Muhammad.

Judaism: Overcoming Destruction

In 587/586 BCE the Babylonians destroyed the Temple in Jerusalem, where the Israelites worshipped their God, and took large portions of the population into exile. In the "ordinary" reality of the ancient world, this meant that Israel's God was indifferent, weak, or defeated. The "non-ordinary" reality of Israel's religion held, to the contrary, that Israel's God was the only deity in the cosmos and determined the behavior of all nations. God had ordained the Babylonians' destruction of the Temple as a reprimand for the Israelites' falling short of God's expectations. But God's commitment to Israel would persist, and forgiveness and reconciliation would follow. The destruction and exile thus demonstrated not divine impotence or apathy, but the opposite: God's strength, engagement, and compassion. The Persians' defeat of Babylon and the rebuilding of the Temple reinforced this view.

To document this "non-ordinary" reality, members of the exilic community collected into a written epic their ancient traditions of the people's relationship with God. Known as the Torah ("teaching" or "instruction"), this text made ancient Israel's "non-ordinary" reality concrete and portable. The Torah's "non-ordinary" reality enabled Judaism to adapt to and transcend the Romans' destruction of the Second Temple in 70 CE.

Christianity: The crucifixion of Jesus of Nazareth

In a year conventionally assumed to be 33 CE, the Roman administration of Pontius Pilate crucified Jesus of Nazareth in Jerusalem. After Jesus had taken his last breath, his followers took his body down from the cross and prepared it for entombment. They assumed, as did others, that he was dead. But some of his followers occupied a "non-ordinary" reality in which Jesus' resurrection was both conceivable and plausible. Because of it, they looked through the material reality to see life beyond death. And the certitude and conviction about that "non-ordinary" reality anchors Christianity, currently the world's largest religion.

Islam: The Death of Muhammad

When Muhammad died in 632, the "ordinary" reality of his death left the Muslim community in disarray. People looked up to Muhammad and found him a trustworthy and noble prophet. Muhammad was understood as the living and walking Qur'an. He would offer commentary on the divine and inimitable text that he was receiving from God. The new believers were unsure how to move on from his death, especially given that he was understood as the "seal of the prophets." During this sad time, the new Muslims assembled around the dead body of Muhammad, and it was here that Abu Bakr, a companion of the prophet and soon to be the first caliph of Islam, said after glorifying God, "No doubt! Whoever worshipped Muhammad, then Muhammad is dead, but whoever worshipped Allah, then Allah is Alive and shall never die." Then he recited Allah's Statement: "(O Muhammad) Verily you will die, and they also will die" (Qur'an 39.30).

Religion and Human Nature

Religion is a distinctly human phenomenon. So far as we know, no other living creatures postulate supernatural agents, devise ways to engage with them, envision multiple realms of time, imagine alternative realities, or speculate on life after death. Religion is natural to humanity.

The anthropologist Richard Sosis suggests that religions contain eight "building blocks," which interact dynamically to produce a distinctive cultural system that can adapt to changing realities. The "building blocks," which provide a helpful framework for understanding Judaism, Christianity, and Islam, are:

1 **Supernatural agents**: beings who can do things to and for humans that humans cannot reciprocate.

2 **Myth**: a foundational story that describes the origins and structure of the "non-ordinary reality" the religion represents. Myths typically include the creation of cosmos, the role of the religion's supernatural agents and founding figures, and the religion's basic types of interaction with the supernatural agents.

3 **Ritual**: structured behavior, usually public, that acts out the patterns of engagement with the religion's supernatural agents. Rituals reinforce and bring social reality to the religion's fundamental teachings and serve to maintain the relationship between the supernatural agents and the religion's participants.

4 **Authority**: different forms of teaching, literature, and leadership that speak on behalf of the religion and legitimate its worldview and behaviors.

5 **Sacred**: an attribute of words or things that makes them unquestionable, foundational, unalterable, and completely distinctive. Sacred words—such as

those in Ultimate Sacred Postulates—ground both community and individual identity and must be recited in a particular way. The idea of the sanctity (or sacredness) of life means that innocent human life cannot be destroyed. Sacred objects—such as scrolls of Scripture—can be handled only in special ways. Sacred time puts constraints on human behavior and defines what participants must or must not do on specified days and times. Sacred space— usually where people encounter supernatural agents—also often requires special behavior, such as bowing, kneeling, removing a hat or shoes before entering, or maintaining a demeanor of respect.

6 **Taboo**: an attribute of an object, class of objects, actions, or class of actions that makes them forbidden to use or perform.

7 **Moral obligation**: required or expected behaviors towards others, initially those in one's religious community, that reflect the cosmic structure and supernatural agents' teachings described in the myth. Charity, caring for the sick, generosity, and forgiveness are the most obvious examples. To live morally is to live in conformity with the cosmic order.

8 **Meaning**: Because of its comprehensiveness, religion provides an indelible structure that enables its participants to make sense of and find purpose in both the ordinary (birth and marriage, for instance) and extraordinary (physical injury, violent death, unexpected financial windfall) happenings in their lives. Religion provides a means to deal with uncertainty, inconsistency, or disruption.

We also should note that what we are calling religion is shaped by different political and governmental structures across the globe. Official state religions typically receive government support for worship and education, and the government may constrain or bar minority religions. Governments also may offer tangible financial advantages to preferred religions. These differences mean that the religion people practice may not be the result of free individual or familial choice.

Review

The category "religion" used in this book has three basic elements:

1 Religion creates "non-ordinary" reality through human engagement with a culture's supernatural agents.

2 A religion's "non-ordinary" reality typically is grounded in a cosmic order that is expressed in Ultimate Sacred Postulates and applies to most areas of human life.

3 There are eight core elements of religion (supernatural agents, myth, ritual, authority, the sacred, taboo, moral obligation, meaning) that—like parts of

speech in language—interact dynamically to create identity, build community, and support a culture's social life. The interaction of the core elements varies by religion and within religions.

Overview of the Book

The book's approach to identifying the elements of the monotheistic heritage is to look first for what is assumed but often unarticulated in each religion's primary texts. What do the basic documents of Islam, Christianity, and Judaism suppose that their recipients or adherents understand without elaboration? What are the "givens" of the tradition? What requires little or no explanation or justification?

Chapter 2 supplies a snapshot of each religion, a concise overview that focuses on basic beliefs and practices, many of which are discussed in more detail later in the book. Each begins with a synopsis of the religion's Scriptures to help readers acquire a preliminary shared knowledge base of the texts that it assumes. Chapter 3 then examines how Scripture functions in each tradition and serves as a means for learning about the One God. Chapters 4–9 explore the basic elements of monotheistic tradition: Creation; Covenant and Identity; Commandment: Ritual, and Ethics; Peoplehood and Community; Gender, Sexuality, and Marriage; Redemption, Salvation, and Life After Death. These elements constitute a shared framework that Judaism, Christianity, and Islam employ in their self-understandings and that shapes the three religions' moral worldviews, ideas about humans' interaction with God and one another, basic notions of right and wrong, family relationships, the sanctity of life, sin, and ultimate redemption.

Chapter 4 explores creation, the idea of a purposeful and ordered cosmos. Questions explored in this overview include the nature of the human person and the disruption of the created order as interpreted in each religion. What is the nature of the human person according to each religion? What are humans empowered to do and not do? The discussion of Covenant and Identity in Chapter 5 centers on the idea of the relationship between God and God's creatures. This chapter illustrates how the idea and institution of covenant is foundational in the monotheistic heritage. The discussion in Chapter 6 of Commandment: Ritual and Ethics explores how humans can follow God and care for one another as God's creatures, and the relationship between and practice of ritual and ethics. Central to this conversation are humans' obligations to God and our obligations to each other. Chapter 7 explores Community and Peoplehood and examines the broad range of community identities within the monotheistic framework and the sectarian and denominational divisions within each religion. Chapter 8 addresses the issue of gender equity in the three traditions. Finally, Chapter 9, Redemption, Salvation, and Life After Death, provides an overview of sin and forgiveness, heaven and hell, and the religions' distinctive expressions of the afterlife.

Chapter 10 offers case studies of the life of the three religions in particular geographic contexts: Judaism in the State of Israel, Christianity in Latin America, and Islam in Great Britain.

Because they all claim authentic descent from a common heritage, Judaism, Christianity, and Islam are—and for their own purposes must be—acutely aware of what precedes and follows them. Islam's claim to correct what it regards as the errors of Judaism and Christianity, and Christianity's claim to rectify what it judges to be Judaism's limitations, necessarily presuppose that each has an understanding of the beliefs, behaviors, and structures they accept, modify, or abandon. Likewise, Judaism's alterations of the Israelite religion of cult and sacrifice assume an understanding of that religious system. All three religions take for granted the Pentateuch as a foundational text. Thus, although each religion is distinctive in its particular beliefs and practices, this biblical monotheistic heritage constitutes the structure of their self-definitions, and their judgments of one another make little sense without it.

The book describes the biblical foundation and shows how it has been—and continues to be—contextualized within the three interrelated traditions. How has it been read, understood and lived by members of these three faiths? How has it shaped the lives of the adherents of each religion? Are there particular points of consensus and dissent among the three? Do Jews, Christians, and Muslims in the contemporary world encounter similar notions of One God? By connecting, re-connecting, separating, and uniting these three traditions, we hope to offer a helpful—and perhaps fresh—approach to understanding monotheism in the world today.

The focus of this book is the big picture rather than detailed coverage of the density or diversity of the expressions of monotheism in Judaism, Christianity, and Islam. Similarly, the book takes theology seriously without itself being theological. Instead, our emphasis is on the foundational claims of the biblical monotheistic heritage. We employ a critical hermeneutic of "monotheism" to integrate history, theology, and critical contemporary debates. We hope this framework will allow the text to explain how each religion—including its most important subdivisions—receives, accepts, adapts, or abandons those parts of the monotheistic legacy it inherits.

2

Brief Overview of the Religions

Judaism, Christianity, and Islam all worship the same deity, the One God of the cosmos. They agree that the One God is the only God that exists. The religions' understandings of God's nature; their ideas of how, when, and with whom God interacts in human history; and their notions of appropriate human responses to God are not identical. They concur in some respects and differ in others. This chapter provides overviews of the essential elements of the three traditions as an entry point into the more thematic discussions that follow. These general descriptions aim to supply a basic vocabulary and framework for each tradition. They do not capture the diversity of opinion and practice within each religion, some of which is discussed in the thematic sections that follow. The chapter proceeds chronologically, beginning with Judaism, then moving to Christianity, then to Islam.

In addition to their affirmation that there is only One God in the cosmos, the three monotheistic religions share the conviction that written Scripture contains the foundational revelation of God's nature and character. To be sure, the religions engage with Scripture in distinctive ways, and each acknowledges additional forms of religious authority and sources of revelation—prophets, priests, rabbis, chains of non-scriptural tradition, for instance. But all three claim a scriptural basis. In the final analysis, the story of the One God begins in and derives from Scripture.

The Scriptures of the three religions—the *Tanakh* (Hebrew Bible) for Judaism, the Christian Scriptures (New Testament) for Christianity, and Qur'an for Islam—interrelate. The authors of the Christian Scripture refer to the *Tanakh* and draw upon it. The Qur'an knows the *Tanakh* and the Christian Scriptures and draws upon both. Often the Christian Scriptures and the Qur'an will refer to or employ ideas, terms, and categories from prior Scriptures without explanation, on the assumption that their readers (or hearers) know what the references mean. The Qur'an does not need to explain who Moses was, and the Christian Scriptures do not need to explain what "covenant" means. Indeed, in many respects, these references to prior Scripture are critical to the religion's self-definition and self-understanding. By appropriating, redefining, and reinterpreting elements of prior Scriptures, these religions explain their distinctiveness.

To reflect the distinctive role of Scripture in all three religions and to provide a common base for learning, each of the following overviews begins with a synopsis of the religion's Scripture. Because the Scriptures vary in literary style, length, and content the overviews vary in length. The Hebrew Bible contains a range of writings—narrative, commandments, prophecy, for instance—that were collected, written, and edited over centuries. The Christian Scriptures and the Qur'an were written in relatively shorter periods of time.

Judaism

The Scripture of Judaism: The Tanakh

The twenty-four books of the Hebrew Bible are arranged into three divisions: *Torah* ("instruction") contains the first five books (Genesis, Exodus, Leviticus, Numbers, Deuteronomy); *Nevi'im* (Prophets) includes the books of Joshua, Judges, Samuel, Kings, Isaiah, Jeremiah, and Ezekiel, the twelve minor prophets (Hosea, Joel, Amos, Obadiah, Jonah, Micah, Nahum, Habakkuk, Zephaniah, Haggai, Zechariah, Malachi); *Ketuvim* ("Writings") includes the remaining books: Psalms, Proverbs, Job, Song of Songs, Ruth, Lamentations, Ecclesiastes, Esther, Daniel, Ezra/Nehemiah, Chronicles. Nearly all the books are in Hebrew, with some passages in Aramaic. The first Hebrew letters of the three divisions (**T**orah, **N**evi'im, **K**etuvim) produce the acronym *Tanakh*.

The contents of the *Tanakh* were produced between the ninth and second centuries BCE, and the basic form of the Torah most likely dates to the fourth century BCE. Scholars estimate that Judaism's canon, the authoritative list of books in the *Tanakh*, was fixed between the mid-first and mid-second centuries CE.

The order of the books in the *Tanakh* is religiously consequential. Although the books derive from a time period covering thousands of years, their order tells the story of the Jewish people's encounter with and relationship to God. It begins with creation; continues with covenant, commandments, Temple, and exile; and ends with redemption and return to the land of Israel. Thus, Judaism positions the books of prophecy in the middle of the *Tanakh's* divisions and concludes with the book of 2 Chronicles, which anticipates the rebuilding of the Jerusalem Temple.

Christianity, by contrast, places the prophets at the end of the collection and concludes what it calls the "Old Testament" with the Book of Malachi, which anticipates the coming of the messiah.

All forms of Judaism regard the *Tanakh*, and particularly the Torah, as essential to the definition and practice of the religion, but have different reasons for thinking so. Classical rabbinic Judaism understands the Torah (the first five books) as God's words dictated to Moses (except for the last eight verses of Deuteronomy, about Moses' death, which tradition says were written by Joshua), and the other books of the *Tanakh* as written by humans but with divine inspiration. Another position is that the *Torah* itself is a human interpretation of a non-verbal encounter with God at Sinai. Finally, some take the *Tanakh* to be a human production that is historically consequential in the life of the Jewish people.

The Patriarchs: The Book of Genesis

In the beginning of everything, God speaks and forms order out of chaos. On the first six days, God creates the cosmos: light, day, night, heaven, earth, seas, vegetation, fruit trees, sun, moon, stars, fish, birds, insects, animals. Also on the sixth day, God creates humans, male and female, in God's image. God blesses the seventh day and declares it holy, because on it God completes the work of creation.

God forms a human (Adam) from the earth's dust and then creates a garden in Eden. God places the human there "to work it and take care of it" and warns Adam not to eat of the tree of the knowledge of good and evil, which is in the center of the garden. God creates living creatures and brings them to Adam, who names them. God then causes Adam to sleep and removes a part of him to create woman. The serpent misleads the woman; she eats the tree's fruit and gives some to Adam, who, on his own, also eats it. They recognize their nakedness and clothe themselves. When God discovers their disobedience, God curses the serpent and rebukes them all. Adam names the woman *Eve*, as the "mother of all the living." God then banishes them from the Garden of Eden. Adam and Eve produce two sons, Cain and Abel. God prefers Abel's offering of the choice fat of firstlings to Cain's offering of agricultural produce, and, in envy, Cain murders Abel. God then curses Cain for the sin of murder.

As the humans multiply, God sees that their behavior is evil and regrets having created them. God resolves to flood the earth and destroy all creation. God tells the one righteous and blameless man, Noah, to build an ark and bring his family and two of every species into it. When the flood subsides, God permits humans to eat animals but forbids the consumption of blood and the shedding of human blood. God then makes an agreement, a covenant, with Noah and all living creatures never to flood the earth again. The sign of the covenant is the rainbow. After the flood, all humans speak a single language and attempt to build a tower to heaven. God confuses their speech, the effort fails, and humanity is marked by multiple languages. The place of the tower is known as Babel.

After many years, God initiates another covenant, with a man named Abram. God calls Abram to leave his home and promises him an heir, nationhood, and the land of Canaan "from the river of Egypt, to the great river, the Euphrates." Abram trusts God's promise. God then certifies the covenant with Abram with a ritual ceremony. Because Abram's wife, Sarai, is barren and ninety years old, Abram, with Sarai's approval, fathers a son, Ishmael, with Hagar, an Egyptian slave. Later, God repeats the covenant, changes Abram's name to Abraham, and promises that Abraham will be the father of many nations. God declares the covenant with Abraham and his family to be "eternal" and their possession of "the whole land of Canaan . . . as an everlasting possession." God makes circumcision of all male children on the eighth day of their life the "sign" of the covenant and says that failure to perform the circumcision removes people from the covenantal relationship. God then renames Sarai to Sarah and promises that she will have a son, named Isaac, with whom God will maintain the covenant. God promises Hagar that Ishmael nevertheless also will be the father of a great nation. At some point later, Abraham and Sarah offer hospitality to three strangers, one of whom predicts that she will have a son.

God then reveals to Abraham the intention to destroy the cities of Sodom and Gomorrah because of their sin. Abraham asks if God will preserve the city for the sake of fifty righteous people within it. God agrees. Abraham then asks if the judge of the earth should not do justice and negotiates with God to reduce the number of righteous to ten. The city is ultimately destroyed.

God then "tested" Abraham by instructing him to offer Isaac as a sacrifice. Abraham follows God's mandate, binds Isaac, and places him on an altar for sacrifice. At the last minute, God rewards Abraham's loyalty, substitutes a ram for Isaac, and again reaffirms the covenant with Abraham.

Isaac grows to manhood, and God enables his wife, Rebecca, who is barren, to conceive. She carries twins, Esau, who is born first, and Jacob. Esau sells his birthright to Jacob. When the time comes for Isaac to transfer the covenant birthright to Esau, Rebecca—because God told her during her pregnancy that the elder twin would serve the younger—concocts a plan for Jacob to deceive Isaac in order to obtain the blessing that should go to Esau. The deception succeeds, but Esau is resentful. As an adult, on his way to reconcile with his Esau, Jacob wrestles with an unnamed "man" until dawn and prevails against him. The "man" wrenches Jacob's thigh muscle on the hip (sciatic nerve) and because Jacob will not release him without a blessing, changes Jacob's name to Israel. The name means "he who strives with God." The story reports that, as a consequence, the Israelites do not eat the sciatic nerve of slaughtered animals.

Jacob ("Israel") has twelve sons, the youngest of whom is Joseph. Jacob loves Joseph more than the others and gives him a special, multicolored cloak. Out of envy and resentment, Joseph's brothers throw him into a pit, and others later sell him into slavery in Egypt. In Egypt, Joseph's gift for dream interpretation propels him to a high administrative office in the Pharaoh's retinue. Because of a famine, the Israelites have to go to Egypt, where Joseph reunites with his brothers. Jacob's twelve sons are the founders of the twelve tribes of Israel.

Moses, Covenant, and Commandments: The Books of Exodus, Leviticus, Numbers, and Deuteronomy

After Joseph's death, a new Pharaoh enslaves the Israelites, treats them harshly, and tells the Israelite midwives to kill all newborn Israelite males. An Israelite woman, Jochebed, creates a watertight basket for her infant son Moses and places it in the Nile River. Pharaoh's daughter rescues Moses and raises him as her son. In his adulthood, Moses kills an Egyptian guard who was beating an Israelite and is forced to leave Egypt. In his exile, Moses encounters the Midianite tribe of Jethro (who is also called Reuel), probably in the Sinai desert, and marries Jethro's daughter, Zipporah. They have two sons, Gershom and Eliezer.

While living as a member of Jethro's tribe, Moses encounters God on a mountain in a "burning bush" (a bush that burns but is not consumed by the fire), and God tells Moses his name, *YHWH*, which means "I am Who I Am" or "I will be Who I will be."

God then commands Moses to lead the Israelites out of Egypt and liberate them from slavery. At an encampment during the return journey, Zipporah circumcises one of her sons (probably Eliezer) to forestall God's (or an angel's) murderous anger at Moses. On his arrival in Egypt, Moses reconnects with the Israelites, particularly his brother, Aaron. Despite evidence of God's power—as when Aaron's walking staff is transformed into a snake that devours the snakes of Pharaoh's magicians, or when God afflicts Egypt with nine of an eventual ten plagues—Pharaoh resists Moses' demands to free the Israelites. God instructs Moses to tell the Israelites to put sheep's blood on their doorposts so that God's agent of death will pass over them, and in that same evening—as a tenth plague—the first-born Egyptian males all die. Pharaoh momentarily relents, and Moses leads the Israelites through the desert to the Red Sea, which God miraculously opens to allow them to cross into freedom.

In the second month of their journey in the desert, God feeds the people with a special divine food called "*manna*." In the third month, Moses leads the Israelites to a mountain in the desert, Mount Sinai, and ascends it to encounter God directly. God instructs Moses to tell the people that if they observe the covenant he is about to make with them they will be a kingdom of priests and a holy people. The Israelites willingly commit to do what God commands. Three days later the people assemble at the foot of the mountain and God speaks Ten Commandments. These forbid idolatry, the worship of other gods, blasphemy; enjoin observance of the Sabbath and respect for parents; and prohibit murder, theft, adultery, false testimony, and coveting what belongs to others. God then gives Moses a set of other commandments that define Israel's ethical, familial, civil, social, legal, and communal life. Moses reports these to the people, and they again affirm their commitment to do what God commands. Moses writes down all the commandments.

The next morning Moses constructs an altar with twelve pillars (one for each of the Israelite tribes) at the foot of the mountain and offers sacrifices. The Israelites again affirm their commitment to follow the commandments. Moses seals the covenant by sprinkling the blood of the sacrifices, which he calls "the blood of the covenant," on the people.

Moses ascends Mount Sinai. God instructs Moses that when he descends, he is to build a Tabernacle—also called a Tent of Meeting—a movable shrine to house God's presence. It will contain the Ark of the Covenant (a wood box overlaid with gold that will hold the stone tablets God will give to Moses). On the top of the Ark were to be gold statues of two *cherubim*, mythical winged creatures who perhaps were understood as guardians of its contents. God commands Moses to anoint Aaron and his sons with oil to consecrate Aaron's family as a caste of priests to offer the sacrifices on the altar of the Tabernacle.

God then writes the Ten Commandments on tablets of stone and gives them to Moses. Moses remains on the mountain for forty days and nights. Fearful because of Moses' long absence, the Israelites build a golden calf to serve as their god. When

Moses descends from Mount Sinai, he discovers the Israelites' idolatry and disloyalty, smashes the stone tablets, and destroys the golden idol. God is enraged and threatens to destroy the Israelites, but Moses dissuades him. Moses carves new stone tablets, and God reaffirms the covenant with Israel. At the foot of Mount Sinai, God issues additional commandments that frame Israel's ethical and ritual life.

As the Israelites approach the land of Canaan, God instructs Moses to send a team of twelve scouts—one from each of the tribes—to assess the land and its inhabitants. The scouts return with a cluster of grapes, pomegranates, and figs and report that the land "flows with milk and honey." They then describe the land's inhabitants as people too strong to defeat. Their report incites the people's anxiety, and they beg to return to Egypt. This angers God, who again threatens their destruction, but Moses secures God's forgiveness. God causes the Israelites to wander for forty years in the desert.

When the generation from Egypt has passed away, the Israelites finally stand ready to enter the land God promised to Abraham. Moses recounts the Israelites' history with God and God's commandments to them and says that God will raise a prophet like himself. He then writes God's teaching, or *Torah*, gives it to the priests, and instructs that it be read aloud every seven years to all Israel, "men, women, and children, and the aliens living in your towns" to evoke and teach them their covenant obligations to God. He predicts the people's exile from the Land of Israel because of idolatry and anticipates its return to the land when it fulfills the covenant. Moses directs the priests to place the Torah next to the Ark of the Covenant so that it can serve as a "witness" against the community. Moses dies before the Israelites enter the land.

Monarchy, Statehood, and Temple: The books of Joshua, Judges, 1 and 2 Samuel, 1 and 2 Kings, 1 and 2 Chronicles, Amos, Hosea, I Isaiah

Joshua becomes the Israelites' leader. Before the people's entry into the land of Canaan, God commands Joshua to make flint knives so that the males can perform circumcision, which they could not do during the exile in the desert. After they do so, the people celebrate the Passover sacrifice. On the eve of his death, Joshua asks the people to reaffirm their loyalty to God. When they voluntarily agree, Joshua makes a covenant for them and writes the events in a book of God's Torah.

The tribes of Israel are then led by figures called judges, who are charismatic leaders. Deborah, a prophetess, predicts Israel's victory over the Canaanites. Partly in response to the invasion of foreign peoples—the Philistines, for example—the twelve tribes of Israel come together and establish a monarchy. The prophet Samuel anoints Saul as Israel's first king, but God replaces Saul with David, whom Samuel also anoints. David's reign is eventually centered in Jerusalem, a city that David conquered.

God declares to David that David's son, Solomon, will build God's house, the Temple in Jerusalem—a fixed location for the Tabernacle, where God's presence is accessible and sacrifices can be given. God establishes with David a covenant that David's line will be Israel's king forever and that God will never abandon David's descendants. Solomon constructs the Temple.

After Solomon's death, a civil war occurs, and ten tribes establish a separate kingdom called Israel, whose capital is Samaria. The tribes of Judah and Benjamin constitute the kingdom of Judah, and its capital is Jerusalem. Both kingdoms must engage with the rise of powerful empires and their cultures. In this period, some of the leaders of both kingdoms worship other deities in addition to the God of Israel.

Prophets, mostly but not only men, speak in God's name and call for exclusive loyalty to God. Prophets such as Elijah, Amos, Hosea, and I Isaiah (the eighth-century BCE prophet whose activity is recorded in the book of Isaiah, Ch. 1–39) criticize the monarchy for disloyalty to God and the people for focusing on the cult's sacrificial rituals rather than care for the poor and the indigent. The prophets insist on the people's complete faith in and reliance on God and predict that God will punish Israel and Judah for their disloyalty to God and their failure to fulfill the commandments.

In the eighth century BCE, I Isaiah tells Ahaz, King of Judah, that God will overcome Ahaz's enemies, that the sign of that promise is a particular young woman who will have a child named Immanuel ("God is with us"), and that the king's enemies will be defeated before the child grows to maturity. I Isaiah also claims that God will judge the nations of the world, establish a new order of reality in which an ideal Davidic king will rule in Jerusalem, God's eternal city, and nations "shall beat their swords into plowshares and spears into pruning hooks. Nation shall not take up sword against nation, nor will they train for war anymore."

In 721 BCE the Assyrian empire conquers the kingdom of Israel and takes substantial parts of its society into exile. Two of Judah's most prominent kings are Hezekiah (727/715–698/687 BCE) and Josiah (640–609 BCE). Both emphasize and enforce the exclusive worship of YHWH. During the Temple's renovation, the high priest Hilkiah discovers a book of the Torah. The book expresses God's opposition to—and anger at—the people's practice of worshipping other deities. Fearful because his ancestors did not adhere to the contents of the book, King Josiah sends the high priest to seek confirmation of the book's authenticity from the prophetess, Huldah. The king then reads "the Book of the Covenant," to the leaders of Judean society—including priests and prophets—and removes any trace of other gods from the Temple. He also destroys all local Israelite altars to other gods and establishes the Temple in Jerusalem as the only place for the worship of Israel's God. The king and the people make a covenant with God to "keep his commands, regulations, and decrees."

Exile and Return: The Books of Jeremiah, 2 Isaiah, Ezekiel, Joel, Micah, Lamentations, 1 and 2 Chronicles, Ezra, Nehemiah, Haggai, Zechariah, Malachi

The kings that follow Josiah lack his skill and integrity, and in 587/586 BCE the Babylonians destroy the Temple in Jerusalem and take the leaders of Israelite society—

royal house, priests, and scribes—into exile in Babylonia. The book of Lamentations articulates the trauma of exile. The prophet Jeremiah, who prophesied from the land of Israel, attributes the destruction to Israel's failures but predicts that after the punishment God will return the Israelites to the land of Israel, rebuild Jerusalem, make a "new covenant" with Israel, place God's Torah within them, and inscribe it on their hearts. The prophet Ezekiel, who prophesied from exile in Babylonia, likewise claims that the Israelites caused the Temple's destruction but that God will maintain the covenant, return a remnant to the land of Israel, and rebuild the Temple. Ezekiel reports a dramatic and elaborate vision of God's heavenly chariot throne and another vision of the "Valley of the Dry Bones," which come back to life. The themes of punishment, compassion, and reconciliation also appear in the prophetic books of Joel and Micah.

In 539 BCE, Cyrus, the King of Persia, invades and defeats Babylon. In response to the exile and the Persian victory, the prophet known as 2 Isaiah (the sixth-century BCE prophet whose activities are recounted in Isaiah, Ch. 40–55) calls Cyrus God's "anointed" and claims that God caused the Babylonian exile because of the Israelites' failure to fulfill the covenant. This means, he says, that Persia's victory over Babylon was God's work, that the Israelites have been punished for their sins, that God has forgiven them, and that they will return to their land. 2 Isaiah sharply ridicules the worship of idols and forcefully expresses the fundamental biblical claim that Israel's God is the only god in the cosmos and shapes the world's history for Israel's sake.

The Persians create an administrative unit around Jerusalem called *Yehud* (the origin of the terms Jew and Judaism) and allow exiles to return and rebuild the Temple. Some do so. The Samaritans and others whose families were not exiled want to participate in the rebuilding, but the returnees reject them. The rebuilt Temple is dedicated in 515 BCE, followed later by the construction of walls around Jerusalem. Ezra, an Israelite priest and scribe from Babylonia, comes to Jerusalem, by some accounts, in 458 BCE. After his arrival, on the first day of the seventh month, Ezra reads the scroll of the Torah of Moses, a document he brought with him from Babylonia, to the assembled people. When Ezra displays the Torah, the people prostrate themselves. Ezra also forces the Israelite men who have married non-Israelite women to divorce them. On the twenty-fourth day of the month, the people gather in Jerusalem, read from the scroll of the Lord's Torah, recount God's works on behalf of the Israelites, confess their sins, invoke God's covenant with the Israelites, and affirm an oath promising to follow God's Torah. This account includes another Israelite leader from Babylonia, Nehemiah, who returns to Jerusalem, builds a wall around the city, and enforces the observance of the Sabbath.

The prophetic books of Haggai, Zechariah, and Malachi affirm the legitimacy and importance of the rebuilt Temple and point to new future. Malachi signals the end of biblical prophecy by elevating the stature of the Torah of "my servant Moses," and promising that the prophet Elijah will appear before Israel's final redemption.

Reflections on Peoplehood and the Nature of God: The Books of Psalms, Song of Songs, Ecclesiastes, Job, Proverbs, Jonah, Ruth, Esther, Daniel, 1 and 2 Chronicles

Some biblical books focus more on basic religious themes and values than on the historical narrative sketched above. The book of Psalms contains poems composed over a wide historical range that express praise for and loyalty to the God of Israel and address basic religious themes. Many psalms are attributed to King David. Song of Songs is an erotic love poem that is read as an analogy of God's relation to Israel. The book of Proverbs suggests that the righteous will be rewarded by God and offers wise sayings about how to manage the natural and social worlds. The book of Job, in contrast, is an extended meditation on the theme of undeserved suffering. In it a heavenly accuser—with God's assent—afflicts a prosperous and thoroughly righteous man, Job, with countless miseries—including the loss of his children—to see if Job will curse God. When Job protests to God about his unfair treatment, he learns—through God's response in a whirlwind—that humans cannot fully understand God's power and motives. Likewise, the Book of Ecclesiastes doubts the existence of a system of divine reward and punishment that is intelligible to humans.

The books of Jonah, Ruth, Esther, and Daniel offer different visions of Israelites engaging with non-Israelites. In the book of Jonah, God twice commands the prophet Jonah to call the people of Nineveh, the capital of Assyria, to repentance. Jonah refuses the first time, but accepts the second. The Ninevites repent and are not punished. The book of Ruth tells the story of a Moabite woman, Ruth, who, after the death of her husband, voluntarily remains loyal to her Israelite mother-in-law, Naomi, and her God. Ruth then marries Naomi's relative, Boaz, and ultimately is the great-grandmother of King David. The book of Esther describes how Esther, an Israelite woman married to the Persian king, saves her people from a plot to destroy them. The first six chapters of the book of Daniel depict Daniel's ability to live a religiously observant life while serving in the government of the king of Babylon. The latter part of the book offers a dramatic vision of the end of history with a brief reference to resurrection of the dead, in which some will have eternal life and others will endure "shame and everlasting contempt." The books of Chronicles are a compressed retelling of Israelite history, beginning with Adam and concluding with the Persian King Cyrus' declaration of the rebuilding of the Temple in Jerusalem.

Judaism: An Overview

The origins of the Judaic tradition reach far back in history. Archaeological evidence for ancient Israel extends over 3,000 years, to the second millennium BCE. Unlike Christianity and Islam, which for most their histories have been state and national religions, Judaism primarily has been a stateless minority religion. Consequently,

Jewish religious thought and practice have adapted to varied cultural, political, social, and religious contexts, while preserving a shared overall structure.

Judaism has no central religious authority and thus no official statement of doctrine. Rather, it is comprised of a set of communal sacred postulates, texts, traditions, and practices that individual Jewish communities and religious authorities interpret and apply differently. This book uses the form of Judaism practiced most consistently from antiquity to the present as a reference point for understanding both Judaism's most common convictions and its internal diversity. As we shall see below, variety in and disagreement about religious belief and behavior are hallmarks of the Judaic heritage.

Basic Judaic Convictions

Judaism, the religion of the Jewish people, is the religion of Torah.

Torah ("instruction" or "teaching") is God's revelation to humanity in general and the Jewish people in particular. Torah teaches the practitioners of Judaism who they are, what God expects of them, and what they can expect of God and one another. It guides their engagement with the world.

Torah has two integrated components.

The first part of God's teaching is contained in the Written Torah (*Torah sheh-bikhtav*), the *Tanakh*. The first five books ("Pentateuch") of the *Tanakh*—Genesis, Exodus, Leviticus, Numbers, and Deuteronomy—referred to as *the* Torah—are foundational because they describe the basic structure of creation, covenant, commandment, and community that constitutes Judaism's religious life. These five books are written in a special way on a parchment scroll and used in Jewish worship. The Torah scroll (*Sefer Torah*) is sacred both as a text and as a holy object.

Alongside the Written Torah, the second component of Torah is called the Oral Torah (*Torah sheh-beh-'al peh*). It contains teachings that Judaism says God told to Moses that were then transmitted orally from Moses to Joshua and onward in a long line of tradition that culminates with the rabbis, the teachers and sages who ultimately became—and continue to be—Judaism's leaders. Judaism calls Moses—the first teacher of Torah—*rabbenu* ("our rabbi"). The Oral Torah is the lens through which the Written Torah is understood. It explains, elaborates, extends, applies, and also supplements the Written Torah. It includes discussions of and arguments about religious practice, interpretations of the *Tanakh*, sermons, and stories about biblical figures and rabbis.

As a tradition transmitted and supplemented from generation to generation, the Oral Torah is continually evolving. It reflects on and animates the Written Torah. It also questions and explains received rabbinic teachings and seeks their reasons, justifications, and potential applications. In this way, the Oral Torah shows Jews how to learn in order to understand God's will, maintain their relationship with God, and bring God's teaching into their own lives. Thus, Oral Torah is a sustained exercise in religious self-awareness and self-reflection. It allows Judaism to respond to new and unanticipated situations. The teachings and methods of Oral Torah are preserved in the literature of rabbinic Judaism. All contemporary forms of Judaism in varied ways continue to probe and develop the content, meaning, and relevance of this religious heritage.

The two parts of Torah, Written and Oral, constitute God's complete, integrated, and comprehensive revelation to the Jewish people.

Basic Judaic Affirmations

Judaism holds that there is only One God in the universe, who created and ordered the cosmos, established the framework for and the meaning of all life, and watches over all lives. God transcends nature and society and cannot and must not be represented in an image. Judaism experiences God as loving, demanding, judging, and forgiving; as a deity who sets the standards of a human life marked by loyalty, love, justice, righteousness, responsibility, charity, community, and peoplehood.

God's name, YHWH, contains four letters from the Hebrew alphabet and is therefore called the tetragrammaton. Because God's name is holy, in Judaism it is not pronounced. In place of the tetragrammaton, it is customary to use the Hebrew term 'Adonai ("my Lord," "the Lord") in worship. Rabbinic literature favors the term HaKadosh, Baruch Hu ("the Holy One, Blessed be He"). Outside of worship, Jews often use the euphemism haShem ("the Name") to refer to God.

Judaism is grounded in the Torah's account of covenant. A covenant is a binding agreement between two parties, and in the ancient Near East different forms of covenantal agreements were used to define relations between nations after wars and between kings and vassals. The Torah draws on this form of agreement, but its claim that a deity initiates a covenant with humans is unique in the ancient Near East.

The Torah presents the covenant in two forms. The covenant with Abraham is a unilateral relationship between God and Abraham, Isaac, and Jacob (whose name is changed to "Israel") and their descendants. God promises to be their god forever and give them the land of Israel as an "everlasting possession." The second form of covenant, formalized at Sinai, articulates, through the prophet Moses, God's commandments (mitzvot). By observing the commandments the Israelites can fulfill God's expectation that they become a kingdom of priests and a holy people (Exodus 19.6). This form of covenant is reciprocal and conditional; falling short of God's standards has negative consequences. Both Abraham and the Israelites at Sinai enter into their respective covenant agreements voluntarily, of their own free will.

The two forms of covenant yield two paths to peoplehood: familial and by adoption. The covenant with Abraham, Isaac, and Jacob means that people inherit covenantal membership from their parents by birth. At the same time, the covenant at Sinai enables people not descended from Abraham, Isaac, and Jacob to enter the covenant by accepting the commandments. Judaism understands the two forms of covenant as mutually reinforcing parts of a single agreement. The core of the agreement is the idea of covenantal kinship, which defines the Jewish people. Covenantal kinship creates Jewish peoplehood through the fusion of birth and choice. Thus, converts to Judaism become members of the Jewish people as if they had been born into the family and then transmit that identity to their children by birth.

The covenant is the foundation of a range of historical and contemporary understandings of Jewish identity. Some emphasize peoplehood or nationality; others focus on religious commitment. Historically, Jews have primarily understood themselves, and been regarded by others, as both: a people or extended family with particular religious beliefs and practices.

The Abrahamic covenant (Genesis 17), God's commandments in Deuteronomy 12.1–11, God's endorsement of Solomon's Temple (2 Samuel 7), and Psalms such as 125 and 147 undergird Judaism's understanding that God selected the land of Israel and the city of Jerusalem as the central location for the worship of God and the full realization of the covenant relationship.

The Oral Torah identifies 613 commandments in the Written Torah. These cover nearly all aspects of life. Among other values, they mandate love of and loyalty to God; respect for parents, the elderly, and the handicapped; care for the poor; honesty in business; fairness in law; and concern for one's neighbor. They address ethical, social, and ritual norms for civility, courtesy, and charity; sacrifice and prayer; the observance of the Sabbath and festivals; dietary conventions; marriage, consanguinity, and family practices; commerce; and ritual purity. They show how repentance and atonement can restore a broken or damaged relationship to God. Twenty-six commandments apply only to life in the land of Israel. The Oral Torah interprets and adapts the commandments to new conditions and contexts.

Most forms of Jewish liturgy affirm the Jewish people's return to the Land of Israel, avow resurrection from the dead, and—in fulfillment of the covenant with David (2 Samuel 7)—anticipate an "anointed" redeemer, a "messiah," from the house of David who will appear at the "end of days." To "anoint" means to pour or smear oil on a person to signify the person's holiness to God. The kings of Israel were anointed when they assumed office. In Hebrew, the term for "anointed one" is mashiach, which is the origin of the English term "messiah." The Greek translation of mashiach is christos, which is the origin of the English term "Christ."

Classical Judaic sources have no fixed or universally accepted doctrine about the nature of the messiah or the future realm that follows the messiah's arrival, which is called the "World to Come." While Judaism's conviction about God's ultimate redemption of the Jewish people is clear and indelible, the commandments focus on concrete action in the present life. Thus, Judaism is primarily a this-worldly religion.

Judaism also holds that entry into the "World to Come"—whatever precisely this may mean—is not limited to Jews. While God's commandments apply only to the Jewish people, Judaism understands God to be the deity of all of humanity. It therefore identifies what it calls the seven commandments of "the children of Noah," the observance of which justifies the entry of the righteous of all nations into the "World to Come." The Noahide commandments forbid 1) denying God, 2) blaspheming God, 3) murder, 4) engaging in illicit sexual relations, 5) theft, and 6) eating from a live animal; they enjoin 7) establishing courts/legal system to ensure fulfillment of these commandments.

Religious and Historical Background

To understand Judaism's form and components, it will help briefly to review key elements of its religion and history.

Tabernacle and Temple

The Torah recounts that after the Israelites affirm the covenant at Sinai, God instructs Moses to build a movable Tabernacle or Tent of Meeting as God's habitat among the people of Israel. Exodus interlinks the covenant, the Tabernacle, the altar, and God's presence:

> I will consecrate the Tent of Meeting and the altar and will consecrate Aaron and his sons to serve me as priests. Then I will dwell among the Israelites and be their God. They will know that I am the LORD their God, who brought them out of Egypt so that I might dwell among them. I am the LORD their God.
>
> EXODUS 29.44–46, NIV, 1984 edition

The Tabernacle's innermost part is called the "Holy of Holies, " which housed the Ark of the Covenant. Just outside the Holy of Holies was a room that contained a seven-branched candelabra (*menorah*), a table with an offering of bread, and a table for the burning of incense. Beyond this outer chamber was an altar.

According to the *Tanakh* (1 Kings 7.51–8.10), Solomon's Temple in Jerusalem became the Tabernacle's permanent location. Ancient Mediterranean peoples regarded temples as the residences of deities, where people had assured access to their god. The *Tanakh* (2 Samuel 7) describes Solomon's Temple as God's house. The Temple made the Israelites' God into a resident deity and was ancient Israel's preeminent religious, cultural, and national institution.

FIGURE 2 *The Israelite Tabernacle (Timnah Park, Israel),* © *Reynold Mainse/Destinations, Alamy.*

Cult and Sacrifice

The Tabernacle housed and supported a religion of cult and sacrifice, which the Torah describes as first practiced in the desert. The term "cult" refers to a set of rituals that, when performed correctly by the proper persons, achieve specific results. The primary goal of the Israelite cult was to insure God's ongoing presence and sustain the covenant relationship. In service of that end, a caste of priests (descendants of Moses' brother Aaron) presented sacrifices of animals and grain on an altar twice daily, with additional offerings for Sabbaths, new moons, and festivals. The sacrifices were gifts to God. Some expressed thanksgiving; others atoned for collective and individual transgressions and repaired ruptures in people's relationship to God. The blood of the sacrificed animals achieved expiation and was sprinkled on the altar and sometimes on the curtain in front of the Holy of Holies to purify God's residence. That the description of the Tabernacle and the procedures of sacrifice occupy over one-third of the Torah testifies to their importance.

Ritual Purity

Religions of cult and sacrifice typically protect their deity's residence against impurity. Impurity is not sin or dirt. Rather, impurity refers to conditions of disorder that corrupt the god's dwelling and alienate the god. Scholars suggest that because Israelite religion conceived God as both eternal and asexual, death and sexuality were barred from God's domicile. Thus, for instance, people who had contact with a human corpse were deemed ritually impure, as were women during and after their menstrual period or following childbirth, and men after a seminal emission. Persons classified as impure had to undergo ritual purification in order to approach God's sanctuary. Depending on the nature of their impurity, people either waited a specified period of time or immersed in water to return to ordinary status. Aspects of ritual purity continue to be practiced in some forms of contemporary Judaism.

Under each of three ancient empires—Persian, Hellenistic, and Roman—Judaism underwent significant adaptation. Let us briefly take these up in turn.

Persia: Temple and Torah (539–333 BCE)

The Babylonians' destruction of the Jerusalem Temple in 587/586 BCE created a crisis. How could the people retain their national culture and relationship to God without the Temple cult that had defined Israelite life since the time of King Solomon? The initial response emerged in the Persian period.

First, as we have seen, leaders of the exiled Israelite community, likely priests and scribes, gathered ancient Israel's national traditions into the Torah. It guided and helped preserve the collective life and identity, religious practices, and national memory of the immigrant Jewish community in Babylonia and oriented their future hope. Second, under the auspices of the Persian state, which conquered Babylonia in 539 BCE, the

Temple was rebuilt, largely by returning exiles, and was rededicated by 515 BCE. The Ark of the Covenant disappeared after the destruction, so the Holy of Holies in the rebuilt Temple was empty. Although ancestral traditions had shaped much of Jewish communal life, the "Torah of Moses," which the *Tanakh* says Ezra read in Jerusalem, would come to inform priestly conduct in the rebuilt Temple and the Jews' lives in their villages and homes, both within and outside the land of Israel.

Hellenism: Synagogue and Statehood (323–63 BCE)

Although many exiles returned to Judea in the Persian period, the majority remained in Babylon. During the Hellenistic period, Alexander the Great (356–323 BCE) conquered and spread Greek language and culture to most of the known world, and Jewish communities developed across the Mediterranean, particularly in Egypt. Temple and Torah began to emerge as the two primary bases of Jewish religious authority. The Torah grew in importance, as did other works, particularly the books of prophecy and the Psalms. Evidence in this period points to a new, lay, non-cultic Jewish communal institution, the synagogue. It served as a meeting place for a range of community functions, including the recitation of the Torah, and would become Judaism's primary religious institution.

In the late third century BCE, the Seleucids, descendants of one of Alexander's generals—who had divided his empire after his death—assumed rule over Judea. In 167 BCE, the emperor Antiochus IV—with the support of a faction of Judean society that wanted to adopt Greek culture—outlawed Jewish religious practice in Judea and desecrated the Temple. A priestly clan, the Hasmoneans (also known as the Maccabees), rebelled, recaptured the Temple, and rededicated it to God. In 140 BCE the Hasmoneans created a Jewish polity that lasted until 63 BCE. They colonized other regions of the land of Israel, including Galilee, which became home to both the Jesus movement and, later, the early rabbis.

The Hasmonean rulers' management of the Temple cult, and their dealings with the larger surrounding Hellenistic kingdoms generated division and opposition groups in Judea. The most consequential were the Pharisees, laypersons who strove to apply priestly practices and behaviors to life outside of the Temple and had their own unwritten non-scriptural traditions; the Sadducees, who held that the Torah was the final authority and who rejected belief in resurrection from the dead; and the Dead Sea sect, a group that opposed Hasmonean cultic leadership and formed a community at Qumran, producing an extraordinary library of biblical and other texts.

Rome: The Oral Torah (63 BCE–400 CE)

Rome conquered the land of Israel in 63 BCE. Its client king of Judea, Herod (74/73 BCE–4 BCE), rebuilt the Jerusalem Temple into one of the architectural wonders of the ancient Mediterranean.

In the first century CE, the Jesus movement, which regarded Jesus of Nazareth as the messiah who had come to usher in the "kingdom of God," appeared.

FIGURE 3 *Herod's Temple, © Pascal Deloche, Getty Images.*

In 66 CE the Jews launched a full-scale rebellion against Rome that led to the destruction of the Second Temple in 70 CE.

After 70, a group known as rabbis ("teacher" or "master") created a religious structure that responded to the Temple's demise. Thought to be the heirs of the Pharisees, rabbis extended and infused the biblical monotheistic heritage into the life of the community. Rabbinic Judaism replaced Temple worship with a framework of prayer and domestic and communal rituals of daily life. Rabbinic tradition (*Avot de Rabbi Natan* 4) reports that *Rabban Yohanan ben Zakkai*, who founded rabbinic Judaism during the rebellion against Rome, taught, on the basis of Hosea 6.6, that deeds of lovingkindness could effect atonement in lieu of sacrifices. Without the Temple and its sacrificial cult, Judaism's center of authority shifted to Torah.

A figure named Simon Bar Kokhba—regarded by some as the messiah who would end foreign domination—led another rebellion in 132–135 CE. Its failure caused the expulsion of the Jews from Jerusalem and its transformation into a Roman city.

The rabbis then moved north from Jerusalem to the Galilee. In about 200 CE, Judah (ca. 135–217 CE), the leader of the Jewish community of the land of Israel, produced the Mishnah, the first collection of teachings of the Oral Torah. The Mishnah contains the first rabbinic statement of Judaism's religious practice (*halakhah*), which transforms the values of Torah—monotheism, covenant, justice, righteousness, piety, and social responsibility—into concrete behaviors and attitudes. Often translated as "law," *halakhah* also can be understood to mean praxis, the proper "way" of doing things.

Collected in the Mishnah are the teachings of rabbis who lived from the second century BCE to 200 CE. Rabbis who date from 70 CE onward are called, in Aramaic, *Tannaim*, "teachers." The Mishnah does not follow the structure of the Torah. Rather, it organizes rabbinic opinions into six major divisions: *Zera'im* ("Seeds"): issues of prayer and agriculture; *Mo'ed* ("Festival"): issues of Sabbath and holiday observance; *Nashim* ("Women"): issues of marriage and family life; *Nezikin* ("Damages"): issues of torts and damages; *Qodashim* ("Holy Things"): issues pertaining to Temple ritual; *Tohorot* ("Purities"): issues of ritual purity, relevant primarily to the Temple.

Rabbis in the land of Israel and Babylonia studied the Mishnah and other early rabbinic teachings. Their commentary is called *Gemara* ("study"). Together, *Mishnah* and *Gemara* constitute the Talmud, Judaism's primary source of rabbinic teaching on halakhic matters. There are two Talmuds. One was produced in the land of Israel by the early fifth century CE and is known as the *Talmud Yerushalmi* or the Talmud of the Land of Israel. The second is the *Talmud Bavli*, the Babylonian Talmud, completed in the mid-sixth century CE, and is the more authoritative of the two. When people refer generically to "the Talmud," they mean the Bavli.

The Talmuds, written in different dialects of Aramaic, follow the order of the Mishnah and transmit teachings attributed to rabbis who lived from 200 CE to 400 CE in the land of Israel and 200–500 CE in Babylonia (called, *'Amoraim*, "interpreters"). They report and discuss different rabbis' judgments and opinions about the meaning and application of discrete Mishnah passages. They also offer biblical interpretation (*midrash*), and religious narrative (*aggadah*). Rabbis in the land of Israel also produced documents of *midrash* and *aggadah*.

Because it was edited later, the Bavli's discourse is more developed than the Yerushalmi's. It exhibits a unique process of rational inquiry, dialogue, and debate in extended animated conversation. Covering 2,711 pages, it explores, explains, interrogates, and elaborates rabbinic opinions and displays the intellectual openness and competitiveness of rabbinic culture. The Bavli is not a code of *halakhah*. Its disputations do not necessarily resolve halakhic questions and often end with two divergent opinions, which invite ongoing discussion and reflection. The quintessence of Oral Torah, the Bavli exhibits Judaism's value of *torah l'shma'* ("learning for its own sake"). Its purpose is to draw people to the study of, and engagement with, Torah.

For most of late antiquity the rabbinic movement was primarily a network of disciple-circles, in which rabbis and their students memorized, recited, transmitted, and interpreted Torah. The study of Torah was the rabbis' central religious obligation and activity, more important than even prayer. It was an elite activity, and rabbis likely in this period were not community leaders. Over time, the disciple-circles developed into academies (*yeshivot*, sing. *yeshivah*). From the late sixth to mid-eleventh centuries the most important of these were in Babylonia. Their leaders, called *Geonim* ("eminences"), were the religious authorities of their day. During this period, the Bavli became increasingly important.

Beginning in the Middle Ages, leading sages produced *responsa*, answers to religious questions from Jewish communities throughout the Middle East and Europe.

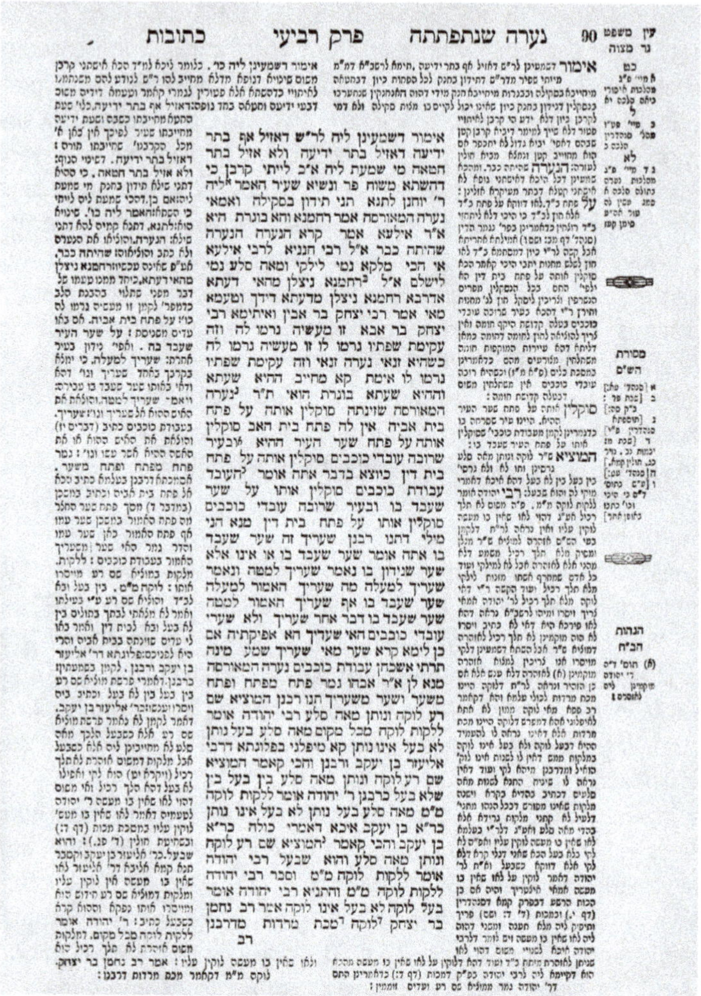
עין משפט נר מצוה 90 נערה שנתפתתה פרק רביעי כתובות

FIGURE 4 *Page of the Babylonian Talmud from the nineteenth-century Vilna edition. The Mishnah and* gemara *are placed in the center of the page, and the commentary of Rabbi Shlomo Yitzhaki (aka* Rashi*), 1040–1105, is on the inner margin. Additional comments and notations are placed on the outer margin. (© Culture Club/Getty Images).*

They standardized the liturgy and began consolidating the Talmud's dialectic into summaries or codes of *halakhah* that systematized Jewish religious practice. The codes rely primarily on the Bavli. Two particularly influential codes are the *Mishneh Torah* ("the Second Torah") of the philosopher Rabbi Moses Maimonides, aka *Rambam* (1138–1204), and the *Shulchan Aruch* ("Set Table") of Rabbi Joseph Karo (1488–1575).

From the Middle Ages until the beginning of modernity, *halakhah* guided Jewish communal life in Christian and Islamic realms across the globe. The three largest of these diaspora communities are the *Sephardim*, who descend from the Jews in

Christian and Muslim Spain; the *Ashkenazim*, heirs of the Jews of France and Germany and, later, Eastern Europe; and the *Mizrahim*, who resided primarily in the Arab world, including North Africa. These communities share the halakhic heritage but with regional and local variations. For instance, the *Shulchan Aruch* contains Sephardic halakhic practices along with glosses of *Ashkenazi* practices, added by Rabbi Moses Isserles (1530–1572). A basic halakhic principle is that rabbis should not offer judgments in another rabbi's community.

Worship

Jewish communal worship requires a quorum (*minyan*) of ten adults (typically males in Orthodox communities) and customarily takes place in a synagogue. In Orthodox and Conservative congregations male worshippers cover their heads with a skullcap called *kippah* or *yarmulke* as a sign of respect to God. Increasingly, women who do not otherwise cover their hair may do so as well. Since antiquity, synagogue interiors face Jerusalem and focus on the Torah scroll (*Sefer Torah*), which is housed in a cabinet *Ashkenazim* call the '*Aron Kodesh* ("Holy Ark") and *Sephardim* call *Heikhal* ("Temple"). Above the Ark/*Heikhal* hangs an "eternal light," which evokes the lights that burned in the Temple and represents God's presence.

In classical Jewish liturgy prayers are said three times daily—morning, afternoon, and evening—with an additional service (*Musaf*) appended to morning prayer on the Sabbath and holidays. These are a modification of the twice-daily periods of sacrifices described in the Torah. The daily and Sabbath prayer book is called a *Siddur* ("order"). The liturgy traditionally is not spoken but is chanted *a capella* by a cantor (*hazzan*) or prayer leader.

The core of the daily liturgy is the *Shema'* and its blessings, which articulate Judaism's basic convictions. The *Shema'* itself is a combination of Deuteronomy 6.4–9, 11.13–21, and Numbers 15.37–41. The passage from Numbers, repeated at Deuteronomy 22.12, instructs people to attach "fringes" to their clothing to remind them to perform the commandments. This is the origin of the *tallit* or prayer shawl worn during morning worship and by some men in the form of a small undergarment.

The passages from Deuteronomy 6 capture the *Shema's* essence:

Hear, O Israel: The LORD our God, the LORD is One. Love the LORD your God with all your heart and with all your soul and with all your strength. These commandments that I give you today are to be on your hearts. Impress them on your children. Talk about them when you sit at home and when you walk along the road, when you lie down and when you get up. Tie them as symbols on your hands and bind them on your foreheads. Write them on the doorframes of your houses and on your gates.

The *Shema'* is followed by the '*Amidah* ("Standing Prayer" or simply "the Prayer"), a set of nineteen blessings that are said silently while standing and then repeated aloud by the *hazzan*.

In all worship services, those marking the anniversary of a death or still in mourning for a relative who has died in the past year rise and recite the mourners' *Kaddish*, an Aramaic prayer of sanctification. In many communities, the entire congregation recites the *Kaddish*.

Judaism's Calendar

The Judaic calendar is lunisolar. It measures the year by the rotation of the sun but counts months by the appearance of the moon. Since the lunar year is 11 days shorter than the solar year, every two or three years Judaism adds an additional month to its calendar so that the lunar months—and Jewish holidays—always occur at roughly the same time in the solar year. Judaism counts years from the time of creation, so, for instance, the years 2019–2020 are the year 5780 in the Jewish calendar. Because the Torah counts days from evening to morning (as God did in the creating the cosmos), all Judaic holidays begin the evening before the day on which they fall. Finally, since in antiquity the appearance of the new moon was determined in Jerusalem, and that message took time to reach distant places, communities outside the land of Israel traditionally add an extra day to each biblical holiday (except *Yom Kippur*) so their observance will fall the correct day.

Holidays

The weekly Sabbath is the most important holiday in Judaism. It is a day of rest on which no work is permitted.

The major annual holidays begin with *Rosh HaShanah*, the New Year, which celebrates God's creation of the world and starts a ten-day period of reflection and repentance ("Days of Awe") that concludes with *Yom Kippur*, the Day of Atonement. The *Rosh HaShanah* liturgy evokes the themes of God's kingship, God's remembrance of each individual's actions, and the new beginning of the New Year. The sounding of the *shofar* ("ram's horn"), a central holiday ritual, evokes God's covenant with Israel. *Yom Kippur* is a twenty-five-hour fast, from before sundown on the evening before the holiday until after sundown on the day of the holiday, during which the community seeks forgiveness from God and from one another for transgressions against them during the past year. The special prayer book for the Days of Awe is called the *Makhzor* ("cycle").

Five days after *Yom Kippur* is the holiday of *Sukkot* ("Booths" or "Tabernacles"), the first of three originally agricultural biblical festivals that were celebrated by pilgrimages to the Temple in Jerusalem. During *Sukkot* participants build and eat in small booths, which symbolize the Israelites' dwellings in their journey through the desert following the exodus from Egypt. Its conclusion is followed by *Shemini 'Atzeret* ("eighth day of assembly"), on which the annual prayers for rain begin to be recited. In the State of Israel, this holiday is combined with *Simchat Torah* ("rejoicing in the Torah"), which celebrates the completion and re-inauguration of the annual reading of the Torah.

FIGURE 5 *Children at lighting of candles in celebration of Hanukkah,* © *Stephen Chernin / Stringer, Getty Images.*

Outside of the land of Israel, *Simchat Torah* is celebrated as a separate holiday on the day after *Shemini 'Atzeret.*

The winter months host the post-biblical eight-day holiday of *Hanukkah*, which commemorates the Maccabees' rededication of the Temple. Its notable features are the lighting of a special eight-stemmed candelabra and the giving of gifts. Next comes the holiday of *Purim*, which recounts and celebrates the story of the Book of Esther.

The spring season is marked by the eight-day festival of Passover (*Pesach*), which commemorates the Israelites' exodus from Egypt. It was once a pilgrimage holiday celebrated in Jerusalem with a special sacrifice, but since rabbinic times, Passover's central ritual is a festive, typically domestic, meal, the *Seder*. The liturgy for the *Seder* is the *Haggadah*, which includes special prayers, songs, rituals, and conversational elements through which families and friends narrate, symbolically reenact, and discuss the story of the Israelites' redemption from slavery. The *Seder* is multigenerational, participatory, and congenial to children. It concludes with the wish, "Next year in Jerusalem." During the holiday leaven is prohibited, and people eat unleavened bread (*matzah*), which represents bread baked in haste as the Israelites left Egypt. Fifty days after Passover is the third pilgrimage festival, *Shavu'ot* ("Weeks" or "Pentecost"), which celebrates God's giving the Torah at Sinai. Finally comes the fast of *Tisha B'Av* ("the Ninth of Av"), the date on which Judaism holds both Temples were destroyed.

Life-cycle Events

Judaism also includes life-cycle events: the *Brit Milah* ("Covenant of Circumcision") for infant male children (and in some denominations a ceremony for infant girls); the *Bar/Bat Mitzvah*, which celebrates the transition to religious adulthood by an adolescent's first recitation of the Torah during worship; and special rituals for marriage and for mourning and remembering the deceased.

Torah as "Virtual Reality"

In Judaism, Torah affects and informs everything people do. Within *halakhah*, even the most habitual and routine act—how one eats, dresses, and does business, for instance—evokes God. The following passage from the *Birkat HaMazon* ("Grace after Meals"), customarily recited at the conclusion of any meal in which bread is broken, illustrates Torah's effect:

> Blessed is The Lord our God, Sovereign of the universe, who sustains the entire world with goodness, kindness, and mercy. God gives food to all creatures, for God's mercy is everlasting.
>
> Through God's abundant goodness we have not lacked sustenance, and may we not lack sustenance forever, for the sake of God's great name. God sustains all, does good to all, and provides food for all the creatures whom God has created. Blessed is The Lord our God, who provides food for all.
>
> We thank The Lord our God for having given a lovely and spacious land to our fathers and mothers; for having liberated us from the land of Egypt and freed us from the house of bondage; for the covenant which God has sealed in our flesh, for the Torah which God has taught us; for the laws which God has made known to us; for the life, grace and loving kindness which God has bestowed upon us, and for the sustenance with which God nourishes and maintains us continually, in every season, every day, even every hour.
>
> RABBI JONATHAN KLEIN, trans.

Nearly all of Judaism's major convictions about God as the sustainer of life, covenant, land, Torah, and God's generous and gracious nature are encapsulated in this short, routinely recited paragraph. Through Torah, Judaism balances "ordinary reality" with "non-ordinary" reality. Wherever Jews happen to live, they experience in their religious practice—bodily and linguistically—God, creation, exodus, covenant, the Torah of Sinai, and the Land of Israel. Whether they are in New York, Shanghai, Cracow, Paris, or Cape Town, they can follow the order of creation and the agricultural rhythms of the land of Israel. They thus dwell in both the empirical reality of the place in which they reside and work and the "virtual reality" of Torah, through which they enact on a daily basis their identity as the Jewish people, the heirs to the covenant of the One God.

Major Judaic Variations

In the diverse settings in which Jews have lived across the globe, their minority religion distinguished them from their neighbors. The uncertainty and instability of Judaism's religious, physical, cultural environments forced it to transcend a number of existential challenges beyond the destruction of the two Temples. Under Muslim rule Jews and Judaism were generally tolerated, though with restrictions and periodic acts of violence. In Christian Europe, however, some New Testament teachings—particularly that the Jews were "Christ killers," responsible for Jesus' crucifixion—generated persistent and widespread negative images of Jews. This hostility is evident for instance, in massacres of Jews during the Crusades; the expulsion of the Jews from England in 1290; the forced exile of Jews from Spain in 1492 and later from Portugal; and anti-Jewish pogroms in Russia and Eastern Europe. The Nazis transformed religious enmity into racism, promoted anti-Semitic propaganda throughout Europe and the Middle East, and committed the state-sponsored, industrial-scale murder of six million Jews in the Holocaust (1933–1945). Regrettably, anti-Semitism has reappeared in sectors of Europe, the Middle East, and the United States.

Christian-Jewish relations have improved and matured over time. For example, the Church of England, in a 2019 document entitled *God's Unfailing Word: Theological and Practical Perspectives on Christian-Jewish Relations*, acknowledged with regret the role of some Christian teachings in the creation and spread of anti-Semitism and called for stronger Jewish-Christian mutual respect, understanding, and collaboration.

Philosophy and Mysticism

Philosophy

Since antiquity, some Jews have understood Torah through the lens of Greek philosophy. Philo of Alexandria (ca. 20 BCE–50 CE) wrote a philosophical commentary on the Torah, which influenced Christian Church Fathers. In the medieval period—particularly within Islamic culture—Judaism again engaged significantly with Greek philosophy. Moses Maimonides, who was both an astronomer and a physician and is regarded as perhaps the most consequential philosopher of Judaism, epitomizes this synergy. His *Guide for the Perplexed*, originally written in Judeo-Arabic, integrates neo-Aristotelian philosophy and Judaic teaching. Arab Muslim philosophy influenced Maimonides, and Christian theologians such as Thomas Aquinas (1225–1274) drew on his work. The philosopher Benedict (*Baruch*) Spinoza (1632–1677) disputed the Mosaic origin of the Torah and laid the foundation for modern biblical criticism. The philosophical study of Torah continues to the present day.

Mysticism

Kabbalah ("tradition") is the term for Jewish mysticism. It represents a heritage of esoteric knowledge and interpretation that claims to include secret teachings about God, creation, Torah, and redemption. *Kabbalah's* primary aims are to perceive God everywhere and achieve intimacy with God. The kabbalistic tradition begins in antiquity with speculation about the prophet Ezekiel's chariot vision of God's presence.

The primary kabbalistic text is the *Zohar* ("The Book of Splendor"), which appeared in the thirteenth century. Allegedly the work of the second-century rabbi Simeon b. Yohai, it likely was written by rabbi and kabbalist Moses de Leon. It envisions God, whom it calls *'Ein Sof* ("the Infinite"), as transcendent, immaterial, and beyond humans' description, comprehension, or direct knowledge. *'Ein Sof* does not relate directly to the created world but reveals itself through ten *sefirot*, emanations or powers, which represent its different aspects, such as wisdom, love, understanding, and glory. What humans come to know about God, they learn through the *sefirot*, which are hierarchical and gendered. Each represents a distinct divine attribute, and their integration and interrelationship represent God's inner life. The Zohar avers that humanity's response to God enhances God's power. By relating to God through the *sefirot*, humans strengthen God's inner life. For instance, the *sefirah* that interacts with the created world is the *Shekhinah*, God's "dwelling" or "presence." It is female. The *Zohar* postulates that the *Shekhinah* is the focus of ritual and that, in particular, Sabbath observance unites the feminine and masculine aspects of God. Versions of the kabbalistic tradition influenced later Jewish messianism and modern Hasidic Judaism.

Judaism in Modernity

In Europe, the forces of the Enlightenment, nationalism, and secularism pulled Jews' and Judaism's integrated covenant-based identity in different directions and led to the development of the major forms of modern Judaism: Reform, Orthodox, and Conservative.

In the eighteenth century, an intellectual and cultural movement known as the Enlightenment, committed to the ideals of reason and human equality, emerged in Western Europe. As Enlightenment ideas became increasingly accepted, Jews—who were Europe's quintessential outsiders—were gradually allowed to enter and integrate into mainstream Western European society and culture.

One form of that integration was the notion that the Jews constituted *only* a religious community. They were loyal individual citizens of the European nations but practiced a religion different from Christianity. The Jewish philosopher Moses Mendelssohn (1729–1786) articulated this idea, which, though Mendelssohn himself never gave up halakhic practice, became a foundation of Reform Judaism.

Reform Judaism emphasized Judaism's ethical teachings, minimized *halakhah*, and streamlined and vernacularized synagogue liturgy and worship. A traditionalist response to Reform is Orthodox Judaism, which acquired an identity as a distinct community within Judaism in nineteenth century Germany. Orthodoxy is committed to *halakhah* and study of Torah. The third major denomination, Conservative Judaism, developed in the United States and has roots both in Enlightenment intellectual ideas and halakhic tradition. A fourth movement is Reconstructionism, a naturalist Judaism founded in the United States.

Alongside these movements, Hasidism ("piety") emerged in the eighteenth century and became popular primarily in Eastern Europe. It drew on kabbalistic traditions, emphasized ecstasy and prayer, and devised a unique form of charismatic rabbinic leadership. While initially standing in opposition to established Orthodoxy, it has effectively co-existed with other traditional forms of Jewish practice and belief so that it is now seen as a quintessential form of Orthodox Judaism.

Judaism and Nationality: Zionism and the State of Israel

Sparked by the ideals of the French Revolution, nationalist movements spread across Europe during the nineteenth century. For instance, Italy was unified in 1861, and Germany became one nation-state in 1871. Zionism, a primarily European Jewish nationalist movement, aimed to solve the problem of Jewish powerlessness and the continual challenges of European anti-Semitism. Zionism understood the Jews to be a nation whose traits included, but were not limited to, religion. It emphasized the Jews' distinctive history and culture and aimed to create in the Jews' ancestral land of Israel a new secular, democratic, Jewish nation-state, with its distinctive language, land, religion, and culture. Its goal was to create a "normal" society—like those of other nation-states—with its own independent political structure that would allow the Jewish people to achieve national self-determination. Zionism assumed a unique urgency in the wake of the Nazi Holocaust. In 1948, following a vote of the United Nations to partition Palestine into Jewish and Arab states, the State of Israel came into being.

Christianity

The Scripture of Christianity: The New Testament

The Christian Scriptures contains twenty-seven books written in Greek by fifteen or sixteen different authors between 50 CE and 120 CE. It can be divided into four groups: Gospels, Acts of the Apostles, Epistles, and Revelation. The narrative structure of the Christian Scriptures begins chronologically with the birth of Jesus. However, the Gospels are not the earliest writings in the New Testament. The epistles (letters) that immediately follow them were written earlier. The Acts of the Apostles is a historical account of the early church, and the book of Revelation is a symbolic text that reveals God's mysteries and describes the end of times. Throughout history and even today

Christians debate the nature of the Christian Scriptures as either the literal word of God or a human text that is divinely inspired. Overwhelmingly today, Christians believe their Scriptures should not be read literally and instead must be interpreted in light of the contemporary world.

The narratives of Jesus' life, ministry, death, and resurrection are found in the four Gospels: Matthew, Mark, Luke, and John. The Gospels, known as good news, contain the teachings and revelations of Jesus Christ. They were all written anonymously and later attributed to followers of Jesus. While the Gospels describe many shared moments about and teachings preached by Jesus, they also each have their own particular emphasis. There are, for example, some stories that are only found in one Gospel and not the others. However, they have become central for how Christians understand Jesus today.

The decision to begin the narrative of the Christian Scriptures with the four Gospels, and Matthew in particular, opens Jesus' story with his genealogy, connecting him directly to David and Abraham. From its first pages the Christian Scriptures want to define Jesus as a descendant of Abraham and David, thus immediately connecting him to the Jewish people. For Matthew, tracing Jesus' lineage from Abraham to Joseph solidifies him within the Abrahamic tradition and connects him to ancient Judaism. Jesus, prior to his birth, is presented as the climax of Jewish history, which begins with Abraham. He is also framed as the fulfillment of Jewish prophecy, labeled "Jesus the Messiah" in the first verse of Matthew. Jesus as the anointed one is within the lineage of King David. These words set the stage for the remainder of the Gospel in particular and the New Testament as a whole. Mark, the second Gospel in the New Testament, follows a similar tone introducing Jesus in light of the prophet Isaiah. The Gospel of Luke opens with the birth of John the Baptist (Jesus' cousin) and follows with the birth of Jesus. Luke makes sure to emphasize that Joseph, Jesus' stepfather, is from the house of David, again reaffirming this Jewish lineage. John, the fourth and last Gospel, follows a similar pattern, contextualizing Jesus in light of Isaiah's prophecy.

The two accounts of Jesus' birth found in Matthew and Luke differ in details, though both agree he was born in Bethlehem (David's birthplace) and that Mary, his mother, was a virgin that became pregnant through the Holy Spirit. Here we return to the theme found in the Hebrew Scriptures of God having power and influence over women's wombs. When Mary learns of her pregnancy from the angel Gabriel, she proclaims her Magnificat, or Song, praising God:

> He has helped his servant Israel,
>   remembering to be merciful
> to Abraham and his descendants forever,
>   just as he promised our ancestors.

LUKE 1.54–55

Joseph, Mary's fiancé, is not Jesus' biological father. Upon learning of his future-bride's pregnancy Joseph decides to leave her quietly, but then an angel of God appears to him in a dream and explains Jesus' origins and destiny as the savior of humanity. This, Matthew reminds us, is in fulfillment of the prophet Isaiah who proclaims, "The virgin will conceive and give birth to a son, and they will call him Immanuel." (Matthew 1:23, citing Isaiah 7.14). Matthew also includes the now well-known visit of the three Magi in his narrative, while Luke highlights the visit of shepherds who arrive to see baby Jesus (after hearing a heavenly voice) and Jesus' birth in a manger. Nativity scenes will combine the two accounts, showing Jesus in a manger surrounded by shepherds, animals, and the three kings. Luke tells us that as a child Jesus was presented at the Temple as a child, following Jewish custom. All four Gospels highlight the role of John the Baptist, Jesus' cousin, whose birth was also miraculous, as a prophetic precursor who announced Jesus' significance in light of Jewish prophecy. When John begins preaching and baptizing people in the river Jordan, the Gospel of Luke tells us people wonder if he is the Messiah. Yet John proclaims, "I baptize you with water. But one who is more powerful than I will come, the straps of whose sandals I am not worthy to untie. He will baptize you with the Holy Spirit and fire" (Luke 3.16). John prepares the way for Jesus.

The four Gospels emphasize Jesus' teachings, his ministry, and the multiple miracles attributed to him. These are key for establishing Jesus as the savior of humanity and the fulfillment of Jewish prophecy. Since the Gospels were written with particular audiences in mind they emphasize different aspects of Jesus' ministry and teachings and should be understood as four overlapping accounts each with its own distinctive voice. His first followers come from his home region of Galilee. Jesus will eventually gather a group of twelve men that will come to be known as his twelve apostles that are distinctive from his other followers who are described as disciples. The number twelve clearly mirrors the twelve tribes of Israel. The overall argument of the Gospels is that Jesus is the Christ who was prophesied in the Hebrew Scriptures.

Jesus grew up in Nazareth in a time when the Holy Land was under Roman rule. We know very little about his early life. At around the age of thirty his cousin John the Baptist is arrested and beheaded. This appears to be what led Jesus to begin his public ministry. One of Jesus' most recognized teachings is found on the Sermon on the Mount, which outlines the Beatitudes, a series of teachings that emphasizes the blessedness of the poor and the reversal of human social structure in the kingdom of God. Jesus often preached about the kingdom of God as a new creation that will follow the transformation of this world and life. At the core of his message is what is known as the Great Commandments of love of God and love of neighbor. Jesus performed numerous miracles throughout his public ministry including feeding 5,000, walking on water, expelling demons, raising Lazarus from the dead (interpreted as a foreshadowing of his own resurrection), and healing multiple individuals.

Jesus' teachings and miracles attracted many crowds and raised the suspicions of Jewish authorities. However, it is the Romans, not the Jews, who will arrest and crucify him for the crime of political insurrection. Jesus' crucifixion becomes a definitive moment for Christians. Prior to his crucifixion Jesus shared a meal with his followers, known as the Last Supper, where he is betrayed by one of his apostles, Judas, who facilitates his arrest. The Last Supper is a pivotal moment in the Gospels, for it is here that Jesus foreshadows his own death, claiming that his blood is the blood of the new covenant. Through Jesus' death and resurrection, Christians come to believe, a new covenant is formed between God and humanity. The very idea of, and language about, covenant connects Jesus' salvific work within the covenant framework found in the Hebrew Scriptures. Jesus' crucifixion has meaning for Christians in that it is not the last word, and is followed by his resurrection on what will be celebrated as Easter. The early Christians are clear in indicating that Jesus was resurrected body and spirit, demonstrating that he has overcome death and can offer his followers eternal life.

One cannot underestimate the significance of the Crucifixion for Christians. Through his crucifixion Jesus offers himself as the ultimate sacrifice on behalf of humanity. He is also the last sacrifice. Remembering the Temple life of Judaism that was characteristic of Jesus' era, for Christians he will come to replace, and end the need for, the sacrificial cult. The notion that the monotheistic God would become incarnate in a human body and suffer and die here on earth is a revolutionary notion even today. Yet for Christians globally, Jesus' suffering on the cross reveals his salvific work. The crucifixion, however, is meaningless without the resurrection. For Christians, Jesus' resurrection demonstrates God's triumph of life over death and the promise of resurrection and eternal life for all of us. On the Sunday after his death some of his followers went to his grave only to discover an empty tomb. Jesus later appears to

FIGURE 6 *Cross and crucifix,* © *Byron Maldonado.*

them, shares a meal, and displays his wounds, demonstrating that he has risen from the dead both in body and spirit. Different Christian churches highlight both moments. Roman Catholics emphasize Jesus's redemptive suffering on the cross. This is clearly seen in their wearing of crucifixes which include Jesus' suffering body. Protestants, on the other hand, wear the plain cross, emphasizing the resurrected body that is no longer suffering. Regardless of the emphasis, one cannot understand the crucifixion without the resurrection and vice versa. Together they have deep spiritual significance for Christians, revealing God's unconditional love for humanity as expressed through his sacrifice and the triumph over that suffering through the resurrection.

The narrative of Jesus found in the Gospels is followed by the Acts of the Apostles, which chronicles the life of the early church. Acts opens with Jesus' ascension into heaven and is quickly followed by Pentecost, a key moment in early Christian history where Jesus' followers receive the gift of the Holy Spirit, one of the manifestations of the Christian God here on earth. Acts describes an emboldened group of early Christians that is persecuted for their teachings. It recounts the death of Stephen, who is considered the first Christian martyr. This account of the first Christian missionaries and their teachings is followed by the twenty-one epistles that are addressed to varying Christian communities that are struggling with multiple theological, cultural, and social issues. The Apostle Paul's voice features prominently in them. Within the letters we find the different stories and struggles of Christian communities as they attempt to negotiate their identity and their faith. The New Testament concludes with the book of Revelation, an apocalyptic (prophesying the end of times) text that is the most symbolic and therefore confusing within the Christian Scriptures. The book describes a vision of the end of times with the final resurrection of the dead and final judgment. Its dramatic and violent imagery has captivated the imagination of Christians and non-Christians alike over the centuries.

Christianity: An Overview

To summarize the basic teachings of Christianity is well beyond the scope and nature of this book. Also, one must make the distinction between what Christians believe and practice versus the official teachings of churches. Most often these are one and the same; however, the manner in which socio-cultural and historical location impacts lived Christianity can create frictions between the official and the everyday expressions of this religion. In addition, as this book argues, the implications of the monotheistic beliefs emerging from Christianity have implications well beyond those individuals who claim to adhere to this religion. Whether it is the civil religion of the United States whose currency includes the phrase "In God we Trust" and whose pledge claims the United States is a nation "under God," or the fact that throughout Latin America and the Caribbean in many countries Holy Week is a national holiday, the impact of Christianity's monotheism is felt far beyond the walls of churches.

The foundation of Christianity is the belief in Jesus the Christ as the Son of God, and that through his crucifixion and resurrection he saved and reconciled humanity from the condition of sin that marks all of us. Jesus is both fully human (Jesus) and divine (as the Christ or savior) and is the second person of the Trinity. Christians profess a Trinitarian understanding of God, who is one (monotheism) yet existing as three persons. The first person of the Trinity is the Creator, commonly referred to as Father; the second is the Redeemer, or Son (Jesus); the third person of the Trinity is the Sustainer or Holy Spirit. Christians recognize the historical Jesus as a human being, and they simultaneously affirm the eternal nature of the Christ as an integral dimension of the Godhead (Trinity). Christians claim that the first person of the Trinity, the Creator, is the God that is described and witnessed in the Hebrew Scriptures. The One God of Judaism is the God of Christianity, yet Christians believe that Christ and the Holy Spirit accompanied this God eternally and are revealed at times within the Hebrew Scriptures. In other words, unlike the beliefs explored regarding Judaism, Christians believe that the God of the Hebrew Scriptures is Trinitarian.

The incarnation is the conviction that the second person of the Trinity became flesh and was the man known as Jesus of Nazareth. Christians believe that there will be a second coming of Christ, and when this happens there will be the final judgment of all people and the full resurrection of all. The purpose of Jesus' incarnation was the redemption of humanity, reconciling our separation from God due to our sinfulness. This notion of God as one yet three is one of the most complex Christian beliefs, and in fact for many Christians is often described as a mystery of faith since words and symbols are unable to capture it. Similarly, the notion of Jesus as a historical human being who is simultaneously the eternal savior God is also difficult for Christians to fully describe, since Christianity teaches that Jesus' divinity did not interfere with his humanity and vice versa.

In addition to the Scriptures, the most basic and direct source for Christian beliefs is found in the creedal statements. The most well-known and significant is the Nicene Creed, dated 325. The name emerges from the Council of Nicaea where the creed was authored. Christians suffered heavy persecution under the Roman Empire in their first few centuries. This all changed in 312. Constantine, emperor of the Western segment of the Roman Empire, won a major battle after a dream that he interpreted to mean that the Christian God would lead him to victory, a victory that would initiate and cement his loyalty to the Christian God. As a result, Christianity eventually becomes the official religion of the Holy Roman Empire. In 325 Constantine convened the Council of Nicaea. This is the first time church leaders, once hidden and disconnected from each other under the cloud of persecution, met together to determine the authoritative Christian beliefs. The Nicene Creed is a product of this. At the core of the Nicene Creed is the testimony that Jesus is God incarnate and the affirmation of the Triune God. It is important to understand that prior to Nicaea there was a lot of diversity of thought surrounding whether Jesus was divine and/or fully human. At Nicaea, as reflected in the Creed, it was determined that while Christians believe in a monotheistic God, that God is triune, existing in three persons and that Jesus is one of those persons.

The Nicene Creed

I believe in One God, the Father almighty,
maker of heaven and earth,
of all things visible and invisible.

I believe in one Lord Jesus Christ,
the Only Begotten Son of God,
born of the Father before all ages.
God from God, Light from Light,
true God from true God,
begotten, not made, consubstantial with the Father;
through him all things were made.
For us men and for our salvation
he came down from heaven,
and by the Holy Spirit was incarnate of the Virgin Mary,
and became man.
For our sake he was crucified under Pontius Pilate,
he suffered death and was buried,
and rose again on the third day
in accordance with the Scriptures.
He ascended into heaven
and is seated at the right hand of the Father.
He will come again in glory
to judge the living and the dead
and his kingdom will have no end.

I believe in the Holy Spirit, the Lord, the giver of life,
who proceeds from the Father and the Son,
who with the Father and the Son is adored and glorified,
who has spoken through the prophets.

I believe in one, holy, catholic and apostolic Church.
I confess one Baptism for the forgiveness of sins
and I look forward to the resurrection of the dead
and the life of the world to come. Amen.

The Nicene Creed affirms belief in One God. However, it also indicates that for Christians Jesus is *of the same substance* (*homoousios*) with God the Father, begotten from God's substance. The determination that Jesus is of the same substance as God emerged from debates over the nature of Jesus that are a result of the lack of communication between Christian communities. There were various voices and theological interpretations in this debate, but key was Arius, a Christian priest who represented the belief that the Son is human and does not have the same status as the Father. Arius and his followers believed that Jesus was a special human being that was closer to God than any other human, but he was not God. Another priest named Athanasius argued, to the contrary, that in order to save us Christ had to be divine. Nicaea reconciled both, claiming that Jesus is both fully human and fully divine, creating a second person in the Godhead. Nicaea also affirmed that the Holy Spirit is the third person of the Trinity, God's Spirit proceeding from the Father and the Son. This last claim will become a point of tension that will lead to a division between Eastern and Western churches. The Western approach affirms Nicaea, while the Eastern approach claims that the Father begets the Son and the Father breathes Spirit. This creedal affirmation indicates the core beliefs that the majority of Christians have shared since the fourth century and continue to embrace today. However, the creeds provide us with a limited and often confusing picture of the totality of Christian faith. They are the core beliefs; however, how those beliefs are interpreted and expressed will vary throughout history and sociocultural location.

In addition to affirming that Jesus is both fully human and divine, the Nicene Creed also contains several fundamental teachings shared by all Christians. The Creed begins by affirming belief in the One God of Christianity who is the Creator. After affirming the divinity of Jesus, the Creed recounts Christ's descent here on earth and incarnation in a human body through the Virgin Mary's impregnation by the Holy Spirit. The Creed then describes Jesus' crucifixion at the hands of Pontius Pilate and his resurrection, and highlights the Holy Spirit and the unity of the Church. It concludes with the importance of baptism for the forgiveness of sins and the resurrection of the dead in the kingdom of God. In essence, in this Creed we have an outline of all the major beliefs that unite Christians.

To speak of Jesus as the Christ is to make a *theological* statement, a statement of belief. On one level, Jesus is the name of a first-century Jew who lived in the Holy Land two thousand years ago. He became a public figure in the last few years of his life, which ended tragically and violently around the age of thirty. These claims are based on *historical* understandings of this man, about whom we know very little today, in spite of the fact that his life and message transformed the very course of human history. In the past few decades there has been an explosion of books, both academic and popular, that seek to uncover the "true" nature and history of a first-century Jew named Jesus. Historical studies strive to uncover the human identity of Jesus. Claiming Jesus as the Christ, however, is to make a *theological* statement about the religious nature of Jesus' life and ministry. Jesus understood as the Christ casts him as the fulfillment of Jewish prophecy, the savior of humanity. He is the Messiah who is prophesied in the Hebrew Scriptures.

Due to his language of the kingdom of God and its presence in the here and now, it is possible that Jesus and his followers were seen as a political threat to the Romans. For Jesus, the kingdom of God was the good news of God's love and compassion. In addition, his fellowship with the outcasts of society created a powerful critique of existing structures of authority in Jewish and Roman communities. The perceived threat of his ministry led to a public crucifixion, and his followers claimed that three days after this event Jesus was raised from the dead. Belief in Jesus' resurrection cemented, for a certain portion of the Jewish community, his fulfillment of the Messianic promise for Jewish peoples. These believers are the earliest Christians. The Jewish roots of Christianity cannot be underestimated. Within the development of the doctrine of the Trinity is the key assumption that the God of the Hebrew Scriptures, Judaism, is the Christian God. One cannot separate the two. When one reads accounts of Jesus in the Gospel, he is often contextualized in light of his religion and its Scriptures. There is a reason why Christians read the Hebrew Scriptures (albeit calling them the Old Testament) in churches. This is due to the fact that for Christians both Testaments speak of the One God.

Fundamental to understanding the belief that Jesus is the savior of all people is the Christian teaching on original sin. The doctrine of original sin is central to Christian beliefs. This teaching is the basis of the belief in Christ's redemptive work: Jesus takes away our original sin: "we were reconciled to him through the death of his Son" (Romans 5.10). Original sin explains the origin of evil and the need for salvation and for the church as mediator of Christ's healing. Christian belief in original sin is grounded in the Genesis 2–3 account of Eve and Adam's transgression. Because they defied God and ate the forbidden fruit of the garden, sin becomes part of human nature. The state of humanity shifts and we are all born in a state of original sin. This leads to a tendency within us to be sinful, a tendency that can only be corrected through Christ's saving work. Ultimately, original sin argues that evil is a part of our world prior to our own personal choices and decisions

Within the Christian Gospels, several of Jesus' key teachings have been highlighted as expressing the core of Christian beliefs as revealed through him. Perhaps the most important is known as the two Great Commandments: "'Love the Lord Your God with all your heart and with all your soul and with all your mind.' This is the first and greatest commandment. And the second is like it: 'Love your neighbor as yourself'" (Matthew 22.37–39). In these two interrelated teachings love of God is intimately connected to love of neighbor. How we treat our fellow human being, these commandments teach, is a reflection of our relationship with the One God. Love of neighbor is not a new concept, as we saw in our discussion of Leviticus 19; however, in making this one of the two core teachings of his ministry, Jesus centralizes and connects love of God and neighbor as fundamental for Christian belief and identity.

While there are moments in the Gospels that depict Jesus giving direct teachings to his followers, many of Jesus' teachings are presented through symbolic parables, short stories with a moral message. Perhaps one of the most well-known parables is the parable of the Prodigal or Lost Son. In that parable, Jesus describes two sons that are given an inheritance by their father. One son takes the money and runs. He spends it frivolously. The older son stays at his father's side. When a famine hits the region the younger son decides to return home. He goes with the commitment of working for his father in order to earn his keep. Before he can get the words out his father sees him from a distance and immediately runs to embrace him. He orders a fine robe for his son and orders a feast. Upon hearing this, the older son is bitter, for he has remained beside his father and has never been treated so luxuriously. To that his father replies, "My son, you are always with me and everything I have is yours. But we had to celebrate and be glad, because this brother of yours was dead and is alive again; he was lost and is found" (Luke 15.31–32).

The story of the Prodigal or Lost Son is ultimately a story about God's love, forgiveness, and eternal offer of grace. The father in the story represents God, and the sons represent humanity. Even though the younger son spent all of his money and left his father's side, his father forgives him. In fact, his father not only forgives him, he rejoices in his return. This does not take away from the love he has for his older son who always remained with him. Nonetheless, the father in this parable is truly moved to have his son return asking for authentic forgiveness. We should also look to the older brother as part of the lesson as well. The older son does not understand his father's ability to forgive, reminding us that for humans, the greatness and giftedness of God's forgiveness is difficult for us to understand.

In addition to the Scriptures and creeds that inform Christian identity and beliefs, there are teachings that also govern how Christians live their lives in relationship with the Triune God. Given that there are a variety of denominations (or churches) within Christianity, there is a lot of variation within Christian teachings and rituals. In some churches, such as the Anglican Church and the Roman Catholic Church, ritual is extremely systematic and ordered. There is little room for any spontaneous religious expression within the order of ritual. On the other end of the spectrum are Pentecostal churches, where religious rituals are much more spontaneous and unstructured. Whether structured or not, Christian worship is always led by a religious leader who is called a priest or pastor. Another thread that unites all Christians is that Sunday is the Lord's Day and therefore the primary day of worship for Christians.

Holidays

There are numerous holidays and seasons that mark the liturgical life (worship and observances) of Christians across the globe. Perhaps the most popularly known and celebrated holiday (even outside of Christianity) is Christmas, where Christians observe the birth of Jesus Christ. The nativity scenes that are so popular across the globe emphasize Jesus' humble birth in a manger. While theologically this is not the most important holiday in Christianity, Christmas is the most popular. Advent is the period that marks the forty days before Jesus' birth, where Christians prepare for Jesus' arrival. The symbol that is most often associated with Advent is the Advent wreath, a circle with four candles, three purple and one pink, that are lit on the four Sundays prior to Christmas. Some Advent wreaths have a white candle in the middle that is lit on Christmas to symbolize Jesus' arrival. Epiphany is the January holiday where Christians celebrate the arrival of the three wise men (in Western churches) and the baptism of Jesus (in Eastern churches).

Easter is the most important holiday within Christianity, for it is here when Christians celebrate the resurrection of Jesus. His resurrection is connected to the Christian hope for the second coming of Christ and the resurrection of all of humanity in the kingdom of God. Lent is the forty-day period of repentance leading up to Easter and begins with Ash Wednesday, where some Christians receive a cross made of ashes on their foreheads to remember their own mortality and also begin this solemn time. Lent is a time of contemplation and self-denial where Christians reflect on the sacrifice and suffering of Jesus on the cross. Fasting is required for Catholics (and observed by other Christians) during Lent on Ash Wednesday and Good Friday. Good Friday is the Friday before Easter and marks the observance of Jesus' crucifixion on the cross. The Sunday before Good Friday, Palm Sunday, is the commemoration of Jesus' entry into Jerusalem prior to his arrest and crucifixion. Palm Sunday also begins Holy Week in Christianity, which culminates with Easter. In addition to Good Friday, Maundy Thursday is also a holy day, commemorating Jesus' Last Supper with his followers. The last central Christian holiday is Pentecost, which commemorates the Holy Spirit descending upon Jesus' followers forty days after Easter.

In light of this study, it would be remiss to avoid the fact that Good Friday, one of the holiest days on the Christian calendar and in some cultures (such as throughout Latin America) more commemorated than Easter, is a day that is plagued with a history of anti-Semitism. Sermons claiming "Jews killed Jesus" or were "Christ killers" laid the foundation for the false belief that caricatured the Jewish community as Jesus' greatest adversary and opponent. The role of the Romans, as the only group with the political power to crucify Jesus, was downplayed in light of this criminalization of the Jewish people as a whole. The Gospel of John is particularly complicit in this mindset, for it repeatedly characterizes the ringleaders behind Jesus' death as "the Jews." And while churches have shifted in their language in the modern era, for example the Roman Catholic Vatican II proclamation in *Nostra Aetate* that Jews are not responsible for Jesus' death, much work needs to be done to dismantle the anti-Semitic elements within the Christian religion.

The fourth century is the definitive era for the establishment of Christian Trinitarian monotheism. In addition, it is the first moment in the history of Christianity when the Church is able to gather as a whole and determine exactly what Christians believe about God, Jesus, and consequently the nature of humanity. This unity will be a short-lived moment in the history of this religion, for divisions and debate will come to characterize Christianity as a whole throughout the majority of its history. We have already alluded to one split within Christianity, the divide between Eastern and Western Christianity in the eleventh century. Western Christianity, the focus of this text, will find a similar division beginning in the sixteenth century with the Protestant Reformation, a Western European movement that sought to return Christianity to its biblical roots. Critical of the manner in which Roman Catholicism had infused Christianity with devotions to saints and Mary, the primacy of the priesthood, and the heavy non-biblical ritualization of Christianity, the Reformation emphasized the centrality of Jesus, believers' direct and individual relationship with God, and a sole emphasis on Scripture. Denominations such as the Lutheran, Methodist, and Presbyterian are direct descendants of this movement, which initiated the numerous expressions of Western

Christianity we encounter today. And yet in spite of the multiple interpretations of Jesus and God, what holds Christians together is the belief in his salvific work as the second person of the Trinity. This Trinitarian understanding of God and the belief that Jesus is God incarnate is what acutely distinguishes Christianity's monotheism from both Judaism and Islam.

Islam

The Scripture of Islam: The Qur'an

The Qur'an is the word of God, from God, without any human interference. It is in the Arabic language. The Qur'an was revealed to the prophet Muhammad to reaffirm the central notion of One God—the absolute unity of God. Although Muslims hold strongly and faithfully to the Scriptures associated with Judaism and Christianity, the Qur'an is understood to be the final, inimitable, and perfect text. Also unlike the Hebrew and Christian Scriptures, which are a collection of texts, the Qur'an is one book. This is important to note before looking at its general narrative. The Qur'an is firmly placing itself with the previous Scriptures but also making clear that it is more complete and

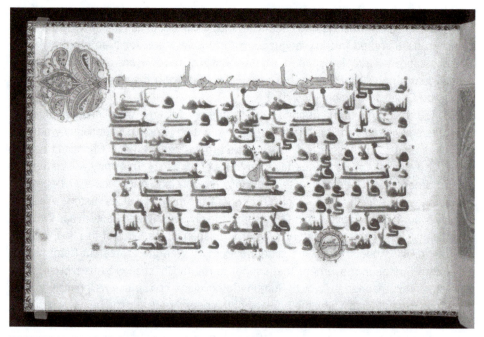

FIGURE 7 *Qur'an, final volume from a sixty-volume set, Spain or North Africa, undated, c. 800–1000. Codex, ink, colors and gold on parchment. Folio: 13.4 x 21.2 cm. Chester Beatty (CBL Is 1411, fol. 1v–2r), © The Trustees of the Chester Beatty Library, Dublin.*

lacks human interference. This sets it apart from the previously revealed Scripture and is a central and running theme in the Qur'an. We cannot separate the Qur'an from its context, so we must appreciate how this distinction helped Muhammad, the prophet or conveyor of this sacred text to people. The Qur'an is understood as guidance for faithful Muslims. It is a sign from God for the common man, the whole of humanity. The Qur'an was revealed between two cities, Mecca and Medina. Over a period of twenty-three years, split between the two cities, the Qur'an was revealed to the prophet Muhammad. It is said that the Meccan chapters of the Qur'an deal more with aspects of belief, and the Medinan chapters point more toward law and social interactions on earth. The Qur'an that one picks up today, whether in Arabic or in its numerous translations, is not set out in chronological order but features the longest chapter at the beginning and the shortest at the end.

The Qur'an's first command to the prophet Muhammad was "Read." To read and understand the Qur'an is to understand life on earth. This has been understood by Muslims to mean that reading and understanding the Qur'an is important. It is through the Qur'an that Muslims understand God in a more refined way. Muslims believe that the Qur'an was revealed at a fixed time in history, but its content is of value for all times. The Qur'an, in all its glory, is understood to be inimitable by Muslims—i.e., no other Scripture is as complete, perfect, and comparable to it. Muslims believe that God protects the Qur'an and will do so until the end of times. Its central theme is monotheism. The Qur'an offers a variety of stories and parables that affirm that there is only One God and all other gods are false. This mirrors the narrative described in the Hebrew Scriptures of the Jewish people struggling with monotheism and falling into belief in false gods. Belief in this One God helps all of creation to live better, but it is a constant struggle because human beings do not see God even though God sees them. Prophets play a role in highlighting this constant monotheistic reminder to creation. The Qur'an recounts the stories of biblical prophets, and they do not differ much at all from the Hebrew Bible. Some biblical figures are even mentioned more often in the Qur'an than in the New Testament (Moses, Jesus, and Mary). The Qur'an makes clear that Jesus is a prophet and cannot be understood as anything else, countering the Christian belief that Jesus is the Messiah, God incarnate, and the fulfillment of prophecy. Similar to the Hebrew prophets, the Qur'an presents stories as warnings to Muslims who do not obey and submit to God alone. It delineates punishments for infidelity and also rewards for righteousness. This theme of a God that punishes and rewards was first introduced in the Hebrew Scriptures.

When Muhammad began telling people about his revelation, they were astounded. The man Muhammad was understood to be illiterate, and the words that he was bringing to his contemporaries were sophisticated and articulate. Many of the monotheists at the time responded by saying that they were in effect Muslim before him, that they already believed in God. It was the additional belief he was proclaiming that he was to be understood as the seal of the prophets and the last messenger that they found hard to believe. The Qur'an does not actually tell Muhammad's story, although it does mention him. This reaffirms Muslims' belief that the Qur'an is centrally about God and that the prophets are merely messengers.

The Qur'an also offers loose parameters for ethics and morality. It is for this reason that the Qur'an is the first and most central source of Islamic law. Although not a legal text, it is said to contain all the information needed to uphold what is good and stay clear of evil. The Qur'an mentions the belief and practices that will help a Muslim live a full life in the belief of God. Across its 114 chapters, the Qur'an points Muslims toward their ultimate destination, which is beyond earth. Life after death is constantly presented in the Qur'an as a way of making Muslims aware of what is yet to come and that life is one big test. Muslims must uphold what is good and stay away from the evil that is instigated and inspired by Satan.

The Qur'anic narrative has also inspired the sciences, philosophy, poetry, and anything that pushes the Muslim mind toward intrigue and wonderment. The Qur'an states time and again that it is a thinking text. Thinking through the text is said to help Muslims with faith, reason, and logic. It also mentions that some may never be able to appreciate what the Qur'an is pushing them toward. There is no compulsion to God, but the Qur'an makes clear that those who do not accept and submit to God are in error.

The Qur'an also points Muslims toward the nature of the earth: God has created not just human beings but also everything that surrounds them. Human beings are advised that they have been created to obey and worship God but to also look after the earth, as custodians. The Qur'an mentions that the entire earth is a place to worship God and that Muslims should seek signs around them to what points toward God's bounty and beauty. Although the Qur'an mentions animals, it singles out the bee and mentions that the insect was also instructed to obey and submit to God. Reflection and care for the environment is essential for Muslim faith and practice.

The Qur'an continues to inspire Muslims in strengthening their faith in God. It roots belief to a Scripture that requires simple acts of reading to complex acts of thinking and critiquing. The way in which Muslims connect to the Qur'an differs from person to person, but its essential position in all their lives cannot be underestimated.

Islam: An Overview

Around a quarter of the world's population is Muslim. How one understands this and the reasons for this differ. Is this due to Muslims having large families or the rise in high numbers of converts to Islam globally? There is no clear answer to this but that the number of Muslims is on the rise. Islam is a religious tradition associated deeply and centrally with Allah (God) and continues an understanding of One God rooted in what was set in motion by Judaism and Christianity. Islam is a world religion that originated in Arabia in the seventh century, by which time the notion of One God was prevalent and widespread. This was a desert land where trade and commerce were thriving between regions.

The word *Islam* is understood in many different ways, but its association with God is paramount. The religion of Islam is a faithful way of life in which submission is peacefully offered in belief and practice to the One unseen God. This binds it to all previous forms of biblical monotheism that connects to the idea of God: namely, Judaism and Christianity. Islam adds a new layer of monotheism to what was already discussed and practiced in pre-Islamic Arabia. Allah (Arabic for "God") was already a part of the culture and society but Muhammad, the last prophet of Islam, brought forward a new form of monotheism. God is at the core of this belief system. Islam's distinction comes from its central commitment only to God. God is understood as an absolute oneness. Nothing is born from God, nor is God born. Muslims use the term *jahiliyya*—ignorance or barbarism—to distinguish Islam from those who do not believe in God. This distinction was very important during the emergence of Islam.

The simplicity of belief in One God is all the more complex because Judaism, Christianity, and Islam have different paths, narratives, traditions, and practices with respect to that One God. The term *hanif* is often used in Islamic traditions to identify pre-Islamic monotheists who were distinct from Jewish and Christian traditions. Abraham would be categorized as a true *hanif* (monotheist). Islam emerged from a society that did value and worship a God, but the outworkings of that idea of One God manifested itself through imagery and, as many Muslims would say, idol worship. The inhabitants of pre-Islamic Arabia could be classified as a form of animistic monotheism— there was belief in God but it was understood and practiced by giving spiritual significance to idols. Consider the Islamic practice of circumambulating the Ka'ba, a cubic structure in the city of Mecca. It is stated in the Qur'an (3:96) that the first place of worship appointed for humankind was in Mecca at that very spot. The god Hubal is said to have had connections to the Ka'ba, and hence there are a number of Islamic traditions which reclaim this practice, which predated Islam, from idol worship and associate it with the One true God. Apart from pagan practices and worship, Judaism and Christianity were very much a part of pre-Islamic culture and society. This is recorded from around the sixth century onward. There were also other forms of monotheism, such as Zoroastrianism. Muslims would evaluate all of these with the conclusion and confirmation of the One God, Allah.

In Islamic thought, human beings understand God through the signs and messages that God provides. These become more distinguished through those individuals that God chooses as prophets. Muslims believe that the first prophet was Adam, and so the origins of Islam were commanded as soon as God created Adam and Eve. Many prophets in Islam are also present in Jewish and Christian Scriptures. Jesus is considered a prophet within Islam. However, Islam as we know it is clearly defined with its last prophet, Muhammad, in the sixth century.

Islamic Convictions

It is important to note at the outset that Islam is not a monolith. Although Muslims globally all connect through the belief in One God, they differ in how they interpret those beliefs and practices. Every attempt will be made to be as inclusive as possible of the various traditions and denominations; the focus of this introduction will remain on attempting to highlight the diversity of Islamic beliefs and practices.

A famous prophetic tradition is found in two of the key books detailing belief and practice in Sunni Islam, the religion's largest denomination. It is said that one day while the Prophet Muhammad was sitting next to his companions, a man came whose clothes were extremely white and his hair was extremely black. There was no sign of travel on him, but no one knew who he was. When he arrived, he rested his knees upon the Prophet's knees and placed his two hands upon his thighs. He then asked the Prophet a series of questions. First of all, "What is faith?" The Prophet answered, "Faith is to believe in Allah, his angels, his books, his messengers, and the last day, and that you affirm the decree, the good of it and bad of it." At this the man said, "You have spoken the truth, now tell me about Islam." The Prophet then responded, "To worship Allah alone and none else, to offer prayers, to pay the compulsory charity, and to observe the fast during the month of fasting." The man then said, "You have spoken the truth. And what is Ihsan?" The Prophet then said, "It is to worship God as if he sees you even though you do not see him." The man then asked, "When will be the Hour?" The Prophet responded, "The answerer has no better knowledge than the questioner but I will tell you of its signs—when a slave lady gives birth to her master and when the shepherds of black camels start boasting and competing in the construction of higher buildings. And the hour is one of five things which no one knows except Allah." The Prophet is then said to have recited Qur'an 31:34: "Indeed, Allah [alone] has knowledge of the Hour and sends down the rain and knows what is in the wombs. And no soul perceives what it will earn tomorrow, and no soul perceives in what land it will die. Indeed, Allah is Knowing and Acquainted." Once the man had departed, the Prophet's companions asked who the man was, and he responded, "That was Gabriel; he came to teach you your religion."

Within Islam, anyone who believes in God and submits to God is called a Muslim. The word *Islam* is often described as "peace," as Muslims believe that they are wholly at peace and with peace through belief in the One God and submitting only to that One God. Muslims believe that God is both merciful and kind. God is at the center of the universes he created be it the earth, moon, sun, heaven and hell. "There is no god but God" is an important testimony that Muslims both believe in and practice. Every aspect and concept that Muslims believe in must be associated with their submission to the One God and accepting God's oneness, or *tawhid* (literally meaning "one"). One of the most powerful invocations that Muslims recite often is "Allahu Akbar"—God is great. In modern times this has become associated with terrorists who have invoked this before attacking. The majority of Muslims today have made attempts to reinvigorate this statement by reassociating it with its beautiful meaning based on what God has blessed them with. This thankfulness is often presented in prayers. Muslims know about God through God, and this comes from the Qur'an (the literal word of God). God creates but is not created. There is no figurative imagery of God, but there are many different ways of understanding God in Islam. These are found in the "99 names of Allah" which are recited by Muslims to remember God. The names of God are often decorated around the home and even included in special amulets to ward off evil. This differs from Muslim to Muslim. God created human beings and commanded them to submit only to God. Through this submission, a believer should discern good and evil. The link between God, humanity, and good actions is an important one in Islam. This means that believing in God requires an action and that action must be good because God loves good actions. It said that God's mercy overrides his wrath. The literal word of God—the Qur'an—begins each chapter, except chapter nine, with the statement "In the name of God, the most merciful, the most kind." The distinction of God above and beyond everything else that is created is affirmed in the Qur'an:

> They regard the jinn as God's equal, though He himself created them, and in their ignorance ascribe to him sons and daughters. Glory to Him! Exalted be He about their imputations! He is the Creator of the heavens and the earth. How should He have a son when He had no consort? He created all things and has knowledge of all things. Such is God, your Lord. There is no god but Him. He is the Guardian of all things. No mortal eyes can see Him, though he sees all eyes. He is benevolent and all-knowing.
>
> Q6:100–103

Angels (*malak*, pl. *mala'ikah*) are God's most obedient creation. They were created before human beings and serve the purpose of bringing God to other forms of creation, especially human beings. God created angels for the same purpose as all of creation—to remember and submit only to Him. But angels play a role different than human beings. There are different angels for different actions and activities. They are said to be made from light, but there are traditions that attest to some angels being made of fire. Some commentators have said that this should not be confusing because fire and light are from a similar nature. Iblis (Satan) falls within the same realm. Jinn, literally meaning "hidden" or "concealed," are another form of supernatural creations that are invisible. Jinn have a similar ultimate role to all creation—to submit only to God. Islamic theology presents quite complicated understandings of Jinn and they are often compared to pre-Islamic understandings of spirits and deities. They have been depicted in colorful ways in Islamic art.

Muslims believe that God revealed himself in many ways—often in books that were revealed to human beings through messengers. The Qur'an is believed to be the central text from God. Muslims also believe in the Tawrat (Torah), which was revealed to the prophet Moses; the Zabur (Psalms of David); and the Injil (Gospel of Jesus). Although these texts still hold signs which show the existence and glory of God, they are deemed unreliable because they are understood to be not as perfected as the Qur'an in terms of their focus on monotheism. The Qur'an gives the example of Jesus to highlight this further:

> And [beware the Day] when Allah will say, "O Jesus, Son of Mary, did you say to the people, 'Take me and my mother as deities besides Allah?' He will say, 'Exalted are

You! It was not for me to say that to which I have no right. If I had said it, You would have known it. You know what is within myself, and I do not know what is within Yourself. Indeed, it is You who is Knower of the unseen. I said not to them except what You commanded me—to worship Allah, my Lord and your Lord. And I was a witness over them as long as I was among them; but when You took me up, You were the Observer over them, and You are, over all things, Witness."

Q5:116–117

Prophets and messengers were used to bring the message of the existence of God to humankind. These were extraordinary human beings who were selected and elected by God. Some of these prophets were given a revealed text, and some were told to speak from a text which was revealed to the prophet before them. Muslims know about these prophets from the Qur'an. Between the first prophet of Islam, Adam, and the last, Muhammad, are a number of prophets, and they are similar to biblical prophets. As Islam was adding a new layer to monotheism yet making itself distinct, the Qur'an makes very clear that all prophets and messengers were human beings, including Jesus.

Discussions continue on the gender of prophets. Can only men be prophets? This question has plagued Islamic theological thought for a very long time. The twenty-five prophets who are extracted from the Qur'an are all male. However, is gender a prerequisite for being elected as a prophet or messenger, given that the Prophet is merely a vehicle to God? The eleventh-century Andalusian scholar Ibn Hazm is known to be one of the key Islamic commentators to speak on the subject of gendering the prophets, and the debate on women prophets in Islam has carried on into the contemporary world. If his theory is to be seriously considered, then Eve and Mary are also prophets because they receive communication from God and, in their own way, make calls toward the oneness of God. These are all the more emboldened questions and debates that Muslims find themselves in today as they make sense not just of female prophets but also of the position of women and other marginalized communities.

Muslims believe that life is a test and that on the great day of judgment (*yaum al-din*, the day of faith/reckoning) everyone will have to answer for their actions. Human beings are tested in good deeds and virtue. Belief in God is said to be not enough but requires acts of faith that uphold good in society and staying away from evil and wrong doing. When judgment is passed, the gates of heaven (*jannat*) and hell (*jahannum*) will be opened for those who have done good and evil. These good acts will lead a Muslim to enter paradise, and those who have carried out evil acts will enter hell. These out of this world locations are understood literally, and their depictions are covered in various chapters of the Qur'an. The angel *Israfil* will blow a terrifying trumpet to herald the end of times, and this will wake everyone, including those in their graves. Muslims continually remember the end of time in order to remind themselves to do good deeds on the earth. There is an Islamic tradition that says the world in which Muslims live is like a droplet in the ocean: the water that drops from the finger is this world, and the rest of the ocean is what is yet to come. Muslims also believe that everything that happens during their lives has been ordained by God. This fits with the idea that God is aware of everything and is the first and last authority on all matters. This test of faith is captured in the following Qur'anic passage: "Had it been God's will, he could have made them all of one religion. But God brings whom He will into His mercy; the wrongdoers have none to befriend or help them. Have they set up other guardians beside Him? Surely God alone is the Guardian. He resurrects the dead and has the power over all things. Whatever the subjects of your disputes, the final word belongs to God. Such is God, my Lord. In Him I have put my trust, and to him I turn in repentance . . . He has ordained for you the faith which he enjoined on Noah, and which we have revealed to you. We enjoined this faith on Abraham, Moses and Jesus, saying, 'Observe the faith and do not divide yourselves into factions.' But hard for the pagans is that to which you call them. God chooses for it whom He will, and guides to it those that repent" (Q42:8–10).

Basic Practices and Worship

Islam emphasizes that practice through rituals is important to strengthen one's relationship with God. Ritual is also an opportunity for Muslims to thank God and to physically condition and discipline themselves. Ritual acts help Muslims do good and ward off evil.

Shahada, the first pillar of Islam, is the testimony that every Muslim must make. It reads, "There is no god but God and Muhammad is the last and final messenger." By reciting this and believing in it, one becomes a Muslim. There is an emphasis on acting on the pillars so this statement must motivate toward good actions for a Muslim. It is important to note that the first article of faith is God and the first ritual pillar is also God. Belief in God must bring together the mind and body in action. The first part of the testimony was not difficult to appreciate by Jews and Christians at the time of Muhammad, but belief in the Prophet being part of faith added a new and different layer to monotheism and to the understanding of God.

Salat (prayer) is said to be performed by everything that God creates in order to show appreciation for all the blessings in their lives. As stated in the Qur'an, "Believers, bow down, prostrate yourself, worship your Lord, and do good so that you may succeed" (Q22:77). The Qur'an talks about prayer in various ways, but it was formalized through the actions of Muhammad. This is ritually done by standing, prostrating, and bowing in the direction of God, symbolized by the Ka'ba in Mecca, which is in current-day Saudi Arabia. The first direction of prayer was the al-Aqsa Mosque in Jerusalem. There is an Islamic tradition saying that the first place of worship to be created on earth was in Mecca and the second was in Jerusalem. The Qur'an mentions a miraculous night journey that Muhammad undertakes to the "furthest mosque." Muslim commentators have said that this is the al-Aqsa Mosque in Jerusalem. Muhammad flies there on the Buraq, an animal-like winged creature that he leaves at the al-Buraq wall (the Western Wall). It is here where Muhammad leads all the previous prophets in prayer. He then travels up the various levels of heaven until he reaches the point where he has a conversation with God about prayer. The initial stipulation is fifty prayers, but as he is returning with this command he meets Moses, who tells him that this is far too many. Eventually Muhammad gets the prayers reduced to five and tells Moses that he is too embarrassed to ask for a reduction.

Although the Qur'an makes clear that prayer is obligatory, it does not detail the method, and this has resulted in the different actions of prayers in different denominations of Islam. Essentially it is a practice that affirms the relationship between human beings and God. Sunni Muslims pray five times a day: daybreak (*fajr*), noon (*zuhr*), mid-afternoon (*asr*), sunset (*maghrib*), and evening (*isha*). Muslims will generally pray in a mosque and are called to prayers by a *muezzin*, who makes the call (*adhan*) from within the mosque. Ritual purification is important. An Islamic tradition holds that purity is half of a Muslim's faith. Muslims should be ritually pure in order to pray to God. Muslims pray at any clean space but often use prayer mats; in mosques, they typically pray on carpets arranged in rows. Only if necessary because of illness will a Muslim pray while seated. Friday prayers are deemed obligatory for Muslims and should be prayed in a mosque. Generally mosques today are segregated spaces, with men and women praying separately. Men are also the imams (prayer leaders). However, today there is a growing number of inclusive mosque spaces emerging throughout the world that are also LGBTQ friendly; more on this later. It is a time for the community to gather together.

Zakat is mandatory almsgiving and therefore more of a tax than charity. In various parts of the Qur'an it states that prayer is worthless if a Muslim is not helping the needy (see Q3:92). The Qur'an outlines who should receive the money: "Zakah expenditures are only for the poor and for the needy and for those employed to collect [zakah] and for bringing hearts together [for Islam] and for freeing captives [or slaves] and for those in debt and for the cause of Allah and for the [stranded] traveler—an obligation [imposed] by Allah. And Allah is Knowing and Wise" (Q9:60). The percentage given then differs within different denominations. Apart from the mandatory tax, Muslims are also expected to give voluntarily, which is often called *sadaqa*. *Waqf* (the charitable endowment of building, plot of land, or other assets) is also an Islamic form of giving.

Sawm is the period of fasting in the Muslim month of Ramadhan. It is the ninth month of the lunar calendar, and Muslims fast from sunrise until sunset. This means no food or drink during daylight hours. Muslims are also prohibited from any sexual activity during this time. The Qur'an states, "O you who believe, fasting has been prescribed for you just as it was prescribed for those before you so that you may attain God consciousness" (Q2:183). It is therefore a time to reflect and concentrate on God's blessings and grace. Menstruating women, those bleeding after childbirth, unsound minds, and intoxication nullify the fast. During the month of fasting, extra prayers are taken—usually in the mosque. Special evening prayers (*tarawih*) in congregation allow Muslims to recite sections of the Qur'an. This is why some Qur'ans are in thirty parts: so that one part can be recited every night during the month of Ramadhan.

The month of Ramadhan [is that] in which was revealed the Qur'an, a guidance for the people and clear proofs of guidance and criterion. So whoever sights [the new moon of] the month, let him fast it; and whoever is ill or on a journey—then an equal number of other days. Allah intends for you ease and does not intend for you hardship and [wants] for you to complete the period and to glorify Allah for that [to] which He has guided you; and perhaps you will be grateful.

Q2:185

Muslims seek the "night of power," *Laylat al-Qadr*, in the last ten days of Ramadhan with extra prayers and steadfastness to God. The actual night is a mystery with Muslims expected to seek it as an act of faith. Ramadhan ends with the great feast, the breaking of the fast, *Id al-Fitr*. It is a time for Muslims to congregate for special prayers, offer extra contributions of charity and exchange gifts.

Hajj is the ultimate pilgrimage that Muslims globally take part in. It takes place in the first part of the last month of the Islamic calendar, *Dhu'l Hijja*. It lasts around seven days and is centered around the Ka'ba. There are a number of ritual acts that Muslims take part in and each one of these is intended to recenter God in faith and practice. As is stated in the Qur'an, "Follow the religion of Abraham, the pure monotheist (*hanif*); he was not one of the idolaters. The first house of worship established for the people was at Mecca, full of blessings and guidance for all peoples . . . pilgrimage (*Hajj*) thereto is a duty the people owe to God—those who can afford the journey" (Q3:95–97). Mecca was a sacred precinct before Islam, too.

Muslims do a number of important rituals during *Hajj*—circumambulating of the *Ka'ba* (the sacred mosque that originates with Abraham), running between the hills of *Safa* and *Marwa* following in the footsteps of Hagar (*Hajar*) in her search for water for baby Ishmael (*Isma'il*), the stoning of the three pillars which symbolize the devil's attempt to tempt Abraham to disobey God in sacrificing his son and finally standing at the hill of *Arafat*, the site where the prophet Muhammad preached his final sermon. The *Hajj* ends with another major feast known as *Id al-Adha*. It commemorates the sacrifice of Abraham of his son Ishmael (Isaac in Jewish and Christian narratives). It is a time when financially able Muslims all over the world will sacrifice animals and distribute the meat to the poor, sacrifice being symbolic of complete submission to God's mercy.

The simple idea of one true God to whom one should submit has always been open to multiple manifestations of that belief. Denominational divisions occurred after the death of the prophet Muhammad. During Muhammad's time, authority lay with him, but after his death the Muslims found themselves asking questions about the way forward. They were united in their belief in God but disagreed on issues of authority. Some argued that a caliph should be elected, and others wanted a caliph to emerge from the prophet's bloodline. This would mean that Ali, the prophet's cousin and son-in-law, would succeed, but that did not happen. The first caliph elected was Abu Bakr (632–634), the second was Umar (634–644), then Uthman (644–656) and Ali (656–661). It must be noted that these were both political and religious leaders, making schism and parties inevitable. The religious ramifications were to be codified in what is now understood as the Shi'a and Sunni divide. The Shi'a got their name from their allegiance to Ali and being called the Shi'a Ali, or the party of Ali.

The differences in ritual practices between Sunni and Shi'a are sharply contrasted when it comes to the concept of intercession. Sunnis tend not to believe in notions of intercession, although this is complicated in some practices; in Shi'a practices this is quite integral, with Ali and other imams understood to hold divine inspiration. The memory and mourning of *Karbala*, where the grandson of the prophet Muhammad, Husayn, was martyred, is an annual pilgrimage that draws attendance from millions of Shi'a, who take part in ritual practices including street processions, sometimes self-flagellation, and also passion plays (*ta'ziya*).

These denominational differences have then given shape to many different rituals that some Muslims perform and some do not. One of these is the *mawlid*, which is a celebration of the birth of the prophet Muhammad in the third month of the Islamic calendar, Rabi' al-Awwal. Those who disagree with its celebration explain that it was an innovation to the faith and instead choose to concentrate only on God. Other practices include pilgrimages to the shrines of accepted saints, often termed as *wali*. A *wali*, friend of God, would be a person (there is no specific gender restriction) who would be seen as exceptional in terms of submission to God. In India and Pakistan there are mystical saints whose graves have become places of veneration. Followers of these saints will visit the graves and will often make special prayers, place flowers on their graves, and on occasion take part in colorful dance rituals. Again, there are some who disagree with such practices because they believe they take the focus away from God.

Some Muslims will also take part in *Tasbih* (to repeat), which entails uttering the praises and glorification of God in short sentences. This is sometimes performed with the assistance of prayer beads. Some Muslims may recite *SubhanAllah* (glory to God), *AlHumdullilah* (praise be to God) and *Allahu Akbar* (God is great) thirty-three times each.

Study Questions: Overview of Religions

What is the role of commandments in Judaism?
How does Torah (Written and Oral) create "virtual reality" in Judaism?
What happened in the Council of Nicaea?
How do Christians believe that God is a Trinity yet One God?
What are the central Islamic convictions outlined in the chapter?
Outline the arguments on women prophets in Islam and their implications
for understanding Islamic convictions.

3

Scripture

The institution of written Scripture as a foundational source of revelation and religious authority—and perhaps authenticity as well—is a defining trait of the monotheistic tradition. This chapter reviews how Scripture is used in the three traditions and some of the major ways the religious interpretation of Scripture maintains its relevance.

Judaism

The idea that God is known through written words is fundamental to Judaism. The *Tanakh* recounts that God's initial commandments are engraved in stone tablets and placed in the Ark of the Covenant. Moses writes God's commandments in a book of the Torah (Deuteronomy 31.24–26) and instructs the Israelite priests to place it next to the Ark of the Covenant. King Josiah reads from "the Book of the Covenant," perhaps a version of Deuteronomy (2 Kings 23.2). Ezra reads the book of the Torah of Moses (Nehemiah 8.1) in Jerusalem.

The Difference the Torah Made

The Torah addressed the challenge of the Temple's destruction, the exile, and the loss of Israel's religion of covenant and cult. It fused the ethical and ritual teachings of prophets and priests into a narrative of the One God's ongoing relationship with the people of Israel. Through the Torah, the Israelites could relate to their monotheistic heritage of covenant and cult anywhere by hearing it, reading about it, thinking about it, and talking about it with one another. In the Torah, the values, practices, and dynamics of Israel's religion become objects of thought, reflection, and imagination. And this kept them alive and pertinent. Over time, the Torah shifted the focus of religious observance from the institution to the individual and the community. Literacy supplemented and effectively replaced lineage as a primary justification of authority. The Torah was what evolutionists might call an emergent phenomenon. It created a religion of attitudes and behaviors that shaped a collective identity.

The importance of biblical books, and of the Torah in particular, increased over time, and hearing and studying the Torah began to become basic elements of Jewish religious practice outside the Temple. Professor Lee Levine observes that in the third century BCE there was communal liturgical Torah-reading and that in the first century CE the Torah scroll was the "holiest object in Judaism outside the Temple and its appurtenances." He also notes that Judaism's text-centered religious practice was unique in the ancient Mediterranean.

The Torah was translated into Greek in the third century BCE, and translations of other biblical books followed later. The Dead Sea Scrolls, which date from the third century BCE to the first century CE, include all the books of the *Tanakh* except the book of Esther. Aramaic translations (*targum*) of the Torah appeared in the first century CE. Non-Jews in antiquity recognized the special character of the Torah scroll. The Jewish historian Flavius Josephus (*ca.* 37–100 CE) recounts an incident in which a Roman soldier burned a Torah scroll and was then ordered beheaded by the procurator Cumanus because of the uproar the act caused. He also reports that the Roman army displayed a Torah in its victory procession after the destruction of the Second Temple. The Christian Church Father John Chrysostom (349–407 CE) criticized his congregants for thinking that synagogues were holy places because they contained Torah scrolls.

The synagogue was Judaism's institutional home and became the prototype of Christianity's church and Islam's mosque. The synagogues of late antiquity contained increasingly elaborate and ornate shrines for the Torah scrolls, and synagogue art drew on Temple symbolism. The focus of prayer towards the Torah and the holy city of Jerusalem links text to land and Temple. As the sense of the Torah's sanctity grew, the synagogue was often called a "small Temple."

The *Sefer Torah* as a Sacred Artifact

Although the books of the Torah initially were preserved in separate scrolls, Prof. David Stern shows that in the rabbinic period they were to be bound in a single scroll, the *Sefer Torah*. Judaism ascribes a sacred status to the *Sefer Torah*, and the scroll's production and treatment decisively demonstrate its uniqueness.

A trained scribe (*sofer*) must write the *Sefer Torah* on specially prepared parchment marked with lines and in a particular Hebrew script. The text must be identical to that of all other Torah scrolls. Worshippers rise in the presence of the *Sefer Torah*. People may not touch the scroll's parchment, including its blank margins, with bare hands, or put any other scroll on top of it. Those reciting the Torah in worship use a pointer called a *yad* ("hand") to keep their place in the text. When the scroll is not in use, *Ashkenazim* cover it with a decorated cloth mantle; *Sephardim* encase it in a wooden cylinder; and both adorn its staves with metal coverings or a crown. Finally, the Torah scroll used in worship must be written without vowels or punctuation. We will examine this trait below.

Torah passages written on pieces of parchment as they would be in a Torah scroll serve purposes other than reading. *Tefillin*, small leather boxes that people—principally Orthodox Jewish males—wear on the forehead and arm during morning prayers, contain passages from the *Shema'* (Deuteronomy 6.4–9; 11.13–21; Exodus 13.1–10,

FIGURE 8 *The* Sefer Torah *and the* yad *used to keep place during the recitation of the text,* © Sean Gallup / Staff, Getty Images.

11–16) that command one to bind God's words as "symbols on your hands" and "on your foreheads." Two of these passages (Deuteronomy 6.4–9, 11.13–21) are placed in the *mezuzah*, an amulet that people affix to the door lintels of their homes to fulfill the commandments to "write" God's words "on the doorframes of your houses." Some people wear a *mezuzah* on a chain around their necks.

Rabbinic teaching asserts that the possession of the *Sefer Torah* is distinctive to the Jewish people and explains God's persisting commitment. Rabbinic Judaism held that one should violate the Sabbath to save the *Sefer Torah* and its wrappings from fire. Because of the Torah's sanctity, even a damaged, worn, or unfit scroll must be buried.

All these practices and teachings mark the *Sefer Torah* as materially sacred; its use in Judaic worship makes that status concrete.

The Torah Scroll in Jewish Worship

In worship, the Torah is recited—with memorized cantillation—on holidays, on Mondays and Thursdays in the morning liturgy, and twice on the Sabbath, fast days, and *Yom Kippur*. The text is divided into portions, and the entire Torah is read in sequence. On weekdays, the portion is divided into three recitations. On most holidays there are five recitations, and on Sabbaths there are seven. Some congregations complete the reading in a calendar year; others divide the portions from each book into thirds and complete the entire reading over three years. When they reach the last portion, in the book of Deuteronomy, congregations celebrate *Simchat Torah*, which entails dancing with Torah scrolls in the synagogue.

When the *Sefer Torah* is taken from the Ark/*Heikhal*, the congregation rises and recites a verse from Isaiah (2.3) that says that Torah shall go out from Zion "and the word of the LORD from Jerusalem" and thanks God for giving the Torah to the Jewish people. The *Sefer Torah* is then carried through the congregation, and congregants touch it with, and then kiss, their prayer books or prayer shawls. Members of the congregation are called up ('*aliyah*) to the podium, and before and after each recitation they recite blessings that thank God for the Torah and the gift of eternal life. Primarily in Orthodox communities, a congregant who knows himself to be a descendant of the Israelite priests is honored with the first '*aliyah*; a descendant of the tribe of Levi (the tribe that assisted the priests in the Temple service) is called second; and a member of the rest of the congregation is called third and for the remainder of the reading's sections. Reform, Reconstructionist, and some Conservative congregations do not necessarily follow this practice; most non-Orthodox synagogues include women in all aspects of the Torah recitation and invite couples to participate in the Torah reading.

In *Ashkenazi* synagogues, the Torah reading concludes with the ritual of *hagbah* ("lifting up"), in which—echoing Ezra and perhaps Sinai itself as well—a congregant raises the open Torah scroll so the congregation can see at least three columns of text. The community then recites in unison a combination of Deuteronomy 4.44 and some words from Numbers 4.37, affirming that "this is the Torah," which the Lord commanded Moses to place before the Israelites. *Sephardi* congregations perform *hagbah* at the beginning of the Torah reading and recite only Deuteronomy 4.44. Next comes the ritual of *gelilah* ("rolling up"), in which a congregant closes the Torah scroll and replaces its wrappings, breastplate, ornaments, or crown.

On Sabbaths and holidays the recitation of the Torah portion is followed by what is known as the *Haftarah* ("conclusion"), typically a selection from the Prophets or from the *Tanakh's* historical books. The *Haftarah* is read from a printed text rather than a scroll and relates to some aspect of the Torah reading of the day or to the theme of the holiday on which it is read. Like the Torah reading, the *Haftarah* is preceded and followed by blessings; these thank God for the gift of prophetic teachings. The blessings recited after the reading of the *Haftarah* ask God to "have mercy on Zion" and invoke messianic themes.

After the recitation of the *Haftarah*, the scroll is returned to the Ark, and just before the Ark is closed the congregation recites the words of Proverbs 3.18 and 17, which describe the Torah as the "tree of life" and affirm its ability to bring happiness, pleasantness, and peace to its adherents. This is followed by Lamentations 5.21, which evokes the theme of the people's return to God. The division of the Torah into portions and the determination of the content of the *Haftarot* were set by rabbinic authorities, and there is some variation between and among different communities.

In addition to the portions from the Torah and *Haftarah*, five other books fom the Tanakh are recited on particular holidays. All congregations recite the book of Esther on Purim and the book of Lamentations on *Tisha b'Av*. Many communities recite the book

FIGURE 9 Hagbah: *displaying the* Sefer Torah *to the congregation,* © *Byron Maldonado.*

of *Qohelet* (Ecclesiastes) on the Sabbath that falls during *Sukkot*, the Song of Songs on the Sabbath that falls during Passover, and the book of Ruth in the morning service on *Shavu'ot*.

The blessings and verses that surround the Torah and *Haftarah* recitations link Scripture to the land of Israel and Jerusalem. The Torah revealed at Sinai goes forth from Jerusalem. These examples from the liturgy illustrate how worship in Judaism evokes the ideas of One God, God's covenant with and revelation to Israel, and the role of the Torah in binding God and the Jewish people to one another.

Giving Voice to the Torah

We noted above that the *Sefer Torah* used in worship must be written without vowels. While this may sound strange, it helps to remember that Semitic languages, which include Hebrew, have consonantal alphabets. Vowels in Hebrew (and in Arabic as well) are graphic symbols—dots and dashes—that emerged as a written system after the consonantal structure was set. In texts other than the Torah scroll, vowels, when used, are marked above, below, or beside the consonants. Thus, in this linguistic system, because different vowels can be applied to the same consonants, a set of consonants can yield different meanings. To get a sense of how this works, imagine that the English alphabet contained only consonants, and consider the following:

th ld ws lvl nd strng

This set of consonants could produce at least the three following meanings, depending on the vowels and punctuation:

The lad was lively and strong.
Thy lady, wise, lovely, and strange.
The load was level and stringy.

This example illustrates both how the meaning of the text depends on the vowels and punctuation and how the context of the reading indicates the correct vowels to use.

To declaim the Torah in worship and give the Torah its voice, the reciter must supply the absent vowel markers to transform the consonants into words. Thus, one must know the text, its proper vocalization, and also the rabbinic tradition of *qere'* ("what is recited") and *ketiv* ("what is written"), in which some words of the Torah are spoken differently from their written consonants. To recite the Torah also requires knowledge of how to break the lines of writing into verses, since the scroll is not punctuated; when to apply accents, stresses, and pauses; and the appropriate melody in which the scroll is chanted.

Between the sixth and tenth centuries, groups known as the Masoretes (which derives from the term *Masorah*, "tradition"), standardized the Torah's text and its cantillation. Because the Torah-writing is both sacred and voiceless, reciting it depends on knowledge of the Masoretic text. The ability to recite the Torah is the mark of religious maturity and responsibility in Judaism and is celebrated in the *Bar/Bat Mitzvah* ceremony. Rabbinic texts claim that the rules for the production and use of the *Sefer Torah* were revealed to Moses at Sinai as part of the Oral Torah.

The ritualized recitation of the Torah in Jewish worship concretely illustrates the fundamental dynamic of Judaism: the integration of the Oral and Written Torahs. In Judaism, Torah cannot come from the text alone. To convey and discover God's teaching—to evoke Torah in the broadest sense—text and tradition require one another. The fusion of the Written Torah and the Oral Torah produces God's revelation.

Torah as Instruction: The Many Lives of Torah

The rituals described above demonstrate the sanctity of the *Sefer Torah*. Everything about it—how it is produced and how it is recited—is exceptional. By declaring

Scripture sacred, Judaism endows it with an absolute and unassailable status. This has two consequences.

First, as a holy object, the Torah in both form and substance is pure, incomparable, inimitable, and autonomous. In this sense, the Torah is in itself what it describes in its text, a permanent, stable, but portable point of contact between God and the Jewish people—a textual Tabernacle or Holy of Holies. The Torah's sanctity is evident in the fact that worshippers rise whenever the Ark/*Heikhal* is open and whenever the Torah scroll itself is being held or carried. During the concluding service of *Yom Kippur*, it is customary to leave the Ark/*Heikhal* open, and in some congregations worshippers approach the Torah scrolls to offer personal prayers for repentance and forgiveness.

Second, Scripture's sacred status means that the text itself is immutable, not subject to change, and thus uniquely dense with meaning. The perspective of the Oral Torah is that nothing about the *Tanakh*—not its letters, its words, its arrangement of verses, for instance—can be irrelevant or pointless. Everything about it is consequential. By showing how the *Tanakh* can be read to uncover layers of significance, the Oral Torah integrates biblical and rabbinic teaching and displays what it sees as Scripture's deep substance and intent.

Consider, for example, the way rabbis integrate verses from across the *Tanakh* to understand God's nature.

A. ". . . he [God] rested on the seventh day" (Exodus 20.11):

B. And does fatigue affect God? Is it not said [in Scripture], ". . . the Creator of the ends of the earth . . . will not grow tired or weary" (Isaiah 40.28), "He gives strength to the weary" (Isaiah 40.29); "By the word of the Lord were the heavens made" (Psalms 33.6)?

C. How then can Scripture say, "and he [God] rested"?

D. He [God] had [Scripture] written about himself [to say] that he created the world in six days and, so to speak, rested on the seventh.

E. [From this] you may reason *a fortiori* [from the stronger case to the weaker one, as follows]:

F. If the one who is not affected by fatigue wrote about himself that he created the world in six days and rested on the seventh, how much more should a human being, of whom it is written [in Scripture], "yet man is born to trouble" (Job 5.7) [also rest on the Sabbath]!

A verse from the Torah says God rested on the seventh day. But verses from other parts of the *Tanakh* say that God does not require rest. As rabbis read it, since the Torah comes from God, this apparent contradiction cannot be an accident; it therefore must be designed to teach something. Indeed, its purpose is to provoke questions and study. So what does the Torah mean? The answer is that God wrote the Torah about himself *as if* God needed rest. This understanding yields a logical argument: Since God, who *does not require* it, rests on the Sabbath, then humans, whom Scripture says *do require* rest, certainly *should do* the same! By describing God in human terms, the Torah, by God's own design, creates a model and a humane and practical reason for God's creatures to observe the Sabbath: they need to rest. Note that the passage draws verses from the Prophets (Isaiah) and the Writings (Psalms, Job) to explain the Torah (Exodus).

A different example, a passage from the Babylonian Talmud, Tractate *Sotah*, 14a, uses scriptural verses to illustrate concretely what it means to follow God.

> **A.** And Rabbi Hamma, son of Rabbi Hanina, said, "What is the meaning of what is written [in Scripture], 'It is the Lord your God you must follow [lit. walk after]. . .' (Deuteronomy 13.4)? Is it possible for a person to follow the Divine Presence? Has it not already been said [in Scripture], 'For the Lord your God is a consuming fire. . .' (Deuteronomy 4.24)? [How can one follow fire?]"
>
> **B.** Rather, [the verse means one should] follow [imitate] the attributes of the Holy One, Blessed be He.
>
> **C.** He clothes the naked, as it is written, "And the Lord God made garments of skin for Adam and for his wife and clothed them" (Genesis 3.21); so should you clothe the naked.
>
> **D.** Just as the Holy One, Blessed be He, visited the sick, as it is written, "And the Lord appeared to him [Abraham] near the great trees of Mamre" [after his circumcision] (Genesis 18.1); so should you visit the sick.
>
> **E.** The Holy One, Blessed be He, comforted mourners, as it is written, "After Abraham's death, God blessed his son Isaac" (Genesis 25.11); so should you comfort mourners.
>
> **F.** The Holy One, Blessed be He, buried the dead, as it is written, "He buried him [Moses] in Moab, in the valley. . ." (Deuteronomy 34.6); so you too should bury the dead.

The passage uses Deuteronomy 4.24 to show that the words "walk after" in Deuteronomy 13.5 must be understood to mean imitating God's attributes rather than literally following God physically. On that basis, it draws together verses from the Torah that illustrate the traits of God that humans can emulate.

Kabbalistic readings of the Torah produced esoteric interpretations that the mystics believed revealed the inner workings of God. The Middle Ages also saw the emergence of individually authored commentaries to the Torah, with different emphases. Among the most influential are the commentaries of Rabbi Shlomo Yitzhaki (aka *Rashi*), 1040–1105, who focused on the *peshat* or plain meaning of Scripture (and also wrote the primary commentary on the Talmud), and Rabbi Moses ben Nahman (aka *Ramban* or Nahmanides), 1194–1270, who produced a kabbalistic interpretation of Scripture. The late rabbinic acronym *PaRDeS* indicates the four levels of meaning Scripture contains: *Peshat* ("simple"), the literal meaning; *Remez* ("hint"), the allegorical meaning; *Derash* ("interpretation"), the interbiblical comparative or midrashic meaning; and *Sod* ("secret"), is the hidden, often, mystical, meaning. Jewish commentaries on the *Tanakh* continued and continue to be produced. Contemporary versions include commentaries that represent Orthodox, Reform, Conservative, and feminist perspectives.

A well-known rabbinic saying about the Torah captures Judaism's engagement with Scripture: "Turn it, turn it, because everything is in it" (*Mishnah Avot* 5:25).

Christianity

The Christian Bible is the most sacred book within Christianity. The word "book" is deceptive, for the Bible is actually a collection of small books. The word "Bible" in fact comes from the Greek word *tabiblia* (little books). The Christian Bible is divided into two major sections, the Old Testament or the Hebrew Scriptures and the New Testament, also known as the Christian Scriptures. There are three elements in referring to a passage in the Bible: the name of the book followed by numbers signaling the chapter(s) and verse(s) that are being cited. Catholic bibles have what is known as the Apocrypha, books that are considered by Catholics to be divinely inspired but are often omitted from Protestant bibles. This is one of the many distinctions you will find between Protestants and Catholics.

The Bible is alien to us in many ways. It was written in Ancient Hebrew and Greek, with parts of the New Testament in Aramaic, which is the language Jesus spoke. This is important to highlight, for many of the quotes we have from Jesus in the New Testament are Greek translations of his words in Aramaic. The books were written centuries ago by authors who had no idea that we would be reading them today. For the majority of Christians in the world they emerge from geographic and cultural spaces that are different from our own. You cannot literally read the Bible today unless you are a scholar of ancient languages, for you are always reading a translation (and thus an interpretation) of the text.

The Christian Bible is a form of religious literature about a group's understanding of God. There are different types of literary modes within the books of the Old and New Testaments and multiple authors. For Christians the Bible constitutes a canon: books that have the highest religious authority within the community of faith. There are many other books that have survived today that are not included in the canon, and thus not in the Bible. There are also books that did not survive. The determination of the canon took centuries to establish by male religious authorities. Bishop Athanasius of Alexandria's list of books as canonical, dated 367, includes all of the books that currently make up the Christian Scriptures and is considered the earliest statement determining the canon. Eventually the official books are canonized as being divinely inspired.

The Gospels

The four Gospels (Matthew, Mark, Luke, and John) tell the stories about Jesus' life, ministry, and death. The Gospels were written anonymously and came to be ascribed to disciples (Matthew and John) and associates of apostles (Mark and Luke) sometime

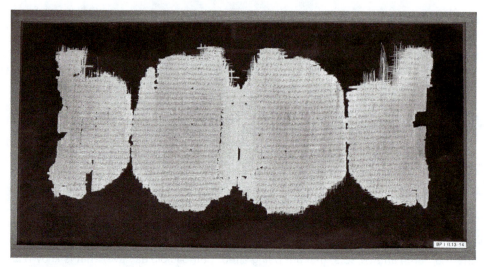

FIGURE 10 *Luke 11.50—12.12; 13.6–24, Four Gospels and Acts, Greek on papyrus 200–250* CE, *Egypt CBL BP 1 ff.13–14, © The Trustees of the Chester Beatty Library, Dublin.*

in the second century. The Acts of the Apostles, written by the author of the third Gospel (Luke), describes the spread of the Christian church from Jesus' death to the death of the Apostle Paul, and is considered the earliest Christian history. Following Acts are twenty-one epistles or letters. The most significant of these letters are attributed to Paul, the first-century missionary who is responsible for the spread of Christianity not only geographically but also to Gentiles, expanding Christian membership beyond adherence to Judaism. By the end of the first century, Christianity had become an increasingly Gentile phenomenon in large part due to Paul. Most of these New Testament books are records of correspondence between a church leader and a Christian community. The epistles address issues of Christian belief, practice, and ethics. They play an important role in Protestant churches and their self-understanding of Christian identity. For Catholics, Paul's letters do not play as significant a role in defining Catholic identity and the role of the Church.

The authors of the Gospels were not eyewitnesses to Jesus' life and ministry; none of them personally knew Jesus. Their stories about Jesus are based on oral traditions and the accounts of others, some of which were written down and became sources for the Gospel writers. While many of these traditions were probably historically accurate, others were certainly embellished or even wholly created in order to emphasize certain aspects of Jesus's character. In addition, the Gospel writers continued to modify and invent stories to underscore their own beliefs about Jesus. Christians told stories about Jesus not to preserve historically accurate records of his sayings and deeds but rather to convey theological truths. Stories were told to convince potential converts that Jesus was the Son of God whose death brought salvation to the world.

The Gospels' authors wrote for particular audiences. The Gospel of Mark was written from a Jewish perspective. At the very beginning of his biography, the author states that Jesus was the Christ (*christos*, the Greek translation of the Hebrew term "messiah"), a title that was meaningful only to Jews. In Matthew, Jesus is unmistakably Jewish: Matthew emphasizes Jesus' connection to two of the most important figures in Judaism, David and Abraham. The Gospel of Luke outlines Jesus' birth, life, death, and resurrection, and Acts traces the spread of Christianity through the Roman Empire. Both books emphasize Jesus' importance for Gentiles. Matthew, Mark, and Luke are known as the synoptic Gospels since they share many of the same sources and stories about Jesus. The Gospel of John is the latest Gospel and differs from the other three. In the prologue (John 1.1–18), John refers to Jesus as the "Word" of God who existed with God from the beginning, and who, in fact, is God. It is only at the end of this mystical reflection that John explains that the Word of God is Jesus.

There are three stages of the Gospels' formation. The first stage is the time of the historical Jesus' life on earth. The second stage is the period of oral tradition (roughly 30–50 CE), in which Jesus' disciples, who directly knew him, preached and taught about Jesus and began to assemble material about him: miracle stories, passion narratives, and parables. Stage three is the time of the written letters and Gospels. Paul's first letter was written around 51 CE. Christians began to record traditions and teachings in writing to keep the record straight, correct distortions, and provide instructions for new converts. The Gospels were written approximately between the years 70 and 100 CE. The Gospels were not written closer to Jesus' death because his first followers thought he would return in their lifetime, and the world and time as they knew it would end. They had no interest in recording his life because in their eyes there would be no future generations to read it. However as those who knew Jesus personally began to pass away, and Jesus did not return, his followers began to document his life and teachings.

The Pauline Letters

In addition to learning that the Gospels were not written by individuals who personally knew Jesus, students of Christianity are often surprised to learn that Paul's letters, not the Gospels, are the earliest writings in the New Testament. Paul was a Pharisee who persecuted early Christians (Acts 8.3). At the time he was known as Saul. Sometime between the years 32 and 36 he had a conversion experience on the road to Damascus. Saul claimed that Jesus spoke to him, and he was then blinded for three days. Upon regaining his sight, he was baptized and eventually came to be known as Paul. Though he was Jewish, he was instrumental in the spread of the gospel to Gentiles. His letters have profoundly shaped Christian churches, particularly Protestant churches. Scholars believe that Paul actually wrote only seven of the letters attributed to him in the New Testament: 1 Thessalonians, 1 Corinthians, 2 Corinthians, Philippians, Philemon, Galatians, and Romans. Six of the letters have disputed authorship and were most likely written by followers of Paul in his name: Ephesians, Colossians, 2 Thessalonians,

1 & 2 Timothy and Titus. They are assumed to be written after Paul's death and differ in style, language, and theology. Paul's letter to the Hebrews is more a homily (sermon), and scholars overwhelmingly agree that it was definitely not written by Paul. The other letters in the New Testament are called the Catholic letters: Hebrews, James, 1 & 2 Peter, 1–3 John, and Jude.

In his letters Paul does not stress Jesus' sayings and stories about him. The majority of these letters are written to specific first-century Christian communities that are struggling with very particular issues and questions. The letters were also a way for Paul to spread his teachings and remain connected to the various churches he established during his missionary activities. Too often the sayings of Paul are quoted out of context or incorrectly applied to the contemporary context. These letters were not written with the intent of being applied to the contemporary world in an ad-hoc manner. Instead, these letters today reveal the issues and struggles of early Christians as they struggled to understand who Jesus was and the implications of his death and resurrection for his early followers.

Apocalypse

The final book within the Christian Scriptures is the book of Revelation. Highly popularized in Hollywood movies, this book is perhaps one of the most misunderstand documents in the Christian New Testament. The book describes Jesus as returning to judge the heaven and earth and initiate the era of the new creation. He battles with Satan, who symbolizes sin and death, so that all can share in the eternal life with God. Satan and his followers will be defeated. The introduction of the book claims that it is written by a man named John on the island of Patmos, who wrote the book after a series of visions. Revelation's heavily symbolic text is written in the midst of the persecution of Christians under the Romans. The Roman Empire is depicted as an agent of the devil. The book centers on the end of time as we know it and the final resurrection of the dead and the final judgment. A New Jerusalem will appear where all will live eternally with God and suffering and injustice will end. While throughout the centuries many Christians have used the book of Revelation as a manner of signposting the end of times, none have come to fruition. Scholars agree that this will always be the case, as this book must be read symbolically and not as a literal guidebook to the end times.

Scripture, History, and the Trinity

The Bible is foundational for the Christian belief in a monotheistic God that is triune. Despite the variations in beliefs and practices among Christians, all forms of Christianity affirm the primacy of Scripture. Where there is great diversity is in the manner in which the Bible is interpreted. Western Christianity, uniquely Roman Catholicism, remained unified until the Protestant Reformation, a Western European movement (1500–1750) that sought to return Christianity to its biblical roots. Perhaps the best-known figure within the Reformation is Martin Luther, a Catholic monk whose Ninety-Five Theses famously outlined what he understood to be Roman Catholic distortions of true Christian practices and teachings. The Lutheran Reformation was initially a German academic movement that became social and political. Luther was condemned as a heretic by the Diet of Worms in 1521. The Protestant Reformation resulted in schisms (divisions) in the Church that led to the formation of various Protestant denominations (or churches), including Lutheranism, Calvinism, and Anabaptism. As a result of this, a Catholic Reformation (once known as the Counter-Reformation) began, and in 1545 the Council of Trent was convened by the Catholic Church to defend its tradition and respond to its opponents. The Reformation is the fundamental moment in the establishment of diverse Western Christianities with widely disparate attitudes.

Several dominant themes of the Protestant Reformation shaped and continue to shape these churches and their understanding of God. The period immediately prior to the Reformations is called the Middle Ages (1050–1500s). This is a time when Catholicism became engaged in philosophical and academic debates about the nature of God that focused on the rational justification and systematization of theological reflection. Theological reflection on Scripture and its meaning became a key source for understanding Christian teachings, identity, and rituals. The most significant figure to emerge in this time period is Thomas Aquinas, whose writings address the relationship between faith and intellect. The University of Paris was founded, and numerous monastic study centers were established by religious societies that combined strict religious observance with intellectual and artistic pursuits. During this period the clergy imposed a firm hierarchical authority, and Roman Catholicism was characterized by an increasing number of popular devotions associated with Mary, the mother of Jesus, and the saints.

The Reformation was in part a response to the increasing devotionalism of medieval Catholicism and the growing authority of the clergy. In response to popular devotions to Mary and the saints, the Reformers emphasized the centrality of Jesus within Christian life. Jesus, and only Jesus, should be the object of devotion. In response to ecclesial authority, the Reformers emphasized that Christians can have a direct and individual relationship with God. Perhaps the most famous mantra that emerged from the Protestant Reformation was *sola scriptura* ("Scripture alone") as the primary source for Christianity. There is no doubt that the Reformers were inspired in part by the publication of the Gutenberg Bible in the 1450s, which marked the beginning of the era of printed books in Western Europe. In response to the Protestant Reformers the Council of Trent affirmed both Scripture and tradition as the foundation of Roman Catholic beliefs. Trent held that the interpretation of Scripture must always be guided by Church authorities and thus affirmed the role of the clergy as mediators of the sacred. This emphasis on tradition was another way of affirming the authority of the hierarchy, who determines what is authentic tradition and what is not. In addition, Trent also affirmed the veneration of Mary and the saints. As a result of these divergent approaches to Scripture, Protestants, even today, tend to rely more heavily on the Bible. In contrast, Catholics rely both on biblical texts and also on devotions, practices, and rituals that are part of the Catholic tradition. The manner in which Scripture is interpreted varies not only between Catholics and Protestants but also among Protestants themselves. Some Protestants read the Bible as the literal word of God. However, the majority of Protestants globally, and Catholics as well, approach the Bible as divinely inspired and thus open to interpretation.

Despite these differences, there is a shared agreement that the foundation for belief in the Trinity is located throughout the Scriptures. Christians cite not only New Testament but also Hebrew Bible verses as the foundation for their belief in the Trinitarian God. Here is a key example of how Christianity incorporated and built upon the Hebrew Scriptures. Within the Hebrew Bible two passages from the book of the prophet Isaiah are often highlighted:

> For to us a child is born,
> to us a son is given,
> and the government will be on his shoulders.
> And he will be called
> Wonderful Counselor, Mighty God,
> Everlasting Father, Prince of Peace.

ISAIAH 9.6

> This is what the LORD says—
> Israel's King and Redeemer, the LORD Almighty:
> I am the first and I am the last;
> apart from me there is no God.

ISAIAH 44.6

Christians interpret both of these passages as prophecies of the arrival of Jesus Christ as the savior who is both human and divine. Christians turn to the creation accounts in the book of Genesis and note that Genesis 1.2 says that "the Spirit of God was hovering over the waters." Christians also highlight that in Genesis, in the creation narrative (Genesis 1), the story of Adam and Eve (Genesis 2–3), and the Tower of Babel (Genesis 11), God persistently speaks in the plural ("Let us create. . ."). Christians acknowledge that Judaism does not believe in the Triune God and would not agree with claims that portions of the Hebrew Scriptures justify the Trinity. Since Christians believe the God of their Old Testament is the God of the New Testament, and thus triune, the fullness of the Trinity was not revealed until the time of Jesus. Christians believe that only until the birth, life, ministry, death, and resurrection of Jesus was God's true nature as a Trinity revealed to humanity.

Scripture in Action

How was the Trinity revealed? Christians point to numerous passages in the Gospels that are later affirmed by Paul in his letters. Within the Gospel of Matthew three key texts affirm the Trinity for Christians. In Matthew's first chapter, verse 23, it is stated "'The virgin will conceive and give birth to a son, and they will call him Immanuel' (which means 'God with us')." Later in Matthew we find the account of Jesus' baptism:

> As soon as Jesus was baptized, he went up out of the water. At that moment heaven was opened, and he saw the Spirit of God descending like a dove and alighting on him. And a voice from heaven said, 'This is my Son, whom I love; with whom I am well pleased.'

> MATTHEW 3.16–17

This moment, where Christians argue the three persons of the Trinity are present, will become the foundation of the Trinitarian baptismal formulas recited by the earliest Christians. The book of Acts has the apostle Peter claim, "Repent and be baptized, every one of you, in the name of Jesus Christ for the forgiveness of your sins. And you will receive the gift of the Holy Spirit" (Acts 2.38). Other moments in Acts show early Christians being baptized in the name of Jesus Christ.

The third passage in Matthew that is important to highlight is Jesus' call to discipleship, where he announces to his followers that they must "Go and make disciples of all nations, baptizing them in the name of the Father and of the Son and of the Holy Spirit" (Matthew 28.19). Here we find Jesus himself proclaiming the Trinitarian baptismal formula. In addition, this is the call to evangelize that is cited by Christians as an affirmation of their missionary activity in spreading Christianity across the globe. Since the first followers of Jesus, this missionary activity, the spreading of the good news of the gospel, has been foundational to Christian identity and fueled violent movements such as the Crusades and the conquest and colonization of the Americas.

Matthew is not alone in highlighting a Trinitarian vision of God. The Gospel of Luke expresses a similar account of Jesus' baptism. The Gospel of John states: "The Word became flesh and made his dwelling among us. We have seen his glory, the glory of the one and only Son, who came from the Father, full of grace and truth" (John 1.14). There are numerous moments in the New Testament letters where Christians locate a Trinitarian understanding of God. 2 Corinthians has the often quoted: "May the grace of the Lord Jesus Christ, and the love of God, and the fellowship of the Holy Spirit be with you all" (2 Corinthians 13.14). In spite of all of the citations and the numerous others quoted by Christians it is important to remember, however, that Jesus never claimed to be God. Titles such as "Lord," "Son of Man," and "New Adam," are used to refer to him. However, ultimately one cannot read the Gospels and the sayings attributed to Jesus and claim that he said he was God. As highlighted above, despite the heavy use of Scripture to justify this Christian claim, the true nature of Jesus and the idea of God as Trinity was determined over two hundred years after the last documents in the Christian Scriptures were written.

The significance of these Scriptures for legitimizing the one Trinitarian God of monotheism cannot be ignored. Scripture also plays a key role in Christian rituals. Whether it is a Roman Catholic mass or a Baptist prayer service, the reading of and reflection upon Christian Scriptures is a key element of Christian worship life. In many worship settings the priest's or pastor's reflection on Scripture, whether through a sermon or homily, are the central feature of Christian liturgical celebrations. The fact that these reflections are so significant highlights the value Christians place on interpreting Scriptures within communities of faith. However, the entirety of the Christian Bible is never read in worship. Instead, churches determine which passages will be read at different times of the year and not every biblical passage is included. This is known as the lectionary. Those Christians who only encounter Scripture in worship settings, instead of in a Bible study or reading the Bible individually, are only exposed to certain portions of the text. The manner in which the Bible as a physical book is treated also varies among Christians. One sees the lifting of the lectionary and the kissing of the Gospels in a Roman Catholic mass and also finds the heavy underlining and writing in the book that can happen in a Bible study. In both settings, however, Scripture's foundational role as containing God's revelation remains a unifying aspect within Christianity.

Islam

The Qur'an is understood by Muslims as the inimitable and most perfect revealed Scripture to understand God. For Muslims, it answers the three ultimate questions of life, "Where did I come from? What is the purpose of life? Where will I end up?" Although Muslims believe in Scriptures attributed to Judaism and Christianity, they believe only the Qur'an has been unchanged and remains the most valid and pure testament from God. Its centrality and significance comes from the strong belief by Muslims that it is the word of God, absolute, unchanged and untouched by humans. The Qur'an plays an essential role in Muslims' understanding of their relationship with God in order to submit perfectly to God. It is not a legal text, but is used as a primary source for Islamic law, which is a later development in Islamic history. The words of the Qur'an are divine, but its interpretation is human. The Qur'an is, then, a thinking text, which requires its believers to ponder its implications. There are two types of approaches that one can take toward the Qur'an—a source-critical approach, interested in how the Qur'an came to be, and a meaning-based approach. Muslims tend to place more emphasis on the latter because they have no question as to the Qur'an's authenticity or origin. The Qur'an is central to all denominations in Islam. However, some variations to the reading of the text occur within the Shi'a denomination. These different readings support the Shi'a imam leadership, as will be discussed in detail later.

Revelation and Muhammad

Muslims believe the Qur'an (literally meaning recitation) is the word of God and was revealed to humankind by the prophet Muhammad through the angel Gabriel. One cannot separate the Qur'an from the prophet Muhammad's life, but what is contained within the Qur'an is separate from Muhammad because it is from God without the Prophet's interference. It is then important to briefly understand Muhammad's life at this stage. What we know about Muhammad comes largely from sources written 100–150 years after his death. The sources (*sira* etc.) wanted to portray Muhammad in a particular way, so the image that the Islamic tradition bestows upon us needs to be considered in this light. This opens up discussions on the "idealist" image of Muhammad versus a historical one. Muslims understand Muhammad as perfect—the greatest example of Islam.

Muhammad was born in 570 CE in Mecca, current-day Saudi Arabia. His father, Abdullah, died about six months before he was born and his mother, Amina, died when he was six years old. Muhammad's life is full of extraordinary events. While a child, he was given to a wet nurse, Halima. It is said that no one was willing to accept Muhammad

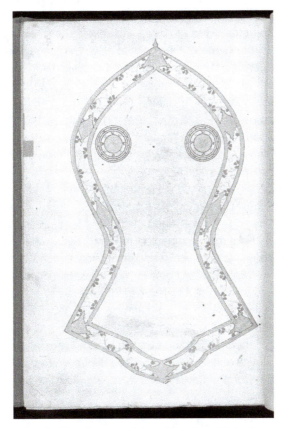

FIGURE 11 *Diagram of the Prophet's sandal outline, from* Fath al-muta'al fi madh al-ni'al *(*Treatise on the Prophet Muhammad's sandals*) by al-Maqqari (d. 1632), manuscript dated 6 Ramadan 1071H, 4 May 1661. Codex, ink and colors on paper. Folio: 30.2 x 21.2 cm. Chester Beatty (CBL Ar 3113 fol. 8r), © The Trustees of the Chester Beatty Library, Dublin.*

when the children were being distributed to wet nurses because they feared that they would not receive much money from a single mother. However, Halima convinced her husband to accept Muhammad, and traditions have it that they were blessed with healthy produce in relation to others. One day Muhammad was playing outside with his foster brother when two men dressed in white cut open Muhammad's chest. A prophetic tradition states that this was the angel Gabriel who came and extracted the "measure of Satan" from his heart. Muhammad is said to have been illiterate. There are varying explanations of this term "illiterate"; for some it meant illiterate and for others it simply meant that he did not have knowledge of other Scriptures. He was known in society as *al-Amin* (the trustworthy one).

When Muhammad was around thirty-five years old, a dispute erupted in Mecca about the placing of the black stone that now sits on the eastern corner of the Ka'ba and is said to date back to the time of Adam and Eve. Muhammad hailed from a tribe, the Quraish, that was charged with looking after the holy sanctuary, the Ka'ba. There were many nonmonotheistic rituals that took place around the sanctuary and people would come from all around to take part in these. It is said that the Ka'ba was renovated after a fire, and so the stone was removed. However, after the renovations the clans could not agree as to which one of them would place the stone back in its place. They agreed that whoever entered through the gate would decide. It was Muhammad who asked for a large cloth. He placed the stone on the cloth and asked each clan leader to hold part of the cloth and place the stone in its rightful position. In a similar event wherein Muhammad plays the role of arbitrator, he is invited to Medina in 622 CE to find a solution between the warring factions of Jews and pagans. It was then that he implemented what has come to be known as the Constitution of Medina, a document hailed for bringing peace and stability to the region.

When Muhammad was orphaned his grandfather, Abdul Muttalib, the leader of the tribe, cared for him, but he died when Muhammad was around eight years old. His uncle Abu Talib then cared for him. Around that time, Muhammad set out on a Meccan caravan trip with his uncle; they stopped off in Bosra, Syria, where they met Bahira, a Christian monk. Initially, Muhammad was left outside to tend to the camels. Bahira insisted that everyone join him inside, and it is there that Bahira told Muhammad's uncle that Muhammad was a prophet. There are two versions of the advice he gave his uncle. In one version, he tells him to guard him from the Jews, and in the other he tells him to guard from the Byzantines. Muslims insist this story verifies that Muhammad is the last and seal of the prophets and that Bahira the monk had access to the true Gospels from God. Critics of this episode declare Bahira a heretical monk who inspired Muhammad and the Qur'an. Some have even argued that he was Muhammad's teacher.

The Qur'an Revealed

When Muhammad was around forty years old, he received a revelation from God that instructed him, simply, to "Read" (*Iqra*). The story goes that one day while Muhammad was meditating in cave Hira on mount Nur (meaning "light"), the angel Gabriel came to inform him that he was the prophet of God. Muhammad was so shocked by this that in fear he ran to his wife, Khadija, who comforted him. There is also a tradition that he was so overcome with this experience that he decided to throw himself from the mountain because he was so depressed—only to be stopped by the angel Gabriel and told that he was a prophet of Islam. This began a twenty-three-year (609–632) revelation cycle during his lifetime which spanned his time in Mecca and Medina. Muhammad's marriage to Khadija (who was fifteen years older than him) bore him six children, two boys (who died in infancy) and four daughters. The marriage lasted twenty-five years. After the death of Khadija, Muhammad had multiple marriages. Muslims state that these were for humanitarian reasons. Some of these women were widowed, and marriage gave them strength in the deeply patriarchal society.

One of the most controversial marriages was to Aisha (613–678), who is said to have been around six or seven years old at the time of their marriage. There have been continued discussions on Muhammad's marriages and Muslims and non-Muslims will offer differing conclusions as it brings into question the issue of child marriages. It is often said that she was around ten years old when the marriage was consummated. Commentators have argued that it was not unusual for premenstrual women to be married off at young ages. These pieces of Muhammad's life have led to intense discussions by Muslims on sexual ethics. Aisha plays a significant role in the *Hadith* canons (the large corpus of sayings and traditions attributed to the prophet Muhammad) in which she narrates a large number of traditions. During a caravan trip, Aisha is accused of adultery. The story goes that she is accompanying Muhammad on a trip but is left behind from the group as she searches for a missing necklace. Safwan ibn al-Muwattal, a member of the army, brings her back to Muhammad. Rumors start to spread that they had both committed adultery. It is said that even Ali, the cousin and son-in-law of Muhammad, was convinced of her guilt. Muhammad is said to have been quite unsure about the issue but receives a revelation from God that vindicates her and reveals divine statements on adultery, which are noted in chapter 4 of the Qur'an, called *al-Nisa* (Women). Aisha was the prophet's most beloved wife after the death of Khadija, and he died in her arms. Muhammad is said to have married around thirteen wives and had two concubines. One of these concubines was Maria al-Qibtiya (Maria the Copt), an Egyptian Coptic Christian slave gifted to him by the ruler of Egypt, *al-Maqawqis*, often noted as Cyrus, the patriarch of Alexandria. Traditions say that Muhammad sent al-Maqawqis a letter of invitation to Islam and was sent a letter back thanking and rejecting the invitation with two maids, Maria and her sister, Sirin. In Islamic traditions, both sisters converted to Islam. The other concubine is Rayhana bint Zayd, who was an enslaved Jewish woman. Muhammad also married Safiyya bint Huyayy, who hailed from the Jewish Banu Nudair tribe, after she converted to Islam.

The Qur'an as we know it was compiled and formalized during the tenures of Abu Bakr, Umar, and Uthman. It is said that it came to be the text as we know it around the 650s. The Prophet is understood to be the living and walking embodiment of the revelation that he was receiving. This meant that he was able to interpret the text and explain its passages to new Muslims. The Qur'an is therefore placed within a particular context of time, and this has been important for Muslims interpreting their Scripture.

Language

Although Muhammad was understood to be illiterate, the society of the time was generally literate. The Arabs of the time were extremely proud of their language, and poets were producing outstanding verse. Muhammad's illiteracy led many to accuse him of being a soothsayer or magician. This was not unusual as there were many of these around, but none of them were producing a text as eloquent as the Qur'an. In 2:23, the Qur'an says, "If you have doubts about the revelation We have sent down to our servant, then produce a single chapter like it." Arabic is then an important language for Muslims even though the majority of Muslims live outside of the Arab world. This has led to some Islamic scholars calling for the compulsory learning of Arabic for Muslims. Although the Qur'an is translated into many languages, Muslims believe the truest form of the revelation is in Arabic. The writing is a mixture of prose and poetry. It is for this reason that there are various ways of reciting the Qur'an which sound quite melodic. Muslims will refrain from calling this singing generally because they want to distinguish the Qur'an as something serious, divine that is recited rather than sung. These passages are recited during the daily prayers that Muslims take part in.

The opening (*Fatiha*) of the Qur'an chapter is recited in every prayer by Muslims:

Praise belongs to God, Lord of the Worlds,
The Lord of Mercy, the Giver of Mercy,
Master of the Day of Judgment.
It is You we worship; it is You we ask for help.
Guide us to the straight path:
The path of those You have blessed, those who incur no anger and who have not
  gone astray.

Q1:1–7

Content

The Qur'an's content is centrally about clarifying God's oneness and what that means to creation in their submission to that One God. Muslims believe it is the single central text in which God directly tells human beings about God. This makes it remarkable. Although the book does deal with many key themes, the first and last are that God exists and that submitting to God brings peace and joy to a believer. God is one and cannot truly be understood by the human intellect. One way of understanding God is through the creation story and all that God created, allowing for mystery and wonderment. Paradoxically, nothing truly embodies God, not even the Qur'an. All revealed texts are, in a way, small signs of God that a believer must struggle with in order to strengthen their faith in that unseen God who sees them but Muslims' emphasis is on the Qur'an. In a push to uphold good and banish evil, there are continuous tropes of judgment—such as heaven and hell—that emphasize to Muslims that they must do good. It is not good enough to believe in God; they must act. The Qur'an uses the stories of the prophets to highlight the struggles that they faced and how belief in God helped. This is where we see biblical prophets and figures emerging. The Qur'an makes clear its distinction from all other Scriptures by asserting that Jesus is one of many prophets, including Adam and Muhammad. The text delves into matters of ethics and morality but does not spell them out clearly. It leaves ideas ambiguous, embedded in long and short tales that require the reader to discern what is right and what is wrong. The Qur'an continues to offer Muslims the core material for thinking through their ultimate role of submitting to God and doing "good." The answers are almost never clear but this is celebrated through the Qur'anic verses which push believers to reflect and question faith.

Originally the Qur'an was transmitted orally. The Qur'an was revealed in stages and over a long period of time, following the life and times of Muhammad. When Muhammad would receive the text, he would tell others and some of them would also memorize it. The Qur'an has 114 chapters and around 6,000 verses; it is often divided into thirty chapters, all with different titles, for example, "The Bee," "The Cow," "The Spider." The Qur'an is full of different stories, often about prophets past, all detailing submission to God that can help humans overcome evil or difficulty. Many of these stories are similar to biblical stories. Muslims believe that the ultimate revelation is held in the seventh heaven, and only small fragments of that complete revelation were revealed, which acts as an explanation for the existence of the various Scriptures that exist within Judaism, Christianity, and Islam, even though they all attest to the centrality of One God.

Exegesis

The Qur'an has been interpreted in a number of ways for centuries. From its original Arabic, many commentators have tried to explain the meaning of the text. These interpretations have been compiled in large volumes of *tafsir*; these are basically books of commentary and explication. Commentators spent considerable time thinking through not only each verse but every word. Muslims will pay close attention to the context in which the passage was revealed and also look to signs within Muhammad's life and sayings to better understand the Qur'an. It is not surprising, then, that there are some exegetes who are branded as either literalists or mystics – this illustrates the varying ways that texts can be read. This diversity of explanation has played a role in diversifying the Islamic *ummah* – the global Muslim community.

Art and Architecture

Arabic calligraphy has always played a key role in Islamic adornment, mainly because Muslims do not depict images of God. Qur'anic passages have been engraved on

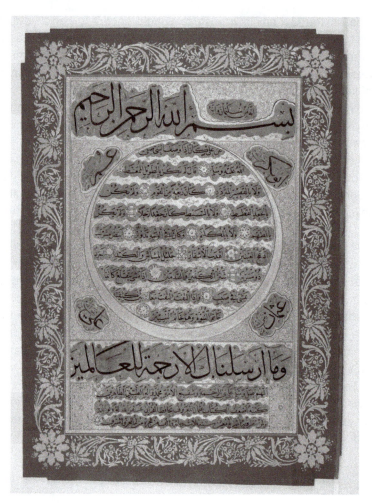

FIGURE 12 Hilya al-nabi *(Description of the Prophet), calligraphy by Hafiz Osman (d. 1698), Istanbul, Turkey, dated 1103H, 1691–1692. Folio, ink, colors and gold on paper. Folio: 44.0 x 32.0 cm. Chester Beatty (CBL T 559.4), © The Trustees of the Chester Beatty Library, Dublin.*

many important buildings throughout the world. These Qur'anic inscriptions can be seen on and in many mosques. The Ka'ba, the main mosque structure in Mecca, now has a black cloth with gold-threaded Qur'anic inscriptions around it. Qur'anic calligraphy can also be seen around the al-Aqsa Mosque in Jerusalem and many other houses of worship. Islamic traditions hold that reciting the Qur'an brings many blessings to Muslims, so they should not only adorn their surroundings but also try to memorize as much of it as possible in order to emulate the living and walking Qur'an—the Prophet himself. A person who memorizes the entire Qur'an is given the title of Hafiz—a person who knows the entire Qur'an, in its original language, by heart.

Hadith

The Qur'an is bound to the life of Muhammad, and so his actions and sayings play an important role in understanding the Qur'an. Muslims have tried to follow the life of Muhammad as best they can, but during the time of Muhammad he emphasized that Muslims should focus on the Qur'an—the word of God. It was largely after the death of Muhammad that narrations of his sayings began to be compiled into books of Hadith. The Qur'an reads, "Obey God and obey the Messenger . . . if you should quarrel over anything refer it to God and the Messenger" (Q4:59). Around the eighth or ninth century, there were a very large number of Hadith in circulation so scholars decided to formulate a way of making sure that only authentic Hadith were added to the canon. There are six Sunni Hadith collections that hold the highest status. Two compilers have been given the status of *Sahih* (most authentic or sound)—they are al-Bukhari (d. 870, who compiled around 600,000 statements and included around 9,000 in his final collection) from Bukhara in central Asia, and Muslim (d. 875, who compiled around 300,000 statements and included around 10,000 in his collection) from Khorasan in north-east Iran. Both were non-Arabs, highlighting the influence on traditions from non-Arabic speakers. The other four compilers were Sunan of Abu Dawud al-Sijistani (d. 889), al-Nasa'i (d. 915), Al-Tirmidhi (d. 892), and Ibn Maja (d. 887). Although the general content of the Hadith is similar in Sunni and Shi'a traditions, the Shi'a focus on the narrative material that came from the prophet's family, from members of Ali's family, and from the Shi'a imams themselves. These emerged after the Sunni collections and they may well have emerged in response to them.

Compilers would try and ascertain the reliability of the narrator before accepting the Hadith. There is a story about a compiler of Hadith who is told about a man who has some new narrations but he finds him speaking to an animal. During this conversation he sees that he is trying to get him to do something and tells the animal that he will get a certain reward. The man does not reward the animal. The compiler leaves. When asked why he rejected the narrations from the man, he responds, "If he is able to lie to an animal, what do you think he will say to me?" This would be in keeping with the traditions that state that Muhammad had earned a reputation during his time as an honest and truthful person, so the compilers of his sayings and actions will have wanted to only include the most authentic of these statements.

There is also another category of sacred, or divine, Hadith: quotes or sayings directly from God to Muhammad through inspiration or a dream. They are called *Hadith Qudsi*. Although they originate from God, they do not hold the same status as the Qur'an because they are not the exact words of God. The narrator of these is always Muhammad, whereas the Qur'an is always the word of God.

The Hadith collections offer added insight to all that was included in the Qur'an. Muhammad's life supported the divine commands. Where the Qur'an talks about fasting, for example, it was the sayings of Muhammad that set the clear times of fasting. If there was a passage of the Qur'an that was unclear, it was within the sayings of Muhammad where it might be further clarified.

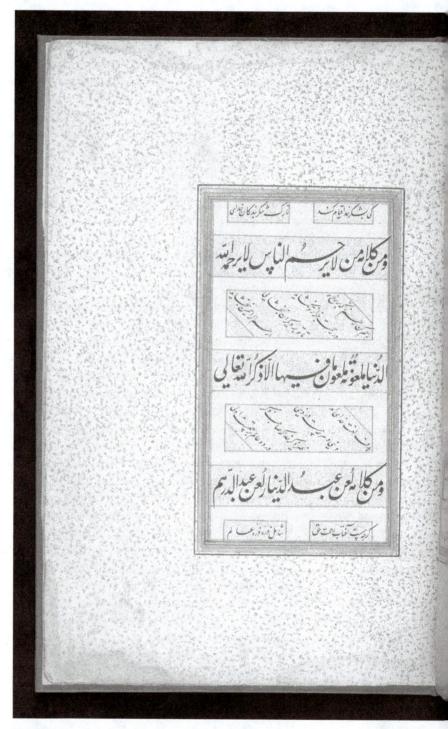

FIGURE 13 Chehel Hadith *(Forty Hadith of the Prophet), selected traditions with additic 1544. Codex, ink, colors and gold on paper. Folio: 24 x 15.3 cm. Chester Beatty (CBL*

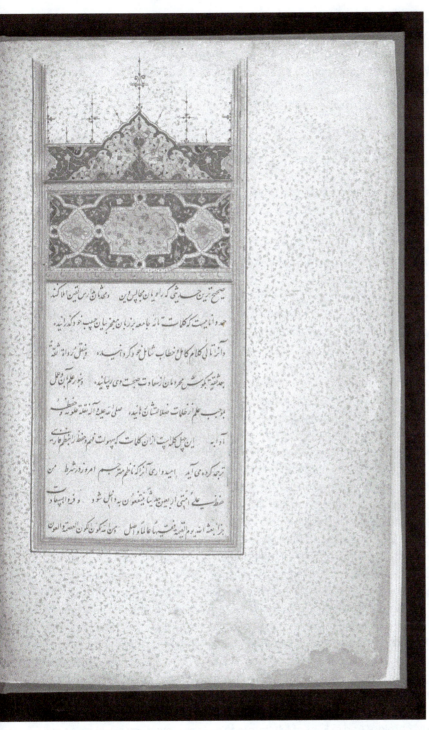

...sian paraphrases by 'Abd al-Rahman Jami (d. 1492), Tabriz, Iran, dated 950H, 1543–...2, fol. 1v-2r), © The Trustees of the Chester Beatty Library, Dublin.

Scripture, especially the Qur'an, then plays an essential role in strengthening the relationship between Muslims and God. It is understood as God's final revelation that allows Muslims to understand God and faith. Islamic Scripture offers no easy answers but in perfect divine order, offers more questions, doubt and gray (rather than clear cut black and white) answers—all the ingredients needed to strengthen faith, devotion, and submission through constant, evolving reflection.

Afterthought: Scripture

It is likely that, in historical perspective, the Bible (*Tanakh* and New Testament) and the Qur'an have affected the lives of more people on this planet than have any other writings. By some estimates, they are the most popular—or among the most popular—books in the contemporary world. Since Scripture is a defining trait of the monotheistic heritage, it is worth asking why Scripture matters. How does it affect what we do and how we do it, our culture and societies?

One way to begin that inquiry is with another question: How did and do heirs of the monotheistic heritage know what God expects of them? In ancient Israel there were two primary bases of cultural, political, and religious authority: lineage and inspiration. Kings and priests, even if initially selected by God, became inherited positions. Alternatively, prophets based their authority on the claim that God either addressed or inspired them. In all three, authority was vested in an individual or family and thus was in some sense personal; people could only listen to them and obey.

Against this background, Scripture was an innovation and a new source of authority. Scripture has unique validity because it both comes from God—whether directly or by inspiration—and is about God. Literally and substantively, God is in, and is known through, Scripture. The physical preservation of God's words and speech in writing objectifies God's revelation and gives Scripture an autonomy and authenticity that transcends social and political institutions and individual rulers and leaders. Because it is from God, about God, and inscribed in a text, Scripture contains the standards that those institutions and persons cannot change but against which they are judged and evaluated. The persistence of the monotheistic tradition is due in part to its Scripture.

Just as Scripture objectifies God's revelation, it also democratizes it. Scripture creates an external memory that is both authoritative and fixed. Thus, Scripture requires ongoing interpretation to demonstrate its relevance. By its very nature, a fixed text—whether it is read or heard—invites particular understandings and interpretations. Because the communities of the monotheistic tradition understand their lives through and in reference to Scripture, new experiences and changing political and social conditions generate fresh readings and ranges of meaning. Thus, in light of the destruction of two Temples, Judaism reads the *Tanakh* as validation of the covenant. In light of Jesus' resurrection, Christianity reads the same books, which it calls the "Old Testament," and writes its own as a prediction of Jesus' coming. And in light of Muhammad's life and experience, Islam sees the Qur'an as a correction of parts of both the *Tanakh* and New Testament.

To continually update the understanding of Scripture and to explore the range of its possible meanings, all three monotheistic religions developed traditions of interpretation. These traditions both enable the critical study of Scripture and constrain potentially dangerous interpretations. Thus, the Oral Torah in Judaism; creeds, tradition, and theology in Christianity; and the *Hadith* in Islam guide the religions and their participants in their understanding of Scripture. Even the versions of these religions that claim to be based solely on Scripture have distinctive ways of reading that deter or deflect random interpretations. The traditional lenses through which these religions read and appropriate Scripture allow it to maintain its authority and relevance.

The centrality of Scripture also enabled the creation of text-based communities in which people gathered to read, hear, and study Scripture, and in which Scripture was a part of worship. This historically unique model began in the ancient synagogue and continues in the church and the mosque.

In the final analysis, perhaps Scripture, more than any other single factor, enacts the basic claim of the monotheistic heritage: that there is only One God in the cosmos. Because God is in Scripture, and Scripture can be and is everywhere, in nearly every language and now online in a range of forms, so the One God is everywhere, communicating and being communicated to diverse peoples in diverse ways.

Study Questions: Scripture

Why is Scripture important to understand Judaism, Christianity and Islam?
How do the Scriptures of the three faiths interrelate?
What connects and disconnects Jewish, Christian, and Islamic Scripture?
Who are some of the key figures in the historical narrative of the Hebrew Scriptures?
How do the Christian Scriptures connect Jesus to Judaism?
How is the Qur'an distinctive from the Hebrew and Christian Scriptures?
Why is Muhammad significant for understanding the Qur'an?

4

Creation

The belief that humanity and the universe around us are created, and thus intentional, ordered, and purposeful, is central to Judaism, Christianity, and Islam. All three traditions value the two creation accounts that open the book of Genesis as fundamental to understanding the created world, though in different ways. For Christianity and Islam, their sacred Scriptures also play a key role in how these religions interpret the shared Genesis accounts. In addition, creation not only relates to how humanity should understand our relationship with the One God, but also how we relate to the world around us.

Judaism

The Torah says that God created the universe and all that is in it by organizing the primordial chaos. Creation, therefore, is an act of ordering. In both its classical and contemporary forms, Judaism exhibits a developed understanding of, and respect and appreciation for, the created order of the natural and social worlds. The rabbinic tradition (Genesis *Rabbah 1*) that God "looked into the Torah and created the world," means both that the cosmos has design and purpose and that the Torah contains essential wisdom about the nature of proper life in the created order.

Creation and Human Nature

The first chapter of the book of Genesis makes clear that the structure of the cosmos is neither accidental nor the result of a crisis but rather is deliberate, purposive, and beneficial. God creates all vegetation, fruit, and animal life and declares them "good" (Genesis 1). God creates male and female human life in God's image. Some rabbinic interpretations focus on the creation of Eve (the female) out of Adam's rib. Others, in contrast, understand the verse that God created them "male and female" (Genesis 1.27) to mean that the original human was androgynous, and God separated the first humans back to create two discrete beings. This interpretation, in turn, yields the rabbinic insight— taken up later in kabbalistic teaching—that the union of male and female in marital life reproduces the original created order. Still other teachings speculate that the union of Adam and Eve was a primal wedding that took place under a cosmic canopy or *chuppah*.

The Garden of Eden, humanity's original habitat, is also the site of its alienation from God. Rabbinic views on this issue are speculative and diverse. Some teachings hold Eve responsible for the expulsion from paradise, but others explore the interactions among Adam, Eve, and the serpent to seek to identify the aspects of humanity that cause alienation between God and God's creatures. Judaism's basic position is that because humans are created in God's image, they have free will and therefore are responsible for their actions and their thoughts. But since humans are not God, they are imperfect and therefore prone to fall short of God's commandments. Humans may sin, but they are not sinful by nature. By fulfilling God's commandments and studying Torah, humans can grow and improve.

Experiencing Creation: The Sabbath (*Shabbat*)

God rests on the seventh day, blesses the day, and declares it "holy." The Torah's designation of a time, a place, or a community as "holy" marks it as distinct from all other comparable times, places, or communities and as particularly congenial to God. On the Sabbath—the quintessence of God's order—people physically and emotionally join with God, rest with God, and experience God.

The Sabbath is Judaism's most important holiday. Only the obligations to save a life, rescue a burning Torah scroll, perform a *Brit Milah*, and, in some cases, mitigate an animal's suffering supersede it. Observing the Sabbath is the fourth of the Ten Commandments and is fundamental to the covenant. God tells Moses to exhort the Israelites to celebrate the Sabbath "for the generations to come as a lasting covenant. It will be a sign between me and the Israelites forever" (Exodus 31.16–17).

The Sabbath is a holiday of radical equality. It invites the Jewish people to follow God and experience the divine cosmic rhythm. The books of Genesis and Exodus link the Sabbath to creation, the book of Deuteronomy to the Exodus from Egypt. Thus, the Sabbath is both universal and particular; it commemorates the creation of the cosmos and the Israelites' discrete redemption. The Sabbath is a holiday of freedom. On it, no work is done. The halakhic tradition developed categories of labor prohibited on the Sabbath, including writing, cooking, washing, carrying money, doing business, planting, building, and demolishing. The commandment of Sabbath rest extends to people's entire households: visitors and employees (both Jewish and not) and also animals. It thereby actualizes the notion that all life comes from God and is entitled to a day of rest from earthly labor.

The holiday extends every week from before sunset on Friday to after sunset on Saturday. Just before sunset, the Friday evening service is preceded by a special liturgy known as *Kabbalat Shabbat* ("Welcoming the Sabbath"), which includes a set of Psalms and the communal singing of the kabbalistic hymn *Lecha Dodi* ("Come, my Beloved"), which welcomes the Sabbath as Israel's "bride."

After the Friday evening service, people return home for the Sabbath evening ritual. It begins with the lighting of candles, with an appropriate blessing. Rabbinic tradition assigned this task to women, but in many families all members participate. This is followed by a festive meal, which begins with the recitation of the *Kiddush* ("Sanctification") prayer over a cup of wine, itself a symbol of joy and blessing. The *Kiddush* begins with the recitation of Genesis 1:31—2:3, and the blessing itself follows:

> Blessed are You, Lord our God, Ruler of the Universe, Creator of the fruit of the vine.
> Blessed are You, Lord our God, Ruler of the Universe, Who made us holy with commandments and favored us, and gave us this holy Shabbat in love and favor to be our heritage as a reminder of creation. It is the foremost day of the holy festivals marking the Exodus from Egypt. For out of all the nations You chose us and made us holy, and You gave us Your holy Shabbat in love and favor as our heritage. Blessed are You God, Who sanctifies Shabbat.
>
> RABBI JESSICA MINNEN, OneTable, trans.

After *Kiddush* people recite a blessing over two braided loaves of bread, called *challah*, which commemorate the double portion of *manna* God gave to the Israelites on the Sabbath in the desert. When people bake their own *challah*, if the baking requires more than ten cups of flour, they perform a ritual called *hafrashat challah* ("the separation of *challah*"). They burn an olive-sized piece of the risen dough as a reminder of the offering made to the Temple priests (Numbers 15:18–21). The meal concludes with the recitation of *Birkat HaMazon* ("Grace after Meals").

People attend synagogue on the Sabbath to pray and listen to the recitation of the Torah and *Haftarah*; they then return home for rest and relaxation or the study of Torah. At the holiday's conclusion is a ritual called *Havdalah* ("differentiation"). It includes blessings over wine, spices, the lighting of a special braided candle, and a benediction that recognizes God for distinguishing between the sacred and the profane, light and darkness, Israel and the other nations, and the Sabbath and the rest of the week. *Havdalah* also evokes the image of Elijah, the prophet who will return to announce the messianic age, of which the peace and fulfillment of the Sabbath is a weekly foretaste.

Sabbath observance varies with denominations and individuals. Some people may only light candles and have an informal Sabbath eve meal. Others may devote the Sabbath day to nurturing family activities away from their work and cellphones. Reform congregations may have a late Friday evening Sabbath service.

Kabbalah and Creation

In 1492—the year Christopher Columbus sailed to the new world—King Ferdinand and Queen Isabella exiled the Jews from Spain. This traumatic event intensified hope for the coming of the messiah and coincided with a new kind of Jewish mysticism developed by Rabbi Isaac Luria (1534–1572) in the town of Safed in the land of Israel. Building on earlier traditions in the *Zohar*, Luria taught that in the beginning, God was all there was. To make room for the created world, God contracted into himself and sent light into the space the divine withdrawal produced. The *sefirot* were the vessels that carried the divine light. The light was too powerful; the vessels shattered; and the shards became the created, material world. Some sparks of the divine light became trapped in the shards, so there was a dislocation within God. Lurianic *kabbalah* proposed that each time a Jew performs a commandment, spark of divinity returns to its original source. When all the sparks are returned, the messianic era will arrive. This teaching made fulfilling the commandments a redemptive act. It influenced Jewish messianism in the seventeenth century, and is evident later in the teachings of Hasidic Judaism.

Creation and the Natural World

The Torah's story of creation envisions the cosmos as an integrated, complex system. Day and night, heavens and earth, land and sea, vegetation and fruit trees, sun and moon, birds and fish, land animals, and, finally, humans are the diverse elements that must work together in order for the system to function and persist. Humanity is the most consequential element of the system. In a classic and often cited rabbinic passage (Ecclesiastes *Rabbah* 7:13), God says that the vegetation of the Garden of Eden was created for humanity and then warns the first human to "not corrupt or destroy my world" because "there will be no one after you to repair it." Because humans—like God—have the capacity to destroy creation, they have a comparable responsibility to maintain it.

The Torah's narrative binds Judaism to nature. In Genesis 1.29–31 God declares green plants the basic nourishment of animals and seed-bearing fruit trees for humans. The major festivals (*Sukkot, Pesach*, and *Shavu'ot*) are all connected to the agricultural cycle in the land of Israel. The Torah identifies animals and birds that are acceptable to eat (see Chapter 6) and to offer as sacrifices, and it prohibits interbreeding species of animals and plants. The Torah also mandates a Sabbatical Year, in which the land of Israel is to lie fallow and rest. In Deuteronomy 20.19–20, God forbids the Israelites during a siege of a city to chop down its fruit trees. This verse is the basis of Judaism's principle of *bal taschit* ("do not destroy"), which prohibits the needless destruction, corruption, or wasteful use of any item that is beneficial to humans. All these commandments presuppose careful attention to nature.

The holiday of *Tu b'Shvat* is illustrative. Known since antiquity as the "new year of fruit-bearing trees," the holiday is the date, the fifteenth day of the Hebrew month of *Shvat*, on which rabbis determined the age of fruit-bearing trees for the purpose of offering a tithe in the Temple. In the sixteenth century Jewish mystics in Safed developed a *Tu b'Shvat Seder*, which includes the seven species the Torah (Deuteronomy 8.8) associates with the land of Israel: wheat, barley, olives, dates, grapes, figs, and pomegranates. Jewish communities now celebrate versions of the *Tu b'Shvat Seder*, often with an ecological emphasis. In the State of Israel, *Tu b'Shvat* is a kind of Arbor Day, on which people plant trees, with a focus on nurturing and preserving the environment.

Multiple contemporary organizations manifest Judaism's concern for nature. The programs of *Hazon* ("Vision"), the Jewish Lab for Sustainability, for instance, include nature retreats for Jewish schools and conferences on ethically produced kosher food. The Jewish Farm School, founded in Philadelphia in 2006, addresses harmful practices in contemporary food production systems and "works to create greater access to sustainably grown foods." In California, the educational farm Urban *Adamah* ("land") donates homegrown organic fruits, vegetables, and eggs through a weekly Free Farm Stand. The Green Zionist Alliance highlights Jewish responsibility to build a sustainable future by supporting the ecology of Israel. *Canfei Nesharim* ("the Wings of Eagles") advocates protection of the environment from a halakhic perspective. Jewcology is a broad-based group of young Jewish environmentalists and activists. The Coalition on the Environment and Jewish Life collaborates with both Jewish and multi-denominational groups on environmental issues.

Care for Animals

In a variety of ways, the Torah makes clear that all animal life in the three realms of creation—land, sea, and sky—are God's creatures, essential to the created order and primary objects of God's concern. God creates them on the fifth and sixth days, and, at God's behest, the first human names them. All creatures that live on the land or fly in the sky are preserved on Noah's Ark during the flood. God's covenant afterwards includes birds, cattle, and wild animals (Genesis 9.10). God gives humans permission to eat animal meat but forbids human consumption of blood.

Multiple commandments in the Torah suggest concern for animals. It is forbidden to sever a limb from a living animal (Genesis 9.4). Sabbath rest (Exodus 20.10) includes domesticated animals, and Israelites must help relieve an animal's burden even if it belongs to an enemy (Exodus 23.5). The Torah forbids the slaughter of an animal and its young on the same day (Leviticus 22.28), yoking two animals of unequal strength to the same plow (Deuteronomy 22.10), and muzzling an animal that is threshing corn (Deuteronomy 25.4).

These biblical commandments underlie the rabbinic principle that forbids any practice that causes *tza'ar ba'alei chayim* ("the needless suffering of animals"). Thus, for instance, the Babylonian Talmud (*Gittin 62a*) holds that people must feed their domestic or dependent animals before feeding themselves. *Halakhah* allows people on the Sabbath to unload an excessive burden from an animal and otherwise relieve its suffering and to feed dependent animals and perform necessary tasks, such as milking the animal. These practices, among others, underscore Judaism's view of humans' responsibility to respect life and exhibit compassion for animals.

Since the Torah permits the consumption of meat, Judaism does not, in principle, advocate or require veganism or vegetarianism but both are permitted. The ritual slaughter of animals and birds fit (*kosher*) for consumption (see Chapter 6) is designed to minimize the animal's suffering.

Many contemporary Jewish organizations promote Jewish awareness of care for animals. The Jewish Initiative for Animals, part of Farm Forward, develops educational resources on how Jewish values can inform the treatment of animals and offers expert advice to Jewish institutions that serve animal products. Concern for Helping Animals in Israel (CHAI) aids animals in Israel through legislation, education, and direct support for animals in need. *Shamayim V'Aretz* ("Heaven and Earth") advocates for veganism. Conservative Judaism has produced *Magen Tzedek* ("Shield of Justice"): An Ethical Certification for Kosher Food, which has strict standards not only for the process of slaughter but also for the treatment of animals who are being raised as food.

Appreciating the Created Order

Judaism developed specific blessings to heighten people's awareness and appreciation of the power and beauty of natural phenomena. Each begins with the traditional formula, "Blessed are You, Lord Our God, Ruler of the Universe," and then adds an appropriate conclusion depending on the focus of the blessing. For instance, the blessing when one sees impressive natural phenomena, such as mountains, deserts, or hurricanes, praises God for doing the "work of creation." The blessing for hearing thunder acknowledges that God's "power and strength fill the Universe." The blessing for seeing a rainbow praises God for remembering and being faithful to the covenant and upholding God's commitment. The blessing for first sight of a beautiful living creature—human or animal—praises God for creating beauty, and, in response to seeing an unusual animal, the blessing thanks God for differentiating the creatures.

All these ideas and practices manifest Judaism's conviction that the created order comes from God, ultimately belongs to God, and that the Jewish people's covenant responsibility is to respect, preserve, and enhance God's handiwork.

Christianity

The foundation of the Christian understanding of creation, humanity's relationship with God, and Jesus' universal salvation is found in the doctrine of creation, the Christian teachings that focus on the creation of this universe by God as based in the Genesis accounts in the Hebrew Scriptures. For Christians the first three chapters of the book of Genesis are fundamental for understanding not only our nature but also God's nature. The book of Genesis opens with two creation stories, accounts that have captured religious and popular imagination for centuries. Whether it is the writings of the earliest Christian thinkers, contemporary debates on intelligent design versus evolution, or a Simpsons cartoon's humorous reinterpretation of Adam and Eve, perhaps no other section of the Hebrew Scriptures and Christian Bible have provoked as much creativity and debate as the first three chapters of Genesis. The first story is found in Genesis 1 and highlights the creation of all of the universe in six days with God resting on the seventh day. Genesis 2–3 tells us the story of Adam and Eve and their betrayal of God and consequent expulsion from paradise. A careful read of both stories through the lens of Christianity follows.

Genesis

As in Judaism, for Christians Genesis 1 emphasizes the idea of a purposeful and ordered cosmos created by God from chaos. As God creates the many elements of this universe and the days go by the narrative culminates with the creation of humanity and the pivotal line in the story found in verse 27:

> So God created mankind in his image,
> in the image of God he created them;
> male and female he created them.

This statement has been a central point of contention and a foundation for Christian understandings of men and women for centuries. The notion that humanity is created in the image of God, distinguishing us from the rest of creation, and the exact meaning of that image, continues to mystify and challenge the religious imagination of Christians. Contrary to the spirit of the passage, male Christian authors have argued for centuries that creation in the image of God as male and female does not necessarily lead to an egalitarian relationship between men and women. Women are seen as possessing the image deficiently, for example, or only in relationship with men. Interpretations such as these have falsely denied the full image of God in women, equated her with bodiliness and elevated man as the ultimate representation of rationality and spirituality, the expression of the image in its fullness. After their creation humans receive dominion over the earth. In the end, like the rest of creation, God claims that this creation is good.

The creation story found in chapters two and three of Genesis, referred to by Christians as the Fall, offers a radically different account of humanity and the cosmos' creation. Unlike the earlier narrative, where humanity appears on the sixth day, this account places humanity at the front and center of creation. The human being is formed the dust in the ground and is placed in the Garden of Eden to care for it, warned against eating from the tree of knowledge of good and evil. God determines that the human being needs companionship, so God places the human to sleep, removes a rib, and from that rib creates another human being and male and female are created. With the opening of chapter three a new actor enters the narrative, the serpent. The serpent convinces the woman to sample from the tree of knowledge, and she in turn gives some to her partner. God enters the garden, finds the two hiding, and realizes what they have done. As a result of their actions, he banishes them from the garden and the nature of their relationship is forever transformed, with woman destined to be subordinate to man. Due to their transgression the egalitarian relationship between man and woman is destroyed, and the man becomes the master of the woman. The Fall results in the end of the intended model of companionship and instead leads to dominion. This was not the intended order of creation. This is a consequence of their actions and therefore a sinful state. Thus the domination of women was not how God intended the relationship between the sexes to be. Genesis 3 does not divinely sanction the subordination of

FIGURE 14 *Adam and Eve, © Getty Images.*

women. In fact, it does just the opposite, presenting gender hierarchy as the product of human sin, and, like all sin, something from which humanity must be redeemed.

Eve is not mentioned anywhere else in the Hebrew Scriptures beyond Genesis 5. In addition, nowhere else in the Hebrew Scriptures are Adam and Eve cited as examples of disobedience. Certain aspects of the Fall help us shed light on the manner in which Genesis 2–3 has been interpreted within Christian theology. Sexist interpretations of the Fall have led (male) theologians to write that

- woman is created second and is thus inferior to man;

- woman is to be man's helper;

- because she comes from man's rib woman is dependent on man and needs him for her existence;

- woman is responsible for allowing sin to enter into the world;

- woman is untrustworthy;

- God allows for man to rule over woman.

These stereotypes will fuel theological speculation on the manner in which woman does (or does not) reflect the image of God. Both Genesis accounts are stories, however—mythic accounts written by a particular community to explain the human condition and humanity's relationship with the divine. Throughout Christian history, however, a patriarchal interpretation of the Genesis accounts has been canonized to legitimize women's secondary status within the Christian tradition. For example, the philosopher and theologian Thomas Aquinas argued in the thirteenth century that woman is always in the image of God, but she reflects this image less perfectly than man. In her individual nature woman is a misbegotten, defective male; however, in collective human nature she is not misbegotten, for she serves the purpose of procreation

Original Sin

The account of humanity's Fall from grace will become the foundation for the Christian teaching on original sin. Original sin is the basis of the belief in and need for Jesus Christ's redemptive works. Jesus takes away our original sin. At the core of the teaching is the attempt to answer the question, "Why do we alienate ourselves from God?" Because of our first parents, Adam and Eve, and their sin and disobedience, we are all born in a state of sin. It is as if their sin is passed on to us in our DNA. This is an important point. If Christians are going to claim that Jesus came to save all humans, all of us need something to be saved from. We all have to have a shared defect that needs to be redeemed. The correction of that flawed state is through Jesus' salvation on the cross. We are not in the state which God intended us to be in. Adam and Eve prior to their sin are how God created us. However, due to their disobedience we are all in a fallen state. In 1 Corinthians 15.45–49 Paul writes:

> So it is written: "The first man Adam became a living being"; the last Adam, a life-giving spirit. The spiritual did not come first, but the natural, and after that the spiritual. The first man was of the dust of the earth; the second man is of heaven. As was the earthly man, so are those who are of the earth; and as is the heavenly man, so also are those who are of heaven. And just as we have borne the image of the earthly man, so shall we bear the image of the heavenly man.

Without the salvific work of Jesus, the heavenly man, we continue to resemble the flawed earthly Adam. This is why Jesus is referred to as the New Adam, or heavenly man, whose obedience corrects the disobedience of the Garden of Eden. One day we will bear that heavenly image instead of being in the image of the earthly man.

While the doctrine of original sin developed gradually, the fourth-century Church Father Augustine of Hippo is considered its classical author. Prior to Augustine there was no consensus or comprehensive approach to original sin. In Augustine, humanity is in a struggle between two wills, as described in Romans 7.18–20:

> For I know that good itself does not dwell in me, that is, in my sinful nature. For I have the desire to do what is good, but I cannot carry it out. For I do not do the good I want to do, but the evil I do not want to do—this I keep on doing. Now if I do what I do not want to do, it is no longer I who do it, but it is sin living in me that does it.

Augustine does not resolve the question of how Adam and Eve were created by God and where the source of their sin that led to fallen humanity comes from; in other words, why Eve and Adam sinned. Sin damages the image of God within us, and only grace can heal us. Wickedness is why we sin (a result of our first parents' sin); it is the result of a change in human nature. Christians believe that Adam and Eve's sin was transferred biologically via procreation. The human was created in a state of original blessedness; Adam and Eve had the ability not to sin. Augustine never gives us the why of their sin. For many Christians their sin is pride, the desire to be like God.

We are now in a dysfunctional state of concupiscence (disordered desire). This disorder is what remains after baptism, and it inclines us toward sin. We are predisposed to sin, though the image of God within us is not destroyed. Grace (God's freely given love), for Christians, heals human nature and we are redeemed through participation in the Church and consequently participation in God. Grace redirects our will toward God. Augustine's teachings transformed the manner in which Christians understood themselves and their relationship with God. His emphasis on original sin forced Christians to see themselves as having lost the glory of their original creation. It also gave Christians a reason to legitimize the claim of Jesus' universal salvation and speak about the human struggle to do the right thing and the temptation or draw one has to do the wrong thing at times.

In Augustine free will becomes the root of sin. Adam and Eve had the freedom to disobey God, and they did. They mistakenly did not realize, Augustine argued, that since we were intended to be in relationship with God, true freedom is actually when we live our lives in obedience to God. Augustine also argued that sexual desire is a result of original sin and is shameful. Prior to their sin Adam and Eve would have procreated without feeling that desire. In spite of Augustine arguing that free will is at the root of our sinfulness, he does not resolve the question of the impulse that led Adam and Eve to sin. In other words, Augustine, and Christianity as a whole, do not fully address why Adam and Eve first sinned. As mentioned, pride is often given as an answer to this question, the desire to be like God. This may not seem like enough to derail the entire order of God's creation. For Paul it is Adam's disobedience, and consequently human disobedience that must be corrected through Jesus: "For just as through the disobedience of the one man the many were made sinners, so also through the obedience of the one man the many will be made righteous" (Romans 5:19).

Salvation

Jesus' crucifixion and resurrection become the fundamental moment within Christian salvation history and our redemption from original sin. The account of Jesus' crucifixion begins with the Last Supper, where Jesus is compared to the Passover lamb. After his crucifixion it is said that three days later he rose from the dead and appeared to his women followers. While Christianity maintains a vision of the human where women are frequently depicted as subordinate, during his crucifixion it is his female followers and his mother, not his male apostles, who stand by him at the cross. Similarly, in the resurrection narratives Jesus appears to women at first, not men. After his resurrection, the Gospels tell us, he is not immediately recognized by his followers. Yet his body bears the wounds of the crucifixion. The Gospels also pointedly highlight that he ate fish with his followers. This small detail was to correct any later accusations that Jesus was just a ghost and not resurrected. Jesus' bodily resurrection will become the foundation for the Christian belief in the resurrection of the body of all humanity at the time of judgment.

Christians assert that Jesus' sacrificial death was a once-and-for-all event that achieved salvation for all of humanity. Within the letter to the Hebrews we find passages that liken this sacrifice directly to the practice of Temple sacrifice in ancient Judaism. Unlike those offerings, his will lead us to God. Hebrews 9.26 states that "He has appeared once for all at the culmination of the ages to do away with sin by the sacrifice of himself." Other sacrifices do not suffice. They will not be able to be sufficient offerings in the face of the enormity of human sin. Only Jesus' sacrifice can be redemptive for all of humanity. He was the ultimate and final sacrifice.

The belief in Jesus' resurrection legitimizes Jesus as God for Christians. The resurrection also symbolizes the renewal of creation, initiating a new era in human history. Humans, saved through Christ, must now allow God's grace to enter into their hearts in order to be saved. Here Christians break with the ancient Judaism that is the foundation of their beliefs. Christians argue that the death and resurrection of Christ are not only necessary, but replace any other paths to salvation, namely obedience to the law in ancient Judaism. Paul clearly indicates this when he writes, "I do not set aside the grace of God, for if righteousness could be gained through the law, Christ died for nothing!" (Galatians 2.21). In other words, if obedience to the Law was all that was necessary to restore our relationship with God, then Jesus truly died for no reason. His death and resurrection become superfluous. Instead, Christians believe, Jesus becomes the necessary precondition for salvation. The Jewish Law is not the path towards righteousness.

Often folded into conversations about creation and sin are Christian discussions about evil and the devil. In popular culture Christians often mistakenly assume that the snake in the garden that tempts Eve and Adam is the devil, though nothing in the passage indicates that this is the case. The character of the devil does appear in the Hebrew Scriptures, most notably in the book of Job. Devil is not a name, however, but a title given to a supernatural entity. Satan is also a title that means "adversary." The name Lucifer emerges in medieval theology as the embodiment of evil and hater of God. In a narrative that is similar to Eve and Adam's, pride forced him to be cast out of heaven into the underworld. In a fifth-century translation of the Bible into Latin—the Vulgate by St. Jerome—the devil is named Lucifer. There are various references in Scripture which have varied meanings: in the book of Job the devil is presented as an angel in God's heavenly court; in the thirteenth century the Fourth Lateran Council of Christian leaders determined that the Devil and the other demons were created by God and were thus good in their nature but they by themselves had turned to evil; for Augustine there are two types of evil: the evil one voluntarily perpetuates and the evil one suffers. God is responsible for the second kind, because God is just and God punishes the unjust (wicked). We are being punished for the collective evil of humanity.

All evil is the result of human will (corruption motivated by desire and lust). This is important to emphasize. Humanity, not God, is the cause of evil. Evil is a lack of good, lack of desire to serve God. God cannot create evil because God is good. You cannot have a Good Creator produce something that is evil.

Christianity teaches that humans were created in an original state of blessedness. However, due to our free will human beings are all now fallen. We are in a disordered state of misdirected desire where we try to find satisfaction in all of the wrong things instead of our true path in God. This disorder is what remains within humanity after baptism, leaving humans with the inclination toward sinfulness. We are now predisposed to sin. Though the image of God within us is not destroyed it is clouded. The only way that we can be redeemed is through God's grace. Jesus' dying on the cross was the ultimate sacrifice on our behalf and is rooted in the sacrificial system of ancient Judaism. The Jewish sacrifice in the Temple is the basis for the Christian belief in Jesus as sacrifice; Jesus "has appeared once for all at the culmination of the ages to do away with sin by the sacrifice of himself" (Hebrews 9.26). Some Christians interpret this sacrifice as atonement. Since Adam insulted God, his sin requires repayment. Jesus, as human and divine, could repay the enormous debt to God. The incarnation of Jesus is repayment for our original sin. These understandings of Jesus as atoning for humanity, as a sacrifice for humanity, and as the final offering in the face of our sinfulness, in addition to their heavy reliance on the book of Genesis, demonstrate the ways in which ancient Judaism truly shaped not only how Christians understood human nature, but also how Christians came to understand God's salvific work within the context of the Trinity.

Creation

As in Judaism, within the Christian tradition there is a link between the doctrine of creation and environmental ethics. Feminist scholars argue that within the Christian tradition sexist interpretations of the Genesis accounts and patriarchal images of God have implications for how we understand not only humanity, but also the rest of creation. Ecofeminist theologians are scholars that link the objectification and exploitation of women to the rest of non-human creation, since women are symbolically identified with nature. The same worldviews that degrade women fuel the disregard and abuse of the environment. Within ecofeminist theology, the *imago Dei* is critiqued as a doctrine that has misinterpreted humanity's relationship with the rest of creation and fueled the abuse on non-human creation. Ecofeminist theologians critique traditional theological anthropologies for divorcing the human from the cosmos in its focus on our "divine image." Today, humanity must resituate itself and accept its appropriate role within creation. Humanity must come to terms with its interrelationship with and dependency on the rest of creation. Humans are not autonomous rulers of creation but are, in contrast, heavily dependent on the created world.

While traditional interpretations of the divine image have fueled abuse of the rest of the creation, this was not the original intent of the Genesis account. Human beings as created in the image of God are representatives of God here on earth. The proper care of the earth is our charge as representatives. We are stewards of the earth. An interpretation of the divine image within this stewardship model implies that both male and female as created in the image of God are God's representatives here on earth. There is a mutual transformation of the manner in which human beings understand themselves and how we name and describe the God that is our Creator. As ecofeminists teach us, this also has deep implications for our relationship with the rest of creation. An ecofeminist analysis re-envisions humanity's relationship with creation as one of care and not dominion. They offer us a different interpretation of creation, one that is nonetheless grounded in Genesis. Within Islam as well, Genesis will play a central role in the manner in which creation is understood.

Islam

A poem by Mirza Ghalib, the most prolific Urdu and Persian poet from Mughal India in the nineteenth century, says, "When there was nothing, there was God. Had there been nothing, God would have been." Everything evolves and revolves around God in Islamic thought. Muslims understand the divine act of creation as a blessing. God creates through pure mercy and blessing. The mercy of God upon creation is highlighted in the creation story.

Adam, Eve, and the Created Order

The creation story in the Qur'an builds on the creation story featured in the Bible. Al-Tabari stated in his commentary on the Qur'an that the story of creation begins two thousand years before the emergence of Adam and Eve. God's most beloved creation was Iblis, who later becomes Satan. God makes Iblis the vicegerent of the earth, a role he executes faithfully for a thousand years. God calls him "the arbiter," but this praise is said to have made Iblis arrogant and ruthless. He creates mischief, enmity, and hate on earth that lasts for two millennia and causes so much bloodshed that "horses waded in the blood."

Because of Satan's evil, when God decides to create Adam and Eve, the first humans, in the Qur'anic narrative, the angels—who are said to be God's most honorable creations—ask him why he is doing so after the previous creation failed:

And when your Lord said to the angels, "Indeed, I will make upon the earth a successive authority," They said, "Will You place upon it one who causes corruption therein and sheds blood, while we declare Your praise and sanctify You?" Allah said, "Indeed, I know that which you do not know."

Q2:30

The angels are then asked about things around them, and they are unable to answer. The answer is imparted to Adam, and this shows the difference between angels and

FIGURE 15 *Adam and Eve expelled from the garden, from* Qisas al-anbiya *(Stories of the Prophets), by Ishaq ibn Ibrahim al-Nishapuri (11thC), Iran, c. 1570. Codex, ink, colors and gold on paper. Folio: 31.7 x 20.0 cm. Chester Beatty (CBL Per 231, fol. 13v), © The Trustees of the Chester Beatty Library, Dublin.*

human beings. This is an important response because it highlights that there are some questions that God's creatures may ask to which they will not receive an answer. The Adam and Eve story comes in different sections of the Qur'an and is not presented fully in any one passage. Creation is where God's first interaction with human beings takes place, and it is the setting of the human condition.

God creates Adam and Eve from what is said in the Qur'an to be dirt from the earth. They are both to be the custodians and vicegerents of the earth. Their submission to God comes through their relationship to the earth. This is why Adam's name is *adim al-ard* (part of the earth, skin of the earth). A commentary of al-Tabari mentions that God created Adam and Eve from his own hands because God wanted to expose Iblis's arrogance and to show creation what had gone wrong with Iblis. Some Islamic traditions comment particularly on Eve's appearance: "She was as big and as comely as Adam, had 700 plaits in her hair, was adorned with chrysolite and perfumed with musk . . . Her skin was more delicate than Adam's and purer in color, and her voice was more beautiful than his."

There is clearly a mix of creations that all seem to be vying for God's attention and love. What is significant is that Eve was created from the same earth as Adam. There are Islamic traditions that talk about Eve being a "handmaiden" to Adam and that God decided to create Eve because he was so lonely. This has led to many conclusions about the relationship between Adam and Eve, but ultimately this story is about God and glorifying God—human actions and activities highlight, once again, the centrality and glory of God, who does not need a companion or another to create. Adam and Eve's only command was to submit solely to God and to stay away from the tree of immortality.

It is said that Iblis was once an extremely knowledgeable being, but he became arrogant with that knowledge. Satan is said to have whispered "evil" to Adam and offers to take him to the tree of eternity and to a place that never decays. It is here that Adam and Eve fall victim to the whispers of Satan, and their nakedness becomes apparent to them (Q20:115–22).

> Then Satan whispered to him; he said, "O Adam, shall I direct you to the tree of eternity and possession that will not deteriorate?" And Adam and his wife ate of it, and their private parts became apparent to them, and they began to fasten over themselves from the leaves of paradise. And Adam disobeyed his Lord and erred. Then his Lord chose him and turned to him in forgiveness and guided [him].
>
> Q20:120–122

It is here that the covenant with God is broken. God had commanded both Adam and Eve to obey only him, but temptation took over. This is where they lose their place in paradise and are told to dwell now on earth.

When God creates Adam and Eve, he asks all other creations to prostrate to them. They all do, but not Iblis. Iblis considers himself superior to Adam because he is made of fire and Adam of the earth with which God created Adam and Eve. It is this disobedience that turns Iblis into Satan. It is submitting to God and obeying God that matters; in a way, everything else is secondary. Whether light, fire, and clay, God's position reigns supreme.

This story resembles others in the Qur'an that provoke thought about the nature of God's creation. They are tales from which much is "read out," from ethics, morality, gender and sexuality. It is only through God's command that he allows Satan the ability to do everything that he can to take Adam and Eve away from the path of submitting fully only to God. The Qur'an is then full of stories of times when human beings lost sight of what full submission only to the One God meant. When this happened, they would be at a loss, and if they repented and turned their sight back to God, they would thrive and prosper. The individual stories of different human beings and their relationship to God shows the diversity of piety and submission in the Qur'anic world.

Adam and Eve are forgiven, but they also become examples of human greed and are arrogant toward God's command: "Then Adam received from his Lord [some] words, and He accepted his repentance. Indeed, it is He who is the Accepting of repentance, the Merciful" (Q2:37). Again, the Qur'an emphasizes bringing back perfection to God. In a different understanding from that of Christianity, Islam holds that Adam's act was not a sin but a mistake that God forgives. The Qur'anic story differs from the Bible as "original sin" does not play a part in Islam and therefore there is no call for a savior in the form of Christ. Adam and Eve are both tempted and the blame is not set on Eve. The greatest sin and the only sin that is not forgiven by God is *shirk*, where Muslims associate anything or anyone with God—the sin of practicing idolatry or polytheism.

Human nature is therefore flawed. Humans may err and make mistakes, but through prayer, repentance, and turning back to good deeds, they can submit to God. It is probably for this reason that some have called Islamic monotheism a radical monotheism. The stories in the Qur'an continually warn against anything that can interfere in the direct link and connection between God and God's creatures and creations. The general gist of the stories command human beings to obey only God. If they err, they should repent, which will bring peace on earth. If they do not repent, a severe punishment awaits them in the hereafter:

> We said, "Go down from it, all of you. And when guidance comes to you from Me, whoever follows My guidance—there will be no fear concerning them, nor will they grieve. And those who disbelieve and deny Our signs—those will be companions of the Fire; they will abide therein eternally."
>
> Q2:38–39

Human beings are also given free will. This has been a point of discussion for many Muslims in the past and present. A Muslim's everyday acts of faith are done within the tension of having free will but also accepting that God knows all things and predestines the beginning and end of all matters.

Some mystics in Islam have argued that Satan should be seen in a different light. Sarmad, a Jewish convert to Islam from Mughal India who was executed in 1661, said, "Go, learn the method of servantship from Satan: Choose one *qibla* (direction of prayer/ submission) and do not prostrate yourself to anything else." Muslim mystics have spent considerable time in thought and action in their religious quest of appreciating all that God has created. *Wajd* is a concept of spiritual ecstasy achieved in the remembrance of God's grace and blessing. This can come from acts of ritual prayer, singing, and dancing. The essence of these actions is to remember God as creator of all things and to nurture inner peace and love. God's love is bestowed upon all things that God creates: it is the earthly path that Muslims tread in their humble attempt to understand this concept. A peaceful, loving, and beautiful *nafs*, often translated as "self," "soul," or even "ego," is a concept that many Muslims, especially the mystics, have highlighted. Muslims spend much time thinking about their actions, which will overcome their sacred struggle over the soul in complete submission to God as creator and Lord. The mystics take this a step further to challenge the idea that men and women are earthly and bound to the ephemeral, but the *nafs* has nothing to do with dust.

The Fruits of the Earth

The Qur'an has many references to the bounties and beauty that God bestowed on the earth God created. From the rivers that flow to the mountains that rise high, they are understood as signs from God to human beings to appreciate the oneness of God. It is through this human-and-earth relationship that God further tests human beings in upholding good. The duties and obligations then extend to the earth and all that it holds. The cycles of the day—the sun rising and sun setting—become a part of Muslims' ritual obligations, as they set their daily prayers around them.

The Qur'an states, "And there is no creature on [or within] the earth or bird that flies with its wings except [that they are] communities like you. We have not neglected in the Register a thing. Then unto their Lord they will be gathered" (Q6:38). Muslims understand this verse to advance a form of "green" Islam, which takes in to consideration the many communities that human beings live alongside. Muslims today are spending considerable time reflecting upon Qur'anic passages in relation to the current ecological crisis.

The significance of water is mentioned several times in the Qur'an. Water is used for ritual ablutions:

O you who have believed, when you rise to [perform] prayer, wash your faces and your forearms to the elbows and wipe over your heads and wash your feet to the ankles. And if you are in a state of *janabah* (after sexual discharge), then purify yourselves. But if you are ill or on a journey or one of you comes from the place of relieving himself or you have contacted women and do not find water, then seek clean earth and wipe over your faces and hands with it. Allah does not intend to make difficulty for you, but He intends to purify you and complete His favor upon you that you may be grateful.

Q5:6

The earth and all that it bears become central in the cycle of Muslim life. The water well by the Ka'ba which is connected by Muslims with the Hajj is called *Zam Zam*, which emerged after the stamping of baby Ishmael's feet when his Mother, Hagar, could not find any food or drink for him, is holy water and is still consumed today. Muslims who perform pilgrimage to Mecca during Hajj and Umra drink and also bring back the water for their loved ones.

Water is not the only created element from God mentioned in the Qur'an. The environment in which Muslims dwell becomes a focus of contemplation and faith. Islamic traditions make several mentions of trees. It is stated in the Qur'an:

> Do you not see that to Allah prostrates whoever is in the heavens and whoever is on the earth and the sun, the moon, the stars, the mountains, the trees, the moving creatures and many of the people? But upon many the punishment has been justified. And he whom Allah humiliates—for him there is no bestower of honor. Indeed, Allah does what He wills.

Q22:18

This verse brings together many different forms of God's creation and reminds human beings that only God has full control over everything that is happening. When Mary is about to give birth to Jesus, she goes to a palm tree and shakes it. She hears a voice: "But he called her from below her, 'Do not grieve; your Lord has provided beneath you a stream" (Q19:24). The prophet Muhammad highlighted palm trees and mentioned that palm trees would be planted for the faithful in paradise. Recently, the Islamic Republic of Pakistan hit its target of planting a billion trees. This was recorded by the World Economic Forum and has been called the Billion Tree Tsunami.

The Qur'an brings the attention of Muslims to gardens too: "Indeed, the righteous will be among gardens and springs" (Q51:15). Paradise/heaven (*Jannat*) is literally understood as a garden. The gardens of the earth are then signs of what could be experienced in the timeless life after death. The Qur'an mentions seven heavens on numerous occasions: "And He completed them as seven heavens within two days and inspired in each heaven its command. And We adorned the nearest heaven with lamps and as protection. That is the determination of the Exalted in Might, the Knowing" (Q41:12). It is said that at the seventh heaven there is the Lote tree (*Sidrathal-Muntaha*) that marks the place where no creation can pass (Q5313).

Animals

Muslims are expected to eat *halal* (permitted) foods. It is stated in the Qur'an, "He has only forbidden to you dead animals, blood, the flesh of swine, and that which has been dedicated to other than Allah. But whoever is forced [by necessity], neither desiring [it] nor transgressing [its limit]—then indeed, Allah is Forgiving and Merciful" (Q16:115).

This then allows the eating of animals which have been slaughtered with the name of God. There are some differences of opinion among Islamic legal Sunni and Shi'a schools when it comes to sea animals in terms of scales and fins. Animals must be alive and healthy when being slaughtered; the throat is cut with a sharp knife and the blood is drained.

An animal is sacrificed during the pilgrimage (Hajj) season. It is a time to reenact the prophet Abraham's sacrifice of a ram in place of his son, Ishmael. In contemporary times, Muslims who can afford to will sacrifice animals. The meat is largely donated to the poor. In the West, Muslims will arrange for animals to be slaughtered in places of need. An organization set up in 2015 by an Australian and Canadian Muslim alliance, the Vegan Muslim Initiative, rereads passages from the Qur'an and advocates that Muslims should stop eating meat and slaughtering animals.

Muslim belief and piety is strengthened through reflecting on the purpose of creation. Why would this all-powerful, merciful God create? These questions have become a part of faith for Muslims as they strive to understand their individual purpose in relation to God and how they act toward all that surrounds them.

Afterthought: Creation

The Torah's narrative is clear that there is only One God, who conceives and constructs the cosmos, the earth, and all living things. The main point of that narrative is that creation is not an accident. This has two consequences.

The first consequence is that humans have free will. Like the rest of creation, humanity's free will is not an accident. From the outset, by God's design, humans control how they will relate to God and to one another. The original humans' exercise of their God-given freedom alienates all humanity from God, which creates the conditions of everything that follows. Had Adam and Eve followed God's commandment, there would have been no additional story to tell.

Humans' alienation from God in turn generates two issues: the cause and nature of the alienation and the actions needed to repair it.

Christianity reads the creation story as the saga of original sin, which it understands as an indelible trait of humanity. Following the model of the sacrifices in the Jerusalem Temple, Jesus' crucifixion saves humans from their sinfulness. Jesus' sacrifice is unique because it is ultimate and generic. It applies once and for all and to all humanity. Jesus' resurrection signals God's alleviation of humanity's sinful condition. To underscore the meaning and promise of the resurrection, most forms of Christianity celebrate Sunday, the day of the resurrection, as "the Lord's Day," instead of the Sabbath.

Judaism and Islam tend to see the creation story more as a chronicle of human weakness and frailty than as original sin. Humans can repair their alienation from God through concrete beliefs and behaviors that are grounded in God's teachings as interpreted by tradition. In Judaism, the Sabbath concretizes and celebrates the order of creation. Jews rest when God rested. Islam's "un-ordinary" day is Friday, the day Adam was created and the day Adam and Eve were exiled from the Garden of Eden.

Because the story of creation depicts Eve as the initial violator of God's teachings, historical Christian understandings of the Genesis story have tended to hold Eve responsible for original sin. Although Judaic and Islamic views of Eve's role are more nuanced, on the basis of the creation narrative all three traditions have perpetuated negative stereotypes of women and created structures that diminish women's roles in the religion's structure.

The second consequence of the creation narrative is that the world is ordered and purposeful. This means that the cosmos is an integrated system designed to sustain life. Living organisms and creatures have diverse characteristics and purposes that make the system work. Humans—created in God's image with male and female genders—have a distinctive role in the realm of the living. A key part of that role is to procreate and populate the earth. In order to do that, humans must respect all forms of life and care for the created order so that it can support and nurture life. On this basis, all three monotheistic traditions express interest in and concern for the environment, including plant and animal life. The monotheistic vision of creation is comprehensive and integrative and highlights humans' responsibility to God, one another, and the order of nature.

Study Questions: Creation

What are some ways in which each religion distinctively interprets creation?
What does the Adam and Eve story teach about the human condition?
What is the connection between the Adam and Eve story and sin?
How does the creation narrative connect Jews, Christians, and Muslims to the environment?
What is the attitude of the three traditions to the created world?

5

Covenant and Identity

It is clear in the biblical narrative that God created human beings in order to have a relationship with them. Covenant is the framework for that relationship. It flows from, realizes, and fulfills the purpose of creation. This chapter explores the varied ways the biblical covenant understanding has come to expression in the three heritages.

Judaism

Covenant is the foundation stone of Judaism. As we have seen earlier, covenant is a pervasive theme in the *Tanakh* and has two forms: 1) familial and eternal with Abraham, Isaac, and Jacob, and with David, and 2) adoptive and reciprocal with Moses.

In Judaism, the covenantal relationship means that God and the Jewish people—both collectively and individually—have a stake in one another, that God does not provoke a breach without reason, and God's frustration with the people is, in principle, warranted, and not arbitrary. The idea of exclusive loyalty and total commitment to God makes the covenantal connection emotionally intense. God expresses disappointment and anger at the people's shortcomings but responds to their repentance with mercy, compassion, and lovingkindness.

Judaism's understanding of the covenant has two major consequences.

First, the covenant means that Judaism is the religion of a people, an extended family. But Jewish peoplehood is unusual because, as discussed above, outsiders who adopt it become relatives as if they had been born into it, and their children inherit that covenantal kinship at birth. The story of Ruth, a Moabite (not an Israelite) who becomes King David's great-grandmother, depicts acceptance of non-descendants into Abraham's heritage.

The determination of which parent transfers covenantal membership has changed over time. In the *Tanakh* familial descent is patrilineal, from the father. Matrilineal (from the mother) descent became normative in the rabbinic period. In Reform and Reconstructionist Judaisms, descent can be from either parent.

Second, the covenant lays the religious foundation for the redemption of the Jewish people. On the one hand, God makes an eternal commitment of land and peoplehood to Abraham and his descendants and of leadership of Israel to King David and his lineage. On the other hand, God warns the Israelites that their failure to adhere to the terms of the covenant will cause their exile from the land God promised and gave them. Combined, these agreements mean that however the Jewish people may suffer the consequences of their shortcomings over the course of history, God will not abandon them. At some undisclosed future time, God's promises will be realized, and God will redeem the Jewish people from exile and restore them to the land of Israel. The covenant affirms that God commits to persevere with the Jewish people while calling them to a life of sanctity and purpose. This understanding undergirds the belief in ultimate redemption, creates the basis for the idea of a messiah from the house of David, and may support the belief in resurrection of the dead as well.

Rabbinic Judaism responded to the destruction of the Second Temple, the devastation of the *Bar Kokhba* rebellion, and the Jews' exile from Jerusalem by affirming that the covenant was still in effect. Ancient rabbis reasoned that because God's ways are inscrutable, the events of history need not signal the end of God's commitment to the Jewish people or God's power over their destiny. What happens in history is less important than how the Jewish people conduct themselves. God initiated the covenant as an act of gracious divine free will, not something the people sought, earned, or merited. Thus, their continued loyalty to God and performance of the commandments maintain the covenant and establish a stable, ongoing relationship with God.

Within this framework, the rabbis could interpret the events of their time in various ways. Some rabbinic teachings, for example, suggest that the transgressions that led to exile were ethical rather than ritual. Other teachings advance the notion that exile illustrates God's love for the Jewish people and that their suffering serves to purify the nation and prepare it for redemption.

The covenant operates along a continuum. It is both particular and universal, familial and voluntary, everlasting and conditional, territorial and portable. Its adaptable framework has charted varied paths to Jewish peoplehood and encouraged Judaism's belief in the possibility of a perfected world marked by the fulfillment of God's covenantal promises.

Circumcision: The Sign of the Covenant

The covenant relationship between God and the Jewish people is actualized in the ritual of the *Brit Milah* (circumcision). The Hebrew word *brit* means "covenant." This ceremony fulfills God's commandment to Abraham (Genesis 17.10–13):

> This is my covenant with you and your descendants after you, the covenant you are to keep: Every male among you shall be circumcised. You are to undergo circumcision, and it will be the sign of the covenant between me and you. For the generations to come, every male among you who is eight days old must be circumcised, including those born in your household or bought with money from a foreigner—those who are not from your offspring. Whether born in your household or bought with your money, they must be circumcised. My covenant in your flesh is to be an everlasting covenant.

People typically celebrate circumcision in the family's home or a synagogue. It begins with the recitation of verses of Psalms and the *Shema'* as the male child is brought into the room. The father places the child on the lap of the child's godfather (*sandaq*), who holds the child during the procedure. As a professional circumciser (*mohel*) removes the child's foreskin, the father—in contemporary practice often together with the mother—recites a blessing that thanks God for the commandment "to bring him (the infant) into the covenant of Abraham our father." The *mohel* recites a blessing over wine, announces the child's name, and places a drop of wine on the infant's lips. Those present respond with the hope that the child's life in the covenant will be characterized by engagement with Torah, by marriage, and by good deeds. A festive meal follows. The ritual also can include a richly decorated "Chair of Elijah," who, on the basis of Malachi 3.1, is identified in Judaic aggadic tradition as the "Angel of the Covenant" and the guardian of Jewish children.

Since the covenantal promise is transmitted to and through the descendants of Isaac and Jacob, Abraham's second-born son and grandson, membership in the Jewish people is a matter of descent, not the result of ritual inclusion. Thus, while circumcision symbolizes covenant membership, in *halakhah* it does not effect it or confer Jewish identity. As Professor Shaye J.D. Cohen notes, according to *halakhah*, children born of a Jewish mother are Jews at birth. *Halakhah* considers a non-circumcised son of a Jewish mother as Jewish. If circumcision poses a health risk, it may be postponed or not performed at all. However, in the case of a non-Jewish male who converts to Judaism, circumcision is transformative and effects membership in the Jewish people.

Cohen observes that within Judaism circumcision has been interpreted in varied ways. Maimonides, for instance, regarded it as representing membership in the community of believers in the unity of God, which included Muslims, who also practice circumcision. By contrast, the *Zohar* holds that circumcision enables the soul to see God and transforms the infant into a Jew.

Some contemporary Jewish groups deem circumcision to be outmoded, painful, or gender-specific and have substituted a baby-naming ritual called the *Brit Shalom* ("the Covenant of Peace") in its place. This rite may not be not recognized by all denominations.

To celebrate the birth of a daughter, many communities engage in an increasingly popular ritual known as *Simchat Bat* ("Rejoicing in the Birth of a Daughter") or *B'rit Bat* ("A Daughter's Covenant"). Often practiced at home, this ritual may include singing, the recitation of blessings and scriptural passages, naming the child, and gifts for the newborn. Orthodox communities conventionally announce the name of a baby girl, along with blessings for her future in the Jewish community, during the Sabbath Torah reading.

Identity

The halakhic definition of Jewish identity—which crystallized during two millennia of diaspora and minority status—is that to be Jewish one must either be the offspring of a Jewish mother or have converted under the auspices of an Orthodox rabbi. In modern times, this definition has been challenged by three new realities: first, large non-Orthodox Jewish denominations in Europe and America; second, the establishment of a sovereign secular Jewish state; and third, the emergence of secular (i.e., cultural, non-religious) understandings of Jewish identity. These realities have introduced fluidity into the religious, legal, and practical aspects of what constitutes contemporary Jewish identity and self-understanding.

Religious Views of Inherited Identity

Judaism's contemporary denominations agree on the principle of matrilineal descent. If the mother is Jewish, so are her children. As noted earlier, Reconstructionist Judaism and later Reform Judaism adopted in addition the concept of patrilineal descent, which applies when only the father is Jewish. In both, if only one parent—mother or father—is Jewish, the child is considered Jewish, with the understanding that he or she will be raised as a Jew and celebrate Judaism's lifecycle ceremonies.

Identity Through Religious Conversion

The Noahide laws make clear that Judaism neither requires nor expects non-Jews to adopt Jewish beliefs and practices in order to find a place in the messianic World to Come. Primarily for that reason, Judaism is not a missionary religion, although it welcomes those who freely wish to embrace it. The Talmud (*Shavu'ot* 39a) understands Moses' words at Sinai—"I am making this covenant, with its oath, not only with you who are standing here with us today in the presence of the Lord our God but also with those who are not here today" (Deuteronomy 29.14–15)—to refer to "coming generations and future converts."

Contemporary denominations agree that conversion requires more than a personal, individual decision; it must entail a communal and official act. But they differ about the nature of the act itself. A halakhic conversion requires study with a rabbi, circumcision for males; the convert's (female or male) immersion in a ritual bath (*miqveh*) in the presence of a "court" of three witnesses, usually rabbis; and an affirmation before that court of the convert's commitment to practice *halakhah*. If a male convert is already circumcised, a drop of blood is taken from his penis. Reform conversion, depending on the officiating rabbi, does not invariably require circumcision or immersion. It asks instead, after a period of study, for the convert's oral and written commitment, in the presence of a three-person religious panel, to be bound to the Jewish people.

The Orthodox and Conservative movements do not accept as valid either non-halakhic conversion or the principle of patrilineal descent. This means that a person considered Jewish by some denominations may not be so regarded by others. For example, Orthodox and Conservative rabbis who will not officiate at marriages between Jews and non-Jews may insist that an individual who understands himself or herself to be Jewish by virtue of having a Jewish father undergo a halakhic conversion.

According to *halakhah*, Jewish identity—either by birth or halakhic conversion—is permanent. A Jew who practices another religion or observes none of the commandments may be deemed an apostate but is still considered to be Jewish. Some Orthodox authorities may regard a convert's abandonment of Judaism as the mark of a false conversion and will no longer accept the person as Jewish. In general, however, within each denomination, a convert to Judaism becomes a "son" or "daughter" of Abraham and transmits Jewish identity by birth to her or—if Reform or Reconstructionist—his offspring.

Civic Identity in the State of Israel

The issue of identity is particularly important in the State of Israel, which offers automatic citizenship to all Jews who choose to live there. For purposes of citizenship, Israel's secular Law of Return draws on but expands the halakhic definition of Jewish identity. It defines a Jew as "a person who was born of a Jewish mother or has become converted to Judaism and who is not a member of another religion." The state offers citizenship to persons who have a Jewish mother or maternal grandmother, a Jewish father or grandfather, to Orthodox converts to Judaism, and to non-Orthodox converts whose conversions took place outside of the State of Israel and meet minimum Israeli government standards of Jewish education and time spent in observance. It also extends citizenship to the spouse, child, and grandchild of a Jew and to the spouse of a child or grandchild of a Jew, whether those family members are Jewish or not. The Law of Return currently does not apply to non-Orthodox conversions carried out within the State of Israel.

The secular legal determinants for Israeli citizenship, however, differ somewhat from those of personal status. In a legal framework carried over from the Ottoman Empire's millet system and the British Mandate, Israel has a two-court structure: secular and religious. Personal status—which includes religious membership, conversion, marriage, and divorce—is controlled by religious courts: Jewish, Christian, Muslim, Druze, Baha'i, etc. Israel does not have civil marriage, and religious courts largely, but not exclusively, handle divorce cases. For Jews, the Chief Rabbinate determines the legitimacy of marriage, divorce, and conversion. In all these matters, the Rabbinate applies the halakhic definition of Jewish identity.

In recent years Israel has experienced increasing numbers of immigrants who are citizens under the Law of Return but do not meet the halakhic norms for Jewish identity set by the Chief Rabbinate. For instance, they may be part of a family in which the father, but not the mother, is Jewish. Because they are not halakhically Jewish, these Israeli citizens—now in the hundreds of thousands—must formally convert to Judaism in order to legally marry in the state. The Chief Rabbinate controls conversion to Judaism, but its process is slow and requires a commitment to *halakhah*, which many potential non-Orthodox converts are not prepared to make.

To circumvent the Rabbinate, thousands of Israelis annually take advantage of a legal loophole that recognizes marriages performed abroad. In addition, many Israelis are opting to be married in Israel—some even by Orthodox rabbis—outside of the Chief Rabbinate, in part as a protest against its policies and control.

The ITIM Institute helps Israelis negotiate the Chief Rabbinate's conversion process. However, some Israelis are now opting for conversions not recognized by the Chief Rabbinate. An organization called *Giyur K'Halakhah* ('halakhic conversion"), for instance, offers conversion approved by some Orthodox authorities, but not the Chief Rabbinate, and has a particular focus on minors. Reform Judaism in Israel also performs conversions, which are gaining adherents. The state recognizes non-halakhic conversions for purposes of civic registration but not personal status. The determination of personal status is a topic of intense and ongoing political discussion in Israel.

Contemporary Identities

In an increasingly global and interconnected world, conventional notions of identity—both collective and individual—are changing. Whereas identity may have been understood as a singular, static marker of a person or group, it now routinely represents fluidity, multiplicity, and choice. Established understandings of Jewish identity—typically framed in terms of "ethnicity" or "religion"—are adapting to these social and cultural changes.

Multiple forms of contemporary Jewish self-understanding—often referred to as "Jewishness"—are secular or cultural. A recent Pew Research survey shows that two-thirds of Jews in the United States self-identify as Jewish primarily by culture and heritage rather than by religion. A substantial number of them have non-Jewish partners, and the children and grandchildren of these marriages—even when they self-identify as Jewish—often affirm multiple heritages. Some see themselves as half-Jewish or one-quarter Jewish and incorporate elements from both sides of their families in their lives. As examples in this book demonstrate, contemporary Jews often manifest their "Jewishness" in conjunction with other forms of identity, such as LGBTQ or feminism. United States' Jewish communities are increasingly diverse, and at least 6%–8% are Black, Latino, brown, and Asian Jews, many of whom claim multiple identities and heritages.

New and diverse interest-driven models of Jewish community are expanding. For example, the organization *Kenissa*, founded in 2016, helps 300 different regional Jewish communal groups from the United States and Canada—such as Jews for Social Justice, Abundant Farm, and Grassroots Shabbat—to innovate and strengthen their effectiveness. Professor Jack Wertheimer notes the development of innovative religious start-ups, which are devising new forms of prayer and engagement and hold communal events in unconventional places, such as nightclubs and theatres. For instance, a national organization called OneTable helps unaffiliated young people aged 21–39 host and join Sabbath eve meals. Families craft Passover Seders that merge the Israelites' liberation from slavery with contemporary political and social issues, and synagogues and individuals participate in special Sabbaths, such as "Pink Shabbat," which focuses on the prevention of breast cancer. Contemporary synagogues also are experimenting with new forms of worship and study that include meditation, yoga, and mindfulness.

All these developments exhibit a personalist approach, in which individuals select the parts of the covenantal heritage that matter to them most.

Classical Judaic texts also have fresh availability. One example is *Daf Yomi* ("daily page"), a popular program developed in 1923 by Rabbi Meir Shapiro, in which participants study one page of the *Bavli* each day and complete the entire 2,711 pages in seven and one-half years. *Daf Yomi* is online, and the internet provides other websites, Facebook pages, apps, and online courses that can promote virtual learning communities of Judaic textual study. Another example is the website and app *Sefaria,* founded in 2011, which contains an array of Judaic texts, many with translations.

There also are multiple international communities that claim covenantal kinship to, and sometimes seek official recognition as, members of the Jewish people. An example is the Ethiopian *Beta Israel* community, which is accepted as Jews by Israel's Chief Rabbinate. In addition, such African groups as the Igbo in Nigeria and the Lemba in Zimbabwe and South Africa claim Israelite or Jewish heritage, as do groups in Cameroon and Papua New Guinea, among other places. In 2005, Israel's Chief Rabbinate recognized as Jews the *Bnei Menashe* community of north-east India to enable their application for Israeli citizenship.

Genetics

Because Jews have been largely endogamous, it has been possible in some cases to use genetic research to trace community identity. But there is no evidence of a "Jewish gene" that links all Jews to one another. In the State of Israel in some cases, particularly for immigrants from the former Soviet Union, genetic testing is being used in an attempt to confirm Jewish heritage and identity. This method, however, has not supplanted traditional halakhic approaches to the issue, which require a study of the individual's family tree on the side of the mother.

Covenant and Holocaust

The Holocaust, a term that means a sacrifice entirely devoured by fire, or, in Hebrew, *Shoah* ("catastrophe"), is a defining event in the history of Judaism and the Jewish people. Between 1941 and 1945, the Nazi regime in Germany murdered two-thirds, approximately six million, of the Jews of Europe—men, women, and 1.6 million children—in a sustained, systematic, state-sponsored, industrial-like genocide. It also murdered large numbers of handicapped people, Roma, ethnic Poles, Soviet citizens, gay males, prisoners of war, Jehovah's Witnesses, and political opponents. To achieve their ends, the Nazis built large concentration and extermination camps with gas chambers, designed to kill as many people—primarily Jews—as possible with maximum efficiency.

Within Judaism, the Holocaust has generated serious theological questions about the nature of God and the viability of the covenant. How could God allow this to happen? Was God powerless to intervene?

One line of response contends that the Holocaust created a fundamental break in the covenant between God and the Jewish people. For instance, Richard L. Rubenstein argues that God is dead, and the covenant is no longer a credible framework for a Judaic understanding of the world. He contends that, in a world that otherwise has no meaning, the Jewish lifecycle rituals and the holidays can provide nurture and sustenance. Irving Greenberg, an Orthodox rabbi, holds that in the Holocaust God broke the covenant and lost the authority to set the terms for any obligatory Jewish attitudes or behaviors. The covenant can persist not by God's command but solely by the voluntary participation of the Jewish people, who should strive to create a world of justice.

Alternatively, feminist theologian Melissa Raphael observes that framing the question about God's role in the Holocaust in terms of God's power employs a patriarchal image that ignores other aspects of God's character. Her study of the testimonies of women survivors suggests that Jewish women's acts of compassion and care for others resisted the dehumanization of the death camps and thereby manifested God's presence.

Eliezer Berkovits argued that, as beings created in God's image, humans have free will, which God does not constrain. Because humans can do evil as well as good, humans, and not God, are responsible for the Holocaust. Freedom entails responsibility and accountability. As stewards of God's creation, humans are responsible to prevent evil and advance good. Finally, there is the view that humans cannot fathom all of God's intentions, and the covenant endures.

This sample of theological responses demonstrates the singularity and distinctive consequence of the Holocaust. It is an event in the history of Judaism and humanity that offers no easy or uniform responses.

The Holocaust provoked international awareness of genocide and was a major factor in the development in 1948 of the United Nations' Convention on the Prevention and Punishment of the Crime of Genocide. Holocaust research pioneered the broader contemporary field of genocide studies. In January 2020, scores of international leaders joined in Israel to commemorate the liberation of the notorious Nazi death camp at Auschwitz. In a January 2020 ceremony at Auschwitz itself, the head of the Muslim World League declared that what occurred there should never happen again.

Christianity

The first followers of Jesus were Jewish and believed that the world would end in their lifetime. Many of the earliest sources we have for Jesus' life depict him as a Jewish apocalypticist (someone who proclaims the end of the world is imminent). After Jesus was carried to heaven in a cloud, two men in white appeared before the apostles, who were staring at the sky, and asked, " 'Men of Galilee,' they said, 'why do you stand here looking into the sky? This same Jesus, who has been taken from you into heaven, will come back in the same way you have seen him go into heaven'" (Acts 1.11). This means that Jesus proclaimed the imminent end of the present age, which would entail the judgment of the world by the Son of Man, the destruction of evil, and the coming of the kingdom of God. In addition, he taught that the Jewish community must repent and return to God. These teachings led his first followers to believe that they were in no way establishing a new religion distinctive from Judaism.

The New Covenant

For Christians, Jesus is the first martyr, who died on behalf of the sins of humanity. At the core of the Christian understanding of Jesus is the sacrifice of the cross and the resurrection. In the Last Supper Jesus substitutes for the Passover lamb. The sacrifice of his body and blood represents a reconciliation with God, creates a new covenant between God and humanity, and replaces the practice of sacrifice outlined in the Hebrew Scriptures. Christians asserted that Jesus' sacrificial death achieved this for humankind as a once-and-for-all event. No other sacrifice is needed. Christ gave himself for human sins to deliver humanity from the present evil age. He creates a new covenant in blood, his blood.

Christians repeat the initiation of a new covenant through Jesus' sacrifice when they read and proclaim his words during the Last Supper both inside and outside of Christian rituals. The Last Supper, the Gospel of Luke clearly tells us, occurs on the day "the Passover lamb had to be sacrificed" (Luke 22.7). Jesus sends his apostles, Peter and John, to make the preparations for the Passover meal. Prior to the meal he breaks bread and states " 'This is my body given for you; do this in remembrance of me.' In the same way, after the supper he took the cup, saying, 'This cup is the new covenant in my blood, which is poured out for you'" (Luke 22.19–20). In the Gospel of Matthew the words vary slightly and Jesus states, "This is the blood of the covenant, which is poured out for many for the forgiveness of sins" (Matthew 26.28). Paul also invokes the importance of the Eucharistic Prayer in 1 Corinthians: "For I received from the Lord what I also passed on to you: The Lord Jesus, on the night he was betrayed, took bread, and when he had given thanks, he broke it and said, 'This is my body, which is for you; do this in remembrance of me.' In the same way, after supper he took the cup, saying, 'This cup is the new covenant in my blood; do this, whenever you drink it, in remembrance of me'" (1 Corinthians 11.23–25). Paul rarely made reference to the events surrounding Jesus' life and ministry, so the fact that he repeats this prayer indicates it was part of the ritual life of the first Christians.

While Christians repeat this prayer many times, they may not realize that it is a direct reference to the covenants found in the Hebrew Scriptures. Jesus' words are saying, in this Judaic context, that he is initiating a new covenant with humanity, through his blood and sacrifice. Too often Christians function without an awareness of the manner in which their rituals, prayers, and theology are influenced by ancient Judaism. The reenactment of this meal will become one of the earliest practices within Christianity and is commemorated on Holy Thursday by Christians across the globe.

Christians who join in Eucharist or Communion reenact the establishment of this covenant on Sundays, sharing a meal with their church community.

This new covenant does not require sacrifice. Jesus is the ultimate sacrifice that replaces the Temple sacrifice of ancient Judaism. His covenant is open to all, even people of different faiths, for at its core is the forgiveness of the sins of humanity. This covenant is also the foundation of the Church as the mediator of God's covenant with humanity. Christians came to believe that Jesus is found in the reenactment of this Last Supper. The Gospel of Luke tells us that shortly after Jesus' resurrection two of the disciples were on their way to Emmaus. They were speaking about Jesus as they walked and Jesus himself approached them. They did not recognize him. When the three arrived in Emmaus the men invited Jesus to stay with them and he agreed. "When he was at the table with them, he took bread, gave thanks, broke it and began to give it to them. Then their eyes were opened and they recognized him" (Luke 24:30–31). The fact that Jesus' followers did not recognize him until the meal indicates that Jesus is found in the breaking of bread. The story also teaches that Jesus in found in this new covenant that was established at his last meal.

Eucharist and Baptism

The word "eucharist" comes from the Greek word for thanksgiving. Not all Christians consider it a sacrament; for some it is an ordinance, an expression of obedience, or an act of remembrance. There are also different ways in which Christians interpret the bread and wine and as the body and blood of Jesus Christ. For some the Eucharist is a memorial to Jesus Christ. Other Christians believe that in the ritual act of consecration, the bread and wine are transformed from physical to spiritual nourishment. The belief in transubstantiation, held by Roman Catholics, holds that at the moment of consecration the substance of the bread and wine literally turns into the body and blood of Jesus Christ, even though the appearance remains the same. The belief in transubstantiation is also why Catholic mass must always be performed at an altar. All Roman Catholic altars contain a relic of a saint and are the focal point of the church structure. They are tables for sacrifice. The book of Revelation says, "I saw under the altar the souls of those who had been slain because of the word of God and the testimony they had maintained" (Revelation 6.9). The Eucharist is said to sustain the Christian community on a regular basis. The blood of the new covenant creates a new relationship between God and humanity, mediated by Jesus. Another connection we find between ancient Judaism and Christianity is the Tabernacle, a locked box that stores the consecrated Eucharist. As consecrated, and similar to its role in Judaism, the Tabernacle in Christianity is the site of God's presence. There are also instances in Roman Catholicism where Mary is referred to as the Tabernacle since she carried the body of Christ within her.

The new covenant breaks the legacy of original sin. Membership in this new covenant is one of the issues that divides Christians. Participation in the church is required by some Christians, while others feel that Jesus died for the sins of all humanity, regardless of participation in Christian life. This diversity is also evident in the

FIGURE 16 *Little girls' First Communion, San Lucas Tolimán, Guatemala,* © *Byron Maldonado.*

diversity of views surrounding Christian baptism. Some Christian churches practice infant baptism—on the argument that the earlier one can perform this ritual the better—as a rite of initiation into the Christian community. Other Christian churches practice adult baptism on the basis that the individual should have a choice and agency in joining a Christian community. For some churches baptism is the sprinkling of water on one's head, while for others it is the full immersion of the body into baptismal waters. Through baptism one is born into the church, where one is washed in the blood of the lamb (evoking the image of Jesus as the sacrificial Passover lamb) through a rebirth. Emerging from baptism, the Christian has now agreed to a new life following the teachings of the church. For some Christians baptism is necessary for salvation. Both baptism and Eucharist are sacraments recognized by all Christian churches. Sacraments are a visual mediation of the divine and are central rites within Christian churches.

Consuming the bread and wine reverses the transgressive eating of the fruit by Adam and Eve, the first sin. This is no coincidence. It is through the act of eating that humans fall into a state of original sin. The Eucharist becomes an act of communion with God and with the Christian community. Eating symbolizes broken relationships and reconciliation; it is an element of the miracles and signs performed by Jesus. Jesus' first miracle occurs at the wedding at Cana, when he changes water to wine (John 2.1–11). Christians often highlight that Jesus' table fellowship with marginalized peoples is a sign of his inclusive compassion for all. The feeding of the 5,000 is one of Jesus' most well-known miracles (Luke 9.10–17). Eating becomes a means to create community, bringing Christians together in fellowship. The Eucharist becomes a symbol of this unique sacrifice and the new covenant. What ultimately makes Christianity distinctive is the new covenant established by Jesus through his death and resurrection.

The Holy Spirit

The Church as mediator of the sacred would be impossible without the third person of the Trinity, the Holy Spirit. The Spirit is, to put it simply, God's presence in the world and in human history. The Holy Spirit has historically been underrepresented within Christian life and thought, in part because there is very little said about the Spirit in the Christian Scriptures. The Spirit is present at Jesus' conception, his baptism, and at Pentecost:

> Suddenly a sound like the blowing of a violent wind came from heaven and filled the whole house where they were sitting. They saw what seemed to be tongues of fire that separated and came to rest on each of them. All of them were filled with the Holy Spirit and began to speak in other tongues as the Spirit enabled them.
>
> ACTS 2.2–4

And yet the Spirit is difficult to pin down and describe. Unlike proclamations surrounding Jesus and God the Creator, which can be contested on the basis of Scripture, Christians constantly and individually lay claim to an experience of the Spirit, which can be difficult to verify or contest. For many, the Spirit is a threat to the authority of institutional churches. Beginning in the twentieth century the renaissance of the Spirit among Christians is evident in the explosive growth of Pentecostal Christianity and charismatic Catholicism across the globe. Both of these Christian expressions emphasize an individual experience of the Spirit, the possibility of possession by the Holy Spirit, belief in speaking in tongues, and more generally a more inward (versus transcendent) understanding of God. The Spirit escapes the authority of the Church because it directly enters into individuals. Belief in the Spirit also has foundations in the Hebrew Scriptures, through the various passages that describe God's Spirit.

Paul

Similar to its role in the Hebrew Scriptures, the Christian notion of covenant characterizes God's relationship with humanity, though now it is firmly established through Jesus Christ's suffering, death, and resurrection. Within the Christian Scriptures Paul is adamant about the distinction between the "old" covenants of the Hebrew Scriptures and the new covenant in Christ. Paul writes:

> Not that we are competent in ourselves to claim anything for ourselves, but our competence comes from God. He has made us competent as ministers of

a new covenant—not of the letter but of the Spirit; for the letter kills, but the Spirit gives life.

2 CORINTHIANS 3.5-6

For Paul the covenant of the commandments is mortal, while the new covenant through Jesus and the Spirit gives eternal life. Paul continues by proclaiming the glorious nature of this new covenant in contrast to the old covenant who "made dull" the minds of the Israelites and puts a "veil" over them. This veil is lifted when you turn to Jesus and are transformed (2 Corinthians 3.14–18). Paul repeats his critique of the commandments in Galatians 3 and instead uses Abraham to illustrate and emphasize the importance of faith. Abraham, Paul argues, lived before Moses and the commandments and instead lived a life of faith. For Paul the Abrahamic covenant cannot be annulled. "Understand, then, that those who have faith are children of Abraham. Scripture foresaw that God would justify the Gentiles by faith, and announced the gospel in advance to Abraham" (Galatians 3.7–8). Paul has to argue this point for, if the commandments were enough, then Jesus suffered and died for absolutely no reason.

For centuries the centrality of covenant language was downplayed and Christians focused more on Jesus' notion of the kingdom of God. Swiss Reformer John Calvin revived this notion of covenant as central to his understanding of the Church. Calvin is seen as a proponent of Federal Theology, a Reformation theology that emphasized covenant. Calvin highlighted the one covenant of grace that was revealed in different ways throughout history and underlies both the Hebrew and Christian Scriptures, unifying them in the Bible. This Protestant emphasis on covenant directly shapes how some Protestants understand their relationship with the government. Puritans in the United States, for example, saw themselves as the New Israel and thus a new covenant people who had arrived in the promised land. Whether emphasized or not, the notion of Jesus as initiating a new covenant is foundational for Christianity, found in Paul's earliest writings, and repeated by Christians in churches across the globe. Underlying this covenant is the notion of redemptive suffering, the belief that suffering saves, which will be modeled after Jesus' suffering on the cross and also lead Christians to believe that suffering can make Christians Christ-like.

Martyrdom

Early Christians suffered severe persecution under the Roman Empire. At the time they were a sect within ancient Judaism who were attempting to convert other Jews in Judea to follow the teachings of Jesus. The Acts of the Apostles recounts when Stephen, a deacon in the Church of Jerusalem, chastised the Sanhedrin for betraying Jesus and was stoned and martyred after being accused of blasphemy. It is written that Paul (at the time Saul) was present for this. Right before his stoning, "Stephen, full of the Holy Spirit, looked up to heaven and saw the glory of God, and Jesus standing at the right hand of God" (Acts 7.55). Right before his death, Christians argue, he affirmed a Trinitarian vision of God. The martyrdom of Stephen unleashed a wave of persecution against the Church in Jerusalem (Acts 8.1). Paul himself will be imprisoned in Rome and beaten, as was Peter. The Roman persecution of Christians began with the Emperor Nero and continued through the fourth century, though was more localized and not sanctioned state-wide. Christians, like some other religious groups at the time, were singled out due to their refusal to worship the Emperor and Roman gods. At the end of the third century the persecution of Christians escalated under the rule of the Emperor Diocletian. The intense persecution lasted until 313, when Constantine legalized Christianity.

Many of the apostles suffered and even died because of their Christian beliefs. They, and those following them who died in the name of Christ, came to be known within Christianity as martyrs. The word "martyr" means witness. As a witness of faith a martyr is a Christian who refuses to renounce her or his faith and would rather face death than deny his/her beliefs. Martyrs inspired faith and conversion in early Christianity. As the second-century North African theologian Tertullian wrote, "the blood of the martyrs is the seed of the church" (*Apologeticus*, ch. 50). As martyrdom spread, small shrines were built near martyrs' graves, which became sites of pilgrimage. The custom of calling on martyrs for prayer arose in this setting as a popular devotion, as a way of being in solidarity with them. The veneration of saints, many of which were martyrs in the early Church, is rooted in this practice.

There continue to be Christian martyrs even today. One example is Oscar Romero, Archbishop of San Salvador. Romero was appointed Archbishop in 1977 in the midst of the Civil War in El Salvador. He was appointed in part due to his conservative views, especially the belief that the role of churches is not to get involved in politics. Romero understood the gospel as a message of peace and reconciliation; he saw the emphasis on social justice and liberation as leading to conflict and threatening Church unity. After being named Archbishop, the repression of the rural poor escalated, and Romero was profoundly affected by their suffering. He was moved to compassion, for he saw the people as a source of grace. The murder of his friend the Jesuit Rutilio Grande profoundly impacted him. Grande had denounced wealthy landowners and defended peasant rights. Romero's sympathy for the poor and oppressed grew, and he began to openly criticize injustice and violence. He saw the Church that encompasses the passion of Christ in the passion of oppressed peoples. He was assassinated while saying mass on March 24, 1980. He is considered a Christian martyr by many and is now on the road to canonization as a saint within the Roman Catholic Church. Martyrs like Romero are testimonies to the manner in which the covenant in blood first proclaimed in the Last Supper remains a central focal point within Christian identity.

Islam

The covenant in Islam is the *din* (roughly translated as "religion" or even "way of life"), which binds human beings with God. God is central to every human life, and with this submission comes peace and a heavenly reward. The Qur'an is understood by Muslims as a reminder of how the covenant is received, forgotten, broken, and renewed. It is the acceptance that God is the creator, most merciful and most kind, that gives life—this is the covenant. It is open to all of God's creation. Life was given to Adam and Eve, but they forgot their covenant with God. The restrictive understandings of the word "religion" in English cannot fully capture what *din* means to Muslims – often Muslims will state that Islam is a 'way of life' – this term reflects a fullness to the word that is limited in the word 'religion'. It is a word that emphasizes covenant at its very core, the covenant between themselves and God that all Muslims hold to strongly. The Qur'an is full of statements that continually remind Muslims of this covenant. The first statement of this covenant appears during the creation of Adam and Eve. The Qur'an states, "And when thy Lord took from the Children of Adam, from their loins, their progeny and made them bear witness concerning themselves, 'Am I not your Lord?' they said, 'Yes, we bear witness'" (Q7:127). The covenant is renewed by Muslims every day in various forms of prayer and communication with God, and one of those acts comes from the first pillar of Islam, which is to testify that there is no god but God and that Muhammad is the last and final messenger. This declaration, or bearing witness, renews the covenant with God and brings Muslims closer together in their collective identity.

God is central to belief and practice. Muslims are expected to continually strive to strengthen this relationship. The ritual acts are a part of this. Muslims also recite a number of additional supplications, *dhikr*, and these are often chanted in different settings. Their purpose is to reaffirm the commitment to God. Even when Muslims forget and are led astray, they should repent and ask God for forgiveness. Mystics will sing God's glory, while others will recite supplications using prayer beads that resemble Catholic rosary beads. The testimony to faith is something that is said often, and reminders of it can be seen in art and architecture.

The term *fitra* ("primordial human nature") means that the essence of human nature is always inclined to submission and worship to God. This is the perfect state of existence, which Adam and Eve experienced but then lost when they erred. However, even though humanity's natural inclination is supposed to be toward worshipping God, there are Islamic traditions that state that human beings are forgetful and arrogant. This leads them to forget about God's position in their life. This is why humans require constant reminders about God's beauty and glory. It is also said that there are some human beings whose hearts have been "sealed" against anything to do with God. These people are understood to be doomed, a tradition that reminds Muslims that they should strive for open hearts toward God. "Then for their breaking of their covenant, We cursed them and hardened their hearts. They distort the meaning of the word, and have forgotten a part of that whereof they were reminded. Thou shalt not cease to discover their treachery, from all save a few of them. So pardon them, and forbear. Truly God loves the virtuous" (Q5:13). The five ritual pillars of Islam are a way of constantly and consistently strengthening the covenant with God.

Natural human forgetfulness and arrogance are the reasons that God has sent many different prophets and messengers to tell people about God. Although there are twenty-five prophets read out of the Qur'an, there were many more. There is a saying of Muhammad that mentions that there were around 124,000 prophets. The Qur'an states, "For every community there is a messenger, and when their messenger comes, judgment shall be rendered between them with justice, and they will not be wronged" (Q10:47).

Muhammad's message of monotheism and belief in God is an extension of Judaism and Christianity. However, it is established on the basis that the covenant has been tainted by the Jews and Christians. Islam does not completely dismiss Jews and Christians as unbelievers because there is much discussion on their position as "people of the Book." The Qur'an alludes to the understanding that Jews and Christians have strayed away from the covenant but not completely abandoned it. This in itself leaves some doubt as to their position with God, especially when Muslims discuss whether Jews and Christians will receive God's forgiveness and blessing. Islamic traditions state that the children of Israel had been the "chosen people" of God, and this is affirmed in the Qur'an, but that they went astray. This is highlighted in the story of Moses being called to Mt. Sinai for forty days. When he returns, he sees that the people had started to worship a golden calf. The covenant is broken with God, and Moses attempts to bring the people back to their covenantal relationship but they refuse. The Jews are given another chance to recompense with Moses' invitation to the promised land, but they refuse and state that they fear the domineering people in the land. For this reason they are banished from the promised land for forty years. Muslims understand this as a reminder of the consequences of breaking the covenant with God.

The covenant with Christians is tainted largely because of the way Christian traditions have ascribed divinity to Jesus. The Qur'an makes clear that Jesus is a human being whom God also selected as a prophet. Even in Islamic tradition, Jesus and Mary are the only two of God's creation who are untouched by sin and evil: it is said by the prophet Muhammad that it is the presence of Satan that makes a baby first cry when born—except for Mary and Jesus. Jesus also performs many miracles, such as restoring sight to the blind, healing the leper, and giving life to the dead, but the Qur'an understands these miracles to be from God and holds that the ultimate power for these miracles is God. The Qur'an states: "'Three.' Refrain! It is better for you. God is only One God; Glory be to Him" (Q4:171) and then "They certainly disbelieve, those who say, 'Truly God is the third of three,' while there is no god save One God. If they refrain not from what they say, a painful punishment will befall those among them who disbelieved" (Q5:73). It is then said that this is not speaking against Trinitarian theology, which does not make God one of three, but it is speaking against the literal understanding of God as three as opposed to one. The Qur'an's comments on Judaism and Christianity are not to render them false but to highlight the connection with them. Additionally to highlight the distinct covenant that Muslims have with God. The Qur'an reads, "And do not argue with the People of the Scripture except in a way that is best, except for those who commit injustice among them, and say, 'We believe in that which has been revealed to us and revealed to you. And our God and your God is one; and we are Muslims [in submission] to Him'" (Q29:46).

FIGURE 17 *Maryam (Mary) with the infant Isa (Jesus), below the miraculous palm tree, from* Qisas al-anbiya *(Stories of the Prophets), by Ishaq ibn Ibrahim al-Nishapuri (11thC), Iran, c. 1570. Folio, colors and gold on paper. Folio: 31.7 x 20.0 cm. Chester Beatty (CBL Per 231.227), © The Trustees of the Chester Beatty Library, Dublin.*

When Muhammad began to preach his message of One God, the communal identity of Muslims was taking shape, but the spread of this message came with a heavy price. One of the earliest converts to Islam was a black slave who was born in Mecca around 580 CE. He was born into slavery and was the slave of Umayyah ibn Khalaf, who tortured him when he announced that he had accepted Islam. There are numerous stories of his firm conviction, belief, and piety as he is dragged around Mecca with many people laughing at him. Bilal continued to declare, "Ahad Ahad" (God is one, absolute). Muhammad heard about this situation and sent his companion, Abu Bakr, to negotiate his freedom. Bilal came to prominence as he was chosen by the prophet Muhammad to make the first call to prayer. Bilal's story is now remembered not only as a lesson for Muslims to stand firm in their belief in the face of any hardship but also as a message about race and ethnicity. The covenant with God challenges racism and bigotry. The prophet Muhammad stated that no believer is superior or inferior to another but only when comparing acts of faith and goodness between believers. This equality is acted out in the pillars of Islam, be it through prayer in a single line or in the simple white cloth that pilgrims wear when they go to Hajj. This is not to say that inequality and racism do not exist within Muslim communities, but there are numerous examples in Islamic traditions that challenge bigotry and serve as reminders to Muslims past and present. The covenant with God, ideally, has helped build a united identity for Muslims, regardless of how they identify themselves. The reality may not always uphold this equality or equity but it is the core of the covenant.

Muslims affirm the covenant with God every day through their beliefs and practices. The collective Muslim *ummah* (global community), which is diverse, is then expected to live life with the constant reminder of that question from God, "Am I not your Lord"; to attest to this means complete submission to God. Complete submission also brings Muslims together in acts of worship, be they prayer or pilgrimage. Muslims are expected to act in kindness and fairness to everyone. The concept of *silah rahmi*, which is generally understood as ties of kinship, demands that Muslims look after each other. The prophet Muhammad taught that those believers who want to prolong their lives and their provisions should give to their relatives and the poor. This comes in addition to giving generally to the poor. This twofold understanding of charity then helps strengthen Muslim community and the important relationships with non-Muslim communities too.

There are certain traditions that Muslims enact in order to strengthen the covenant. Often when a baby is born, a close male relative recites the call to prayer in the ear of the newborn. It is to awake the baby to God. Something sweet and solid is often placed in the mouth of the newborn. This comes from emulating a tradition of the prophet Muhammad of chewing and feeding of dates to the newborn. Some Muslims may also shave a baby's head, weigh the removed hair and give a related amount in charity. A special feast known as the *aqiqa*, which may include sacrificial meat, is enjoyed by family and friends. These traditions may vary from family to family and community to community, but they give an insight on some traditions that mark the introduction of new Muslims into the community of believers. In this way, the covenant with God should strengthen community building as it upholds the important divine command of "doing good."

Muhammad, as the final seal of the prophets, plays an essential role in how Muslims understand the covenant. Muhammad offered a *sunna*, which was his teachings and acts—a beautiful pattern of life that would strengthen the relationship between believer and God. Although the Qur'an does not explicitly mention circumcision, it was a practice associated with the prophet Muhammad. Muslims will generally circumcise male babies as soon as they possibly can after birth. There are parties held to celebrate this time, and it is often seen as part of one's initiation as a Muslim and one's connection to God. The discussion is intense when it comes to female circumcision, which is generally not accepted by the vast majority of Muslims due to its detrimental effects on women.

The term "covenant" is not often used by Muslims but it is central to belief and practice. It is the connection that every Muslim has with God as they bear witness to God as creator. This relationship effects everything that Muslims do in their lives as they submit only to God. Muslims believe that the first covenant was made with Adam, who is the first prophet in Islam. It is with Adam and Eve that God's relationship begins but it was due to both of them erring and forgetting the covenant that they fell from grace. It is God's forgiveness and mercy that allows the covenant to be re-strengthened when Muslims err and forget. In summary, Islamic traditions highlight that the covenant between God and human beings began through the creation of Adam and Eve. But due to forgetfulness and ascribing connections to God, revelation and prophecy continued from prophet to prophet and ended with Muhammad. Some Muslims will exclude Jews and Christians from this covenantal connection but the Qur'an, in its typical thought provoking way, confuses this assumption:

> They are not [all] the same; among the People of the Scripture is a community standing [in obedience], reciting the verses of Allah during periods of the night and prostrating [in prayer]. They believe in Allah and the Last Day, and they enjoin what is right and forbid what is wrong and hasten to good deeds. And those are among the righteous. And whatever good they do—never will it be removed from them. And Allah is Knowing of the righteous.
>
> Q3.113–115

Afterthought: Covenant and Identity

A covenant is an agreement that reflects a shared understanding about something in particular. Agreements are always specific and always have conditions. God's covenant with Noah and all living things, for instance, stipulates only that God will not flood the earth again. It is not a general commitment against divine destruction.

God makes a covenant of land and loyalty with Abraham that extends forever to his descendants, whom God also defines. It is important to note that while the covenant with Abraham is eternal, Abraham has to agree to it. It is not imposed on him against his will. He believes God's promise, and his descendants demonstrate their acceptance through the ritual of male circumcision. Likewise, the Israelites at Sinai affirm their acceptance of the commandments through the ritual of sacrifice. These formal acts of acceptance—somewhat like marriage vows—make the covenant concrete and the relationship real.

All relationships are particular and specific. Whether they are between two individuals or among many participants, relationships by their very nature are exclusive; some people are in them, and some are not. All relationships have insiders and outsiders. Relationships thus are the basic ingredients of the diversity of human experience. Although relationships can be imposed, such as between nurses and patients or guards and prisoners, the more durable ones are grounded in free choice and assent. That is how the monotheistic covenants work.

God's covenants with the Israelites are both exclusive and inclusive. In principle, only the descendants of Abraham, Isaac, and Jacob inherit the terms of the covenant and experience its consequences; but outsiders, through conversion, also can join the family.

Early Christianity took up this idea and altered its terms. Through his experience of the resurrected Jesus, the apostle Paul argued that Gentiles—that is, non-Jews—could become heirs to Israel's covenant by believing in the resurrection. If they believe in the resurrection as Abraham believed God's promise to Abraham, they can become heirs of the Israelite covenant by faith rather than by birth. The ritual that affirms this form of the covenant is baptism, which, in a sense, gives birth to a new "covenanted" person. Paul did not deny the covenant with Abraham. Rather, he created a means for non-Jews to become its beneficiaries as well.

This new covenant is no less exclusive than the Israelite covenant. Only those who agree to it benefit from it. To be a recipient of the new covenant, one must believe in the resurrection and undergo baptism. Thus, while the terms of covenant membership are changed, the structure of the agreement is not. Like the Israelite covenant, there are insiders and outsiders, but now the conditions for membership and inheritance are correct belief rather than familial descent. Pauline Christians are a theological peoplehood, in which correct belief replaces family ties.

Islam asserts that Jews and Christians did not fulfill their covenants with God, and claims that God's original covenant was with all humanity, beginning with the creation of Adam and Eve. In the Qur'an, Adam and Eve acknowledge God as their sovereign and creator. This means, the Qur'an explains, that at the time of resurrection humans cannot plead ignorance of their obligation to submit to God. Due to forgetfulness and ascribing connections to God, revelation and prophecy continued from prophet to prophet and ended with Muhammad. Although God's covenant is universal, those who do not believe in and submit to God have violated the covenant.

In all three monotheistic traditions, covenant is a consequence of creation, and humans' exercise of free will leads to their relationship with God.

Study Questions: Covenant

Why is the covenant important in Judaism, Christianity, and Islam?

Why is circumcision important to understand covenant and identity? What are some of the current debates on this issue?

What is the relationship between identity and community?

Is it possible to be Jewish, Christian or Muslim without community? Highlight some of the issues in your answer.

What is the significance of suffering and memory for identity?

What is the relationship between covenant and sin in Christianity?

How do Christians understand 'the kingdom of God'?

Do the different understandings of covenant in the three religions make it easier or more difficult for them to connect? Discuss.

6

Commandment:

Ritual and Ethics

Commandment, ritual, and ethics all refer to the areas in each religion that focus on human behaviors and actions in this life. For Jews, Christians, and Muslims our actions have consequences for our relationship with God and are a reflection of that relationship. In addition to requiring certain concrete behaviors, each religion has significant variance in terms of how they interpret certain actions as expected or reflective of the believers' relationship with the One God.

Judaism

Ritual and Ethics

The values and behaviors that guide and define how the Jewish people should relate to God and treat others—both inside and outside their community—derive from the framework of creation, covenant, and commandment. The commandments reflect God's will and nature. Their purpose is to create, nurture, and sustain a way of being human and a human community that reflect and embody Judaism's understanding of the reality of God.

As creatures with free will, humans are responsible and accountable for what they do and think. In Judaism, therefore, fulfilling God's commandments should be intentional, not accidental; it entails both attitude and action. The Talmud ('Avodah Zara 3a) says it is better to act in response to God's commandment than to act on one's own. Rather than merely instructions to be obeyed, the commandments aim to stimulate attention and mindfulness within the framework of the covenant. In Judaism, how one regards and treats other human beings—and the rest of God's creation as well—testifies to the character of one's relationship to God.

The Torah's claim that human beings are created in God's image undergirds core Judaic values of the sanctity of life, the dignity and equality of each human being, and the maintenance of family and community. The Torah articulates these values in its call "to love the Lord your God" (Deuteronomy 6.5) and "love your neighbor as yourself" (Leviticus 19.18). The commandments make the values concrete. They integrate ritual and ethics, behaviors that Western thought typically separates as two categories of action. Saving human life outweighs all other obligations. Likewise, caring for the less fortunate, the elderly, the disadvantaged, and the stranger; treating people equally before the law; observing the Sabbath; respecting laborers and workers; practicing honesty in business; studying Torah; and turning enemies into friends—all are responses to God's call. Some representative examples are discussed below.

Tikkun 'Olam

Tikkun 'Olam ("repair the world") has its roots in the Mishnah and Talmud, where it serves to justify halakhot that ease the conditions of disadvantaged persons. The term acquired a mystical meaning in Lurianic Kabbalah, where it referred to the return of the displaced sparks. In contemporary Judaism—particularly its more liberal forms—the term refers to social action for the broad betterment of society, to organized Jewish communal activity on issues of social justice, particularly gender equity, respect for minorities, and care for the poor.

Tzedakah

The Hebrew word conventionally translated as "charity" is tzedakah, which derives from the Hebrew word tzedek ("justice"). Tzedakah is a duty to God to care for God's creatures. Helping those in need—whom the Torah defines generically as the poor, the orphan, the widow, and the stranger—strengthens human community. Judaism does not regard poverty as a virtue, and it does not leave care for others to a whim. The obligation to practice tzedakah applies to everyone, even those who receive it. The High Holiday liturgy includes tzedakah, along with repentance and prayer, as actions that can effect forgiveness of sin.

Judaism's conviction about the centrality of tzedakah is grounded both in God's commandment and in the Israelites' experience of oppression and disenfranchisement. For example, Deuteronomy 10.17–19 states:

For the Lord your God is God of gods and Lord of lords, the great God, mighty and awesome, who shows no partiality and accepts no bribes. He defends the cause of the fatherless and the widow, and loves the foreigner residing among you, giving them food and clothing. And you are to love those who are foreigners, for you yourselves were foreigners in Egypt.

These passages evoke both compassion and empathy and make clear that tzedakah includes both the giving of alms and the treatment of everyone as equal participants in the human community.

Since *tzedakah* is an obligation and not a supererogatory act or dependent on one's mood, people may assure themselves that their gifts actually are used to help the poor before donating. Rabbinic Judaism developed organized, communal charity in ways designed to preserve the dignity of the poor. Moses Maimonides devised eight levels of *tzedakah*; the lowest is giving unwillingly, and the highest is enabling the recipient to become independent and self-sufficient. The centrality of *tzedakah* helps explain the extensive development of Jewish charitable organizations and their substantial financial contributions to both Jewish and non-Jewish causes, such as hospitals, universities, and social welfare programs.

Lashon ha-ra' ("Evil Speech")

Because of its focus on the importance of community, Judaism judges speech that harms another person to be a serious transgression. *Halakhah* developed categories of prohibited speech, which include talk that is hypocritical, obscene, dishonest, misleading, malicious, or embarrassing. Of all these, one category stands out as particularly destructive: *lashon ha-ra'*, speech that uses truth for the purpose of harm, confusion, or falsehood.

A quintessential example of *lashon ha-ra'* is the report of the scouts Moses sends to explore the promised land to prepare the path of the Israelites' entry into it (Numbers 13–14). The scouts' language ignites the Israelites' fears and provokes emotions that make them doubt God, look backward rather than forward, desire a return to Egypt, yearn for slavery, and wish for death—just when they stand at the very entrance to freedom and redemption. God is outraged at the people's response and threatens to eradicate them. Moses intercedes. He invokes God's mercy and "great love" and asks God to "forgive the sin of these people." God replies, "I have forgiven them, as you asked" (Numbers 14.19–20). This language is central to the liturgy of *Yom Kippur*, Judaism's day of stocktaking and rectification. That the generation of Israelites victimized by *lashon ha-ra'* wanders the desert for forty years and does not enter the promised land suggests the gravity of the offense.

The rabbis judge *lashon ha-ra'* harshly because it corrodes community. The agent of duplicity, of innuendo, of sly implication, of saying one thing to mean its opposite, *lashon ha-ra'* corrupts and undermines reliable communication, which is essential to any human community and collective life.

Business Ethics

As this-worldly religion, Judaism takes business seriously. It does not oppose success in commerce. Rather, its basic concern is the impact of commercial practices on the quality of collective life. Jewish business ethics are consistent with the shift in contemporary business management from a focus solely on profit to a concern for service, to attention to the interests of customers as well as shareholders.

The basic principles of Jewish business ethics reflect the Torah's insistence on the primacy of fairness, honesty, and equality as the foundations of human community.

Multiple verses from the Torah constitute what might be considered the building blocks of Jewish business ethics. Leviticus 19.13 addresses workers' rights and requires that employers pay their workers on time when the work is done. Withholding payment assaults the integrity of work. Leviticus 19.14 opposes misleading and incomplete disclosure. Leviticus 19.35–36 and Deuteronomy 25.13–15 mandate accuracy in weights and measures so that customers get what they pay for. Leviticus 25.17 insists on fair prices and opposes deceptive speech in business transactions. Deuteronomy 19.14 prohibits violating or transgressing another's business "territory." Exodus 23.8 and Deuteronomy 16.19 prohibit bribery, and Leviticus 19.17 warns against tolerating wrongdoing.

Taken together, these principles address a host of contemporary business practices and issues. On their bases, Judaism advocates an environment of mutual respect between employers and workers, and timely compensation for hard work. Price fraud, false financial records, defective merchandize, unfair competition, false packaging and labeling, and theft of intellectual property all fall into the category of prohibited activities. The commitment to fairness makes profiteering unacceptable, and the commandment against tolerance of wrongdoing justifies corporate "whistleblowing." All these values envision a business environment that focuses on both the merchant and the customer and that puts the quality of human relationships at the forefront of Jewish business ethics.

Violence and War

Violence—whether individual or collective—is the planned, intentional, and premeditated inflicting of harm by humans on other humans in order to weaken, dominate, or destroy them. Violence typically is physical, but it also can be manifest in speech.

Judaism's approach to violence is pacific but not pacifist. Preserving human life is the primary obligation, and the prophetic tradition envisions a redeemed world of peaceful coexistence among nations. At the level of individual and communal behavior, the Torah advocates peace and civility and prohibits unprovoked violence. It opposes human sacrifice, murder, rape, theft, and kidnapping. While Judaic teaching constrains violence, the obligation to preserve life includes one's own. Judaism therefore opposes suicide and justifies self-defense.

Collective violence, whether sponsored by states or terrorist organizations, is primarily about territory, ideology, control, or all three; it requires planning and organization and therefore is inevitably political. Since for nearly two thousand years Jews had no national political or military power, they experienced persecution and violence far more as victims than as perpetrators. Consequently, classical Jewish religious views on war tend towards the theoretical. The Mishnah distinguishes between wars of choice and necessity but discusses them primarily in terms of who is obligated to fight and if warfare is permissible on the Sabbath. Rabbinic teachings also focus on ideas such as the Torah's commandment (Deuteronomy 20.10) to attempt to negotiate peace before engaging in war, exempting indefensible locations from battle, delaying a siege until the enemies attack, and keeping one gate of a target besieged city open so civilians can escape. In general, rabbinic tradition downplays and discourages Jews' use of violence.

The founding of the State of Israel established a Jewish polity with the capacity for national self-determination and collective self-defense. Either in response to an attack or in an effort to prevent one, Israel has fought eight major wars and defended itself against continued acts of terrorism. The code of conduct of the Israeli military applies international, secular, legal standards for behavior in war. Some Jewish groups within and outside Israel have been critical of Israeli military action.

Within the Orthodox sector of Israeli Jews, some individuals and groups have emerged that, on the basis of their interpretation of Jewish messianism, favor aggressive political and even military action to possess of all the land the Torah says God promised to Abraham. In the context of Israel's enemies' persisting threats or acts of war and terrorism, genocidal rhetoric, and negative indoctrination of the young, some members of these Jewish groups have engaged in terrorist activities, primarily against Palestinians, but also against some Jewish Israelis. These acts of violence have been overwhelmingly condemned by most parts of Israeli society and judged and punished by successive Israeli governments.

Commandments and Daily Life

The comprehensiveness of the commandments means that Judaism tends to ritualize everyday living. The daily rituals aim to remind people that they live in a world God created and lead them to be mindful of their thoughts and actions. Perhaps the best example of this tendency toward ritualization is *kashrut*, Judaism's dietary system.

On the basis of the Torah's commandments, rabbinic Judaism developed a comprehensive dietary program that defines which foods are "fit" (kosher) to consume. The Torah specifies that only ruminants, plant-eating land animals that have a cloven hoof and chew the cud—cattle, sheep, goats, deer, and bison—may be eaten. Chicken, turkey, duck, and goose are kosher, but birds of prey or scavengers are excluded. Permitted aquatic animals must have scales and fins, so shellfish and seafood with skin instead of scales—eels, for instance—are not kosher. Rodents, reptiles, and insects are forbidden.

The land animals and birds permitted for human consumption must be slaughtered by a ritual slaughterer (*shokhet*), who severs the animal's trachea and esophagus in one quick and exact motion with a very sharp extremely smooth knife. The practice is alleged to cause immediate unconsciousness. Animals that died a natural death or were killed by other animals or hunters are not permitted. Since the Torah forbids consuming blood, all of it must be drained; this procedure is supplemented by salting, soaking, and sometimes broiling the meat. If a spot of blood appears in the fertilized egg of a permitted bird, the egg will be discarded.

Jacob's night-long, name-changing wrestling match (Genesis 32.22–25) stands behind the exclusion of the sciatic nerve, and Leviticus 3.17 prohibits eating the fat surrounding the vital organs and the liver, the same fat that Genesis says Abel offered to God. Finally, to be kosher, slaughtered animals and birds must be inspected and declared free from disease or organic imperfections.

The Torah also—Exodus 23.19 and 34.26, and Deuteronomy 14.21—forbids boiling a kid in its mother's milk. Expanding this ordinance, *halakhah* prohibits cooking or consuming *any* meat products—animal or fowl—together with dairy products. In practical terms, this separation creates the need to have two sets of kitchen, cooking, and dining utensils, one for meat, the other for dairy, because the utensils acquire the status of the food with which they are used. During Passover, because the practice of *kashrut* includes not consuming leaven or keeping it in the home, many observant families maintain a separate set of leaven-free Passover kitchen utensils.

Jewish observance of *kashrut* varies across a spectrum. Some follow *halakhah* comprehensively; others, for instance, keep a kosher home and avoid prohibited foods outside.

Christianity

Among Christian scholars the terms "moral theology" and "theological (or Christian) ethics" refer to reflection on moral issues based on Christian theological presuppositions. At the foundation of these moral systems is the assumption that God, who is good, created the world we live in, and this world has a moral order. In Christianity, teachings in the area of morality and ethics operate under the assumption that due to our fallen humanity we are in constant need of guidance and correction. Sin plays a key role in Christian constructions of morality and ethics. For Roman Catholics, human reason helps humans discern the moral order through what is called natural law. Protestant Christianity has a similar understanding of the order of creation. Ultimately, the field of ethics and morality forces believers to interrogate how their belief in God shapes the way they act. At the foundation of Christian morality and ethics are the two Great Commandments: love of God and love of neighbor (Matthew 22.36–40). Christianity regards these two commandments—which are cited frequently—as the foundation of Jesus' teachings and holds that they must be understood together. Love of God and love of neighbor are interconnected. How Christians treat their fellow human beings is intimately connected to their relationship to God. One cannot separate the two.

Charity

The importance of charity is connected to the Great Commandments. At the core of Christians' understanding of charity is service to one's neighbor. In Mark's account of the Great Commandments, Jesus agrees with a man who states "You are right in saying that God is one and there is no other but him. To love him with all your heart, with all your understanding and with all your strength, and to love your neighbor as yourself is more important than all burnt offerings and sacrifices" (Mark 12.32–33). To be charitable is the ultimate expression of one's faith. Charity must be grounded in love, for love "always protects, always trusts, always hopes, always perseveres" (1 Corinthians 13.7). Christianity understands charity as a moral virtue. Also of note in the Markan passage is the notion that the two Great Commandments supersede and replace the cult of Judaism.

Christians will also speak of God's charity toward humanity through Jesus' suffering and death on the cross. Love and charity thus refer to both God's actions and ours. Our expressions of love and charity, while mirroring those of Jesus, are incomparable to his selfless outpouring. Charity tells us something about the nature of God. It also tells us something about the nature of the poor, who give us privileged access into the sacred through God's preferential option for the poor, the belief that the poor have a privileged place in God's heart and consequently in Christian commitments.

Matthew 25 continues with this theme. At the time of judgment, Jesus claims, people will be separated as a shepherd separates sheep from goats. Those on the right will enter into the kingdom of God. "For I was hungry and you gave me something to eat, I was thirsty and you gave me something to drink, I was a stranger and you invited me in, I needed clothes and you clothed me, I was sick and you looked after me, I was in prison and you came to visit me" (Matthew 25.35–36). When the people ask Jesus if he was ever in any of these situations he replies, "Truly I tell you, whatever you did for one of the least of these brothers and sisters of mine, you did for me" (Matthew 25.40). He then turns to those on the left and condemns them, for they did not reach

FIGURE 18 *Good Friday procession, San Lucas Tolimán, Guatemala, © Byron Maldonado.*

out in the face of hunger, prison, or thirst. When they ask when they rejected Jesus in any of these situations he replies, "Truly I tell you, whatever you did not do for one of the least of these, you did not do for me" (Matthew 25.45). Jesus identifies and defines the disregard for the marginalized and the oppressed as a rejection of him. Christian ethics therefore will always operate under the assumption that how Christians live their lives and treat their fellow human beings is a reflection of one's faith and love of God. In addition, as this text emphasizes, how Christians treat their fellow humans has implications for them in the afterlife.

The Catholic Social Tradition

Within Roman Catholicism the Catholic Social Tradition is perhaps the best example of the interconnectedness of ethics and Christian understandings of God. Catholic Social Tradition (hereafter CST) focuses on the intersection of faith, social issues, and everyday life. At the foundation of CST is the Catholic notion of the common good. The CST's teaching on the common good emphasizes that our morality cannot be dominated by individualism. The individual exists in community, and our moral decisions must always be governed by more than self-interest. The basis of the common good is God's assertion in the book of Genesis that humans are created in the "image of God." Yet God in the Christian tradition is triune. The CST reminds Catholics that the Christian God is one that does not exist in isolation but in relationship, a relationship with humanity, but also in God's nature there exists the relationships that create the Trinity. The Trinity is the foundation for Christian understandings of community and consequently of the Church itself. Through humans' relationship with God, their fellow human beings, and the rest of creation, they reflect the image of God within them.

This is not an uncritical and romanticized understanding of relationships. Not all relations reflect the image of God. Instead, relationships are judged against the norm of Jesus' concrete life, ministry, death, and resurrection. Guided by Jesus' teachings, believers grow in the image of Christ and consequently the image of God. Hierarchical relationships that privilege certain sectors of humanity contradict Jesus' inclusive vision of community. Within CST, therefore, human salvation is social. The common good highlights this communal model. Therefore, individual personal salvation is inextricably linked to the salvation of all of humanity. Salvation is incomprehensible without connecting it to the salvation of others.

Similarly, sin can also be social. Social sin exists within Catholicism, and documents within the CST combat this, as seen in the 2018 document by the United States Conference of Catholic Bishops entitled *Open Wide Our Hearts: The Enduring Call to Love*. The document opens by defining racism and connecting it to sin. Racism, the bishops argue, is sinful because it violates justice. The letter defines justice as right relationship with God, God's creation, and each other. Then enters the theological justification against racism, grounded in our egalitarian creation as humans in the image of God. Ultimately, to be a racist is to deny the full humanity of your fellow human being. We can be consciously racist but we can also be unconsciously racist. The document presents racism as something that can live personally in our hearts but also structurally in institutions. The document is a call to conversion, a conversion of the heart that will lead to social change and the reformation of our institutions and society. We are called to humility for only then will our hearts be open to the long road of conversion. Part of embracing this humility is acknowledging the original sin of racism in the United States. In connecting Christian teachings to a social sin, this document exemplifies the CST's commitment to the common good.

The foundation of the common good generates a morality that is the basis of CST. After all, the belief that humans are social in nature has moral implications. Because CST has a communitarian basis, its morality is grounded in the positive obligation toward others. Often when people hear the words "duty" or "obligation," they think of things they "have" to do. This is not the attitude CST embraces. Catholics' obligation toward others is something they want to do. They want to be in solidarity with their fellow human being and to empower them. Catholics embrace the fact that their love of God is reflected in their love of neighbor. This positive obligation is not only at a personal level but also at a societal level. Civil, political, and economic rights entail duties—duties of solidarity toward others.

The distinction between the individual and the social, as well as the personal and societal, is seen in the distinction between acts of charity and social justice work. Charity is directed at the effects of injustice. The intention of acts of charity is to respond to immediate needs. The classic example of this in the Catholic Tradition is Mother Theresa of Calcutta. Acts of charity address human suffering but not the root causes of that suffering. Social justice, on the other hand, refers to social change in institutions and political structures. Acts of social justice examine those root causes of injustice and involve public, collective action. This is also seen in the distinction in Christianity between individual sin (which refers to personal acts) and social sin (which refers to societal sin). Examples of social sin are racism, sexism, and economic injustice.

Black Liberation Theology

In this spirit Liberation Theologies have been challenging Christian churches for over fifty years about the centrality of the oppressed in Jesus' teachings. Liberation theologians offer a new way of being the Church, one that they root in the gospel's message that the Church should be part of both denouncing and transforming unjust social structures. Liberation theologians argue that these movements are rooted in grassroots churches. Liberation theologies argue that the oppressed and the marginalized must be the starting point and center of theological reflection. They are global theologies that emerge from distinctive populations and often highlight one dimension of oppression as the focus of their scholarship.

Black liberation theology in the United States emerged from Black Protestant Churches during the Civil Rights Movement and was also influenced by the Black Power movement in the 1960s. These theologians challenged Christian churches and the broader society to confront the racism that has defined the United States since even before the founding of the nation. Without a commitment to the struggle against racism and oppression, churches preach an empty message that is devoid of the gospel. Christianity as a whole must be critical of the contemporary social order, and as part of this order must also be self-critical. Churches must emerge from, be an advocate for, and make an option for, the oppressed.

Liberation theologians depict Jesus as the Messiah of the poor, marginalized, oppressed, and crucified. Jesus today is incarnate among the marginalized. For black liberation theologians, since racism is the most extreme expression of oppression in the United States, this means that Jesus is black. And, if Jesus is black then God is black. This is perhaps one of the most challenging and revolutionary claims made by black liberation theologians. In proclaiming that Jesus is black they are not only reminding us of his own humble origins and accompaniment of the marginalized, they are challenging the pervasive global notion that Jesus and God are white. One only has to look at the history of Western art and visit churches across the globe to see this, in spite of the fact that we know that Jesus was a Jewish man from the Middle East, not a Western European, as he is overwhelmingly depicted.

Churches must open themselves to the realities of the crucified Christ today, which is best exemplified in the martyrdom of the suffering. Liberation theologians as a whole claim that the Church of the marginalized is the Church in solidarity with the oppressed, committed to make the kingdom of God a reality in the here and now. It is not an alternative to the institutional Church but a realization of the true vocation of the Church. Liberation theologians also consistently emphasize that liberation is in the here and now, not just in the future. Such a vision of the Church empowers the oppressed to evangelize the Church. Connected to martyrdom is the image of the poor and suffering as crucified peoples. The crucified peoples are the suffering servant today.

The parable of Lazarus and the rich man (Luke 16.19–31) reaffirms the centrality of the marginalized through the lens of economic poverty. The central theme of this passage is the avoidance of the love of money. The Pharisees, who are listening to Jesus speak, are depicted as lovers of money that mock Jesus for his teachings. Like the Pharisees, the rich man in this parable is a lover of money who values material wealth over people. He refuses to share his wealth with the poor, who are personified in the figure of Lazarus. After their death, however, the fate of the two men is reversed. It is the poor man who is at Abraham's side and the rich man who is condemned to Hades. This parable reinforces a Christian teaching that the paradigms of rich and poor, oppressor and oppressed, will be radically reversed in the kingdom of God. The message of the parable is God's solidarity with the marginalized and the forgotten. The fact is that the rich man does not triumph, but the poor man does. These teachings show that within Christianity good deeds are rewarded. They also show that solidarity with the marginalized is an avenue to God. This ritual of solidarity becomes a means of expressing one's Christian faith.

Violence

Within Christianity, bodies matter. They not only matter because of the human bodies people encounter in their everyday lives, or because how people treat their fellow human beings reflects, for Christians, the life of faith. More consequentially, bodies matter because of the incarnation. Jesus was incarnate in a human body. The Eucharist embodies Jesus' ultimate sacrifice for humanity for it is an act that brings the Christian community together to remember how God suffered and died to save humanity. The celebration of the Eucharist, whether it is viewed as a sacrament, a symbol, or a memorial, reminds Christians that part of the Christian life is denouncing unjust violence toward their fellow human beings. Just as Jesus' message in Matthew 25 reminds Christians that what they do unto others they do to God, so too is the Eucharist a constant reminder of the ethical charge Christians have to live a life of charity, love, faith, and hope in solidarity with the forgotten of this world.

While within Christianity there is a tradition of denouncing unjust violence, within Christianity there is also violence that is justified. Christianity has a complicated relationship with violence, for it proclaims that Jesus saved humanity through his violent death on the cross. In addition, the tradition of martyrdom correlates suffering and death with holiness. The just war theory within Christianity is a classic example of justified violence. The purpose of the theory is to justify when it is appropriate for Christians to engage in war, in other words the ethical justification for war. Perhaps the most influential Christian writer on the just war theory is Thomas Aquinas, who addressed not only when wars are justified but also what acts of war are justifiable. For Aquinas there are three principles that legitimize a just war. The war must be waged by an authoritative body, most often interpreted as the State. This is in part to assure the common good. The second principle is that a war cannot be motivated for selfish reasons and must have a purpose beyond self-interest. The intention behind the war must be a just one. Third even though war is ultimately linked to violence, the ultimate goal of a just war is peace. Later schools of Christian thought have added other elements to the just war theory, including self-defense, to control an aggressive nation or tyrant, as a last resort, and only in cases when success is likely. A war that is just, however, does not allow all forms of unchecked violence.

In spite of the just war theory Christianity teaches that violence is evil and must only be a last resort. This may seem, and in fact is, hypocritical in light of the history of violence one finds in the religion. One only has to look at the Crusades, the Inquisition, the Conquest of the Americas, and the trans-Atlantic slave trade, for example, to point to moments when Christian institutions and Christian countries have acted in violent and horrific ways. Violence occurs between Christians, as we have seen in the violence between Catholics and Protestants in Ireland that only ended in the late twentieth century. Or we can look at the surge of white supremacist Christian groups globally that have emerged in the twenty-first century. The counterpoint to this is the strong tradition of pacifism and non-violence within the Christian tradition, most publicly recognized in the United States through the work of Martin Luther King Jr. and the Civil Rights Movement.

There are no simple answers to the relationship between Christian ethics and violence. Many scholars of Christianity have pointed out that the biggest shift in Christianity occurred in the fourth century, when Christianity ceased to be a persecuted religion and became a religion that was able to and in fact did persecute. Christians are often quick to deny the violence that non-Christian religions have associated with the cross. Perpetuators of violence in the name of Christianity, as well as non-Christian detractors highlight when Jesus claims, "Do not suppose that I have come to bring peace to the earth. I did not come to bring peace, but a sword" (Matthew 10.34). This Scripture passage, like so many, is often misquoted out of its broader context to legitimize Christianity as violent. Christianity, like all religions, has a violent side and a history of violence. This has been and will remain a tension between the ethics of love and justice at the heart of the Christian message.

Islam

Islamic traditions focus the attention of believers on doing good through submission to God. This has led to much moral and ethical debate within Muslim communities from the very beginning. The notion of good is highlighted throughout the Qur'an and the practice and teachings of Muhammad, but its meaning and action comes from reflection, question, and critique. It could be said that more of the division within the ummah is due to the theological differences than to any other matters. Ethical behavior must be rooted in definitive text—primarily in the Qur'an, the word of God. The beliefs highlighted earlier in this book cannot be separated from the pillars, or actions, that Muslims must maintain. This means that belief and behavior must both be refined. Muslims will often remind themselves and others of upholding the best *akhlaq* which is translated as virtue, morality, and manners. These are the virtues that Muslims believe define Islam. God stated in the Qur'an, "You are the best community brought forth unto mankind, enjoining right, forbidding wrong, and believing in God. And were the People of the Book to believe, that would be better for them. Among them are believers, but most of them are iniquitous" (Q3:110). Islamic traditions highlight two types of human obligations, or duties, to God. One is known as *fard ayn*: the individual duty, or command, that every Muslim has to God. This would include rituals such as fasting, praying, giving alms, and pilgrimage. The other, *fard kifaya*, is understood as a duty, or command, for the entire community. It is not necessary that everyone take part in *fard kifaya*, but a sufficient number of individuals from the community must. An example would be attending funeral prayers.

The notion of enjoining right and forbidding wrong has been a part of faith for Muslims since the very beginning. Muslims have defined the community as distinct from others, a task that early Muslim jurists attempted to make sense of. The Shari'a (literally, a watering place, a well) is the divine legislation of God, but it is *fiqh* that is human understanding and jurisprudence of Shari'a. Early jurists attempted to create a science of understanding as they aimed to create the ideal Islamic society and life—their aim was to get closer to this perfect watering well that would nourish the soul of the believer, but the jurists were also aware that their attempts would always be imperfect and need revising. There is a common misconception that Islamic law is rigid; this is not the case. The law was constantly evolving during the medieval period but became more static around the tenth century.

In his time, Muhammad was able to explain what was right and wrong, and his prescriptions differed from person to person. Salman al-Farsi, who was a companion of the prophet, asked the prophet one day whether people were permitted to use animal fat, cheese, and fur. Muhammad answered, "Permissible is that which God has made lawful in his Book and the unlawful is that which he has forbidden, and that concerning which He is silent he has permitted as a favor to you." It was after his death that caliphs and governors were expected to offer legislation and think through difficult problems and challenges of society. The tension today is looking at this historical Islamic law through contemporary eyes. These Islamic principles of ethics are also judged through notions of ethics and morality in what could be categorized as "secular" settings. The issues of today, especially in view of constantly developing global human rights law, have left it at odds with historical Islamic law. Bridging the two is a challenge for Muslims around the world today.

The primary source of ethics is Allah, as understood through the Qur'an and, once again we must reiterate that it is not a legal text. It is this divine text which the global *ummah* (community) attempts to understand in order to uphold moral standards. Only around five hundred verses of the Qur'an make clear stipulations on what is lawful and prohibited. Apart from Qur'anic statements and its interpretation, early Muslims adopted some local customs which they found not to interfere in belief in Allah. These adoptions were on occasion accepted by Muslims, but only informally. The rationale was that if it was helping in enjoining good, then it was good. Islamic jurists during medieval times differed with this on the basis that these customs were not prevalent in any written text. The prophet Muhammad's actions and sayings are also consulted in understanding the *Shari'a*. In our current times, the Shari'a is often oversimplified in that we associate it with matters that are plainly and simply "right" or "wrong". But the methods of early Muslim jurists from across different denominations were both complicated and sophisticated. Early jurists were reflecting on intricate details of legal capacity from human beings to animals. Their statements of law were connected to faith, which made them open to further reflection. This nuance and deliberation is often not appreciated when Islamic law is compared to other forms of law.

Muadh Ibn Jabal (605–639 CE) was a companion of the prophet Muhammad who was known for his knowledge. He was sent to govern Yemen by Muhammad, who put the following question to him before departure: "According to what will you judge?" "According to the book of God," replied Muadh. "And if you find nothing therein?" "According to the Sunna of the prophet of God.'" "And if you find nothing therein?" "Then I will exert myself [exercise *ijtihad* and *qiyas*] to form my own judgment." Muhammad was pleased with this reply. The prophet Muhammad said that his community will "never agree on error"; from this saying, the Islamic concept of *Ijma*, meaning consensus, derives. *Ijma* does not mean unanimity but has a more blurred edge of general agreement in disagreement. This philosophical space was essential in developing ethical frameworks within all denominations. Another method of jurisprudence is *qiyas*, which is analogical reasoning from sources of the Qur'an and prophetic traditions (*sunna*) on new circumstances. This source of law required rational and logical reasoning to take place. *Ijtihad* is independent creative reasoning. Jurists made clear that a person who carries out *ijtihad* (a *mujtahid*) needed to fulfill the requirements of acceptable criteria such as knowledge of theology, Arabic language, and general principles of jurisprudence. The concept of *maslaha* is the making of a decision in the public interest. Al Ghazali, an eleventh-century Sunni polymath, argued that there were five essential public-interest matters that needed to be preserved for human well-being: religion, life, intellect, offspring and property. There has been a lot of debate on all of these issues, and the way in which they have or have not been adopted within different Islamic denominations is complicated because of issues of authority. These will be discussed in chapter seven.

Marriage (*nikah*) in Islamic law is understood as a contract. When Islam emerged, it was also a social safeguard for a woman to be married to a man. Marriage at that time was between a man and a woman. Jurists spent considerable time thinking about issues of marriage and divorce. They promoted marriage, a legitimate avenue for satisfying sexual desire, in order to keep believers from perceived immorality, and they suggested that believers lower their gaze in order to remain concentrated on God. There was much discussion about who a man or woman could and could not marry, such as two persons who were suckled by the same milk-mother. Marriage was allowed between a Muslim man and a woman who was Jewish or Christian, but a Muslim woman was prohibited from marrying a Jew, Christian, or nonbeliever because there was concern that any children born might not be Muslim. Contracts bound the husband and wife, and it was expected that the husband would offer *mahr* (dowry) to the wife, which she held exclusive rights over. This was to give the wife more control in the marriage. Divorce was generally allowed, but the jurists always advocated for much reflection before severing ties. This led some jurists to opine that after the husband uttered the words "I divorce you," a three-month waiting period (*'iddah*) was needed. Reconciliation could occur during this waiting period. Some Muslims use the formula of instant triple divorce (*talaq*), which has raised some serious concern in contemporary times.

These very general historical forms of union highlighted above are today being challenged in many different ways. Muslims have not embraced same-sex marriage publicly, but much has happened and continues to happen privately. Marriage between a man and woman and the flourishing of family was understood to be an important public good, but the urges, feelings, emotions, and actions that took place between lesbian, gay, transgender, and queer members of the ummah were often overlooked. The contemporary conundrum, which will be discussed later in this book, highlights how this issue is reaching a pivotal point among Muslims globally today.

There are generally five principles of actions for a Muslim, obligatory *fard*, recommended *mandub*, allowed *mubah*, reprehensible *makruh*, and forbidden *haram*. This shows that things are not black and white between obligatory and forbidden. During early Islam the development of Islamic legal schools began to take shape, with key figures leading them. In Islamic Sunni law, they are Abu Hanifa of the Hanafi School (d. 767), Malik Ibn Anas of the Maliki School (d. 801), Ahmad Ibn Hanbal of the Hanbali School (d. 855), and al-Shafi'i of the Shafi'i School (d. 820). The Shi'a denomination has its own schools. Within their legal canons, one finds all sorts of issues discussed. They can largely be differentiated into two categories: *ibadat* (worship—prayer, ablutions, fasting, pilgrimage) and *muamalat* (interactions—marriage, divorce, inheritance, trade, commerce, criminal justice).

A *mufti* is a person qualified to offer a legal statement (*fatwa*) on an issue. They are often asked to comment on a particular matter and they consult the Qur'an and sunna and then offer an authoritative opinion. Fatwas are always understood to be advisory. The primary source of anything deemed lawful or prohibited is the Qur'an. This is not as simple as one might expect or be told—the text needs human interpretation and that can lead in many different directions. The interpretations of the Qur'an for ethical behavior are as varied as there are Muslims in the world. Generally, a *qadi* (judge), appointed by the government, could uphold or dismiss the statements of a *mufti* in a law court. Islamic law also offered many different penalties for crimes. One of the most infamous of these is the penalty for illicit sexual relations: a hundred lashes, but only if the transgression is satisfactorily proven. The challenge in modern times for Muslims globally is how to bridge between the historical Shari'a and current social norms. Who is taking the position of *mufti* or *qadi* in modern Muslim communities in both Muslim and non-Muslim countries? Some Muslims are resistant to any kind of change or development to the historical law. They believe that to evolve is to adopt Western ways and means accepting colonialism. It is the drive to implement the historical Islamic ethical codes that impelled extreme groups such as the Taliban and ISIS to react against modern nation-states and call for an Islamic state.

However, it must be noted that Islamic traditions and law are particularly focused on individuals and not necessarily on organizing states and society. Muslims continually strive to uphold goodness through justice. A personal quest which affects society and community but not the other way round. The Qur'an states, "O you who have believed, be persistently standing firm in justice, witnesses for Allah, even if it be against yourselves or parents and relatives. Whether one is rich or poor, Allah is more worthy of both. So follow not [personal] inclination, lest you not be just. And if you distort [your testimony] or refuse [to give it], then indeed Allah is ever, with what you do, Acquainted" (Q4:135). Muslims have always embraced the development of ethical standards. This has meant thoughtful reflection on issues which have not been raised before.

One concept that gets much attention in a world of rising acts of terrorism is *jihad*. The literal translation of the word is "striving." This is often misunderstood as *qital*, which is used in the Qur'an for actual fighting and killing. The concept of *jihad* is bound to ethical behavior, upholding good. In Islamic traditions it is often split into two

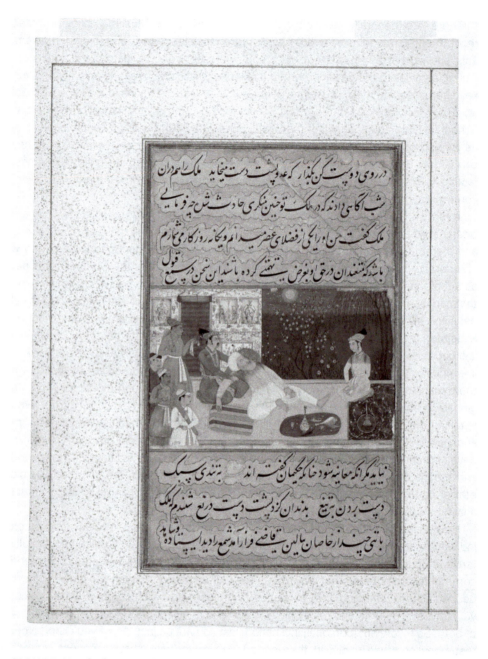

FIGURE 19 *The king angrily wakes up the drunken judge, from the* Gulistan *(Rose Garden) by Sa'di (d. 1291), manuscript produced for Mughal emperor Shah Jahan (r. 1628–1658), Agra, India, dated Jumada I 1038H, December 1628 – January 1629. Folio, ink, colors and gold on paper. Folio: 35.4 x 26.4 cm. Chester Beatty (CBL In 22.90), © The Trustees of the Chester Beatty Library, Dublin.*

meanings—the greater *jihad* being about oneself: upholding all good within oneself in terms of virtue and morality. This extends from the philosophical understanding that God loves beautiful things and that every Muslim should be driven toward the beautiful within themselves and society. This leads to the lesser *jihad*, which was in medieval times also about physical acts of fighting. It is not about unruly killing but about upholding a spiritual struggle which could lead to a just war.

Understood in the context of early Islam, it was not uncommon for tribal battles and fighting to take place. Muslims fought battles, too, but these were understood to be about upholding belief in One God. The early Muslims, including the prophet Muhammad, had to deal with the danger of being killed. Tribal rivalry which led to battles was a part of society. Such discussions and actions "in the way of God" were not dissimilar to what is today regarded as just war theory, or just war doctrine, which has some roots in ideas and notions presented within Christianity and Judaism. Islamic concepts of martyrdom involve acts of heroism that establish and uphold God's greatness. Very few Muslims would agree that suicide bombing is Islamic. Current-day Muslim terrorists have claimed that their acts should be understood in such a way, too, but the majority of Muslims globally do not agree. Some Muslims think that Qur'anic passages instructing Muslims not to harm or kill innocent people conclude that these are not martyrdoms but in fact suicides. This is disputed by the likes of current-day Al-Qa'ida, or ISIS fighters who interpret jihad in their own way.

Many Muslims have commanded jihad through the pen too. The war of words and ideas has been illustrated in different interpretations of what is deemed as "Islamic" and this has included the way in which jihad is understood. Jihad is a complicated term that is often oversimplified to mean killing. It is a term that Muslims interpret differently but drives their sacred struggle to realign their focus on God and upholding good.

Afterthought: Commandment: Ritual and Ethics

Commandment is a consequence of covenant. Relationships have expectations that establish reliability. Those expectations are most effective when they are concrete, specific, and clear. If you and your partner agree that you will always be on time for dinner, and one of you repeatedly comes late or doesn't show, the credibility of the relationship and the reliability of the communication are damaged.

In the Torah, the expectations of covenant are framed in terms of commandments. The commandments stipulate God's expectations of the Israelites, and they are spelled out in detail. The covenantal commandments are comprehensive in scope. They include what scholars call "prosocial" behaviors and we call "ethics." These are acts of kindness, fairness, concern, generosity, and practical assistance to a full range of classes of living beings: family members, neighbors, strangers, enemies, the poor, the disabled, immigrants, and animals. They also include what we now call ritual, which includes behaviors directed at God, such as worship and thanksgiving, confession of

God's oneness, and actions that effect community, such as celebrating the Sabbath, observing dietary rules, and practicing ritual purity.

In the realm of ethics, all three religions place a major focus on charity. Whether understood as an obligation or as a spontaneous act of love and generosity, charity is a defining trait of the monotheistic tradition. The institutionalized charities of the industrial world, and likely many governmental policies to diminish poverty, derive from this core monotheistic value. Charity, in turn, is grounded in the biblical ideas of humans as God's creations and the sanctity of human life. All three religions prohibit suicide.

At the level of individual action, all three religions reject unprovoked violence on others. Murder is prohibited and never justified. And while all three religions accept martyrdom in defined circumstances, none argues that people should seek death by allowing themselves to be murdered. The three traditions understand but struggle with the reality of violence in war and contemporary terrorism. To invoke the language of biblical prophets, it is impossible to "speak truth to power" if truth is controlled by the powerful. In large measure, violence within and between the monotheistic religions results from a fusion of—and perhaps a confusion about—religion and politics.

In the realm of ritual, all three religions operate along a continuum. Orthodox Judaism is the most ritually intense and comprehensive form of the religion, and Reform Judaism is the least. In Roman Catholicism, the ritual actions of the sacraments—such as baptism, the Eucharist, and marriage—produce indelible results. Although some Protestant denominations may have a somewhat less literal understanding of these rituals, they all regard them as transformative. On the matter of ritual in worship, Roman Catholicism has a highly structured and formalized liturgy. Most Protestant worship is less structured and focuses on Scripture reading, a sermon, and congregational hymn singing. Similar differences can be found within Muslim denominations from within the varied strands of Shi'a to Sunni and many others in between.

What is the role of God's commandments to the practice of ethics and ritual? How do practitioners of the three religions know they are fulfilling God's expectations?

As we have seen, the commandments constitute Judaism's *halakhah*, its realm of religious practice. The performance of specific commandments actualizes, reinforces, and affirms the covenant. Comprehensive in scope, the commandments assume knowledge and intention and thus are better understood as calls to considered action rather than as directions to be thoughtlessly followed. The Oral Torah continually modifies and adapts them to new circumstances.

Islamic law, as with the word *halakhah* (the "way"), also focuses on particular, concrete actions as evidence of a believer's submission to God. Belief in God leads to questions of ethics and morality. For this reason, Muslims would argue that it is not a set of rules; thus to impose it on Muslims through state laws has been difficult and ineffective. *Shari'a*, understood as Islamic law, addresses the issue of how Muslims are to meet God's expectations. Jurists struggled with texts in order to understand divine law—the ideal forms of submission that would strengthen the covenant between a Muslim and God.

Christianity takes a different approach to the question of commandments. Jesus' teaching highlights what some might call the ethical dimension of the Torah's commandments by emphasizing two: loving God and loving your neighbor as yourself.

The apostle Paul understood the commandments as "law," rules to be obeyed. He argued that, because people are sinners, it is impossible for them to fulfill them. He further suggested that God gave the commandments to show people that they could not fulfill them and thereby to prepare them for Jesus' coming. The resurrection eliminates the need for the commandments because, in baptism, the believer is united with the risen Christ and reborn knowing how to fulfill the commandments without being told. A changed human nature, as it were, makes proper ethical behavior intuitive. Most forms of Christianity hold that God's grace alone repairs the rupture between God and humanity, and that repaired relationship leads people to the right actions.

This review suggests that the difference between the two approaches to commandments is procedural rather than substantive. No form of Judaism, Christianity, or Islam advocates murder, suicide, cruelty to the poor, or disrespect for elders, for instance. There is no fundamental disagreement among them on God's desires for proper human conduct. The issue is what motivates and enables humanity's right attitudes and right actions.

Study Questions: Commandment: Ritual and Ethics

What is the connection between space, ethics, and ritual in the three traditions?
What makes charity 'good' in the three traditions?
Define charity in Judaism, Christianity, and Islam.
Are ethical positions as numerous as Jews, Christians, and Muslims or
    are they fixed? Discuss for and against.
What is the relationship between ritual and ethics in the three traditions?

7

Peoplehood and Community

Community and peoplehood are fundamental concepts within the study of religion. At their core, religions consist of communities, and those communities are the spaces and places where we find these lived and practiced beliefs and rituals. Similarly the theme of peoplehood is intimately tied to the sense of identity within religious traditions. Both terms contain the connotation of insider and outsider, defining not only who is a part of a religious community, but also who is not. While peoplehood and community are key themes within the study of monotheism in Christianity, Islam, and Judaism, how these categories play out in these traditions varies. This chapter provides an overview of the manner in which peoplehood and community play a role in these religions in their own distinctive manner. Special attention will be paid to the divisions within the tradition, when appropriate, and the categories, sects, and/or denominations within each religion.

Judaism

Judaism is a relentlessly communal religion. Its two mutually reinforcing covenantal bases of identity, its religious decentralization, and its extended geographic diversity contributed to the development of Jewish communities that differ from one another religiously and culturally.

Religious Variation in Judaism: Ancient and Medieval Times

Samaritanism

The Samaritans, who emerge in the second century BCE, are the descendants of a group of Israelites. Samaritanism is a variant of biblical monotheism that accepts only Mt. Gerizim, a mountain near the city of Nablus, as God's sacred center and the place for sacrifices. Samaritanism claims to be the original religion of Israel, practiced continually by those who remained in the northern kingdom of Israel after the Assyrian destruction and exile in 721 BCE. There is a Samaritan Pentateuch, which resembles the Torah. Samaritanism excludes the Prophets and Writings from its canon. During the Second Temple period, the returned exiles from Babylonia regarded the Samaritans as outsiders because it was believed they had intermarried with people brought to the northern kingdom by the Assyrians and that they worshipped both the God of Israel and other deities. The Hasmonean leader John Hyrcanus destroyed the Samaritan Temple in 112/111 BCE, and it has never been rebuilt. The Israeli Chief Rabbinate requires Samaritans to have a halakhic conversion to be deemed Jewish. Contemporary Samaritans live either near Mt. Gerizim or in Holon, near Tel Aviv. The Samaritans continue to sacrifice lambs on Mt. Gerizim on the first night of Passover.

Karaism

Beginning in the early eighth century CE, a movement known as Karaism disputed the religious claims and practices of rabbinic Judaism. The term likely derives from the Hebrew root *kara'* ("to read"). Karaism holds that God's revelation to Israel is contained only in the written text of the *Tanakh* and denies the validity of the Oral Torah and behaviors that derive from it. Karaites claim to determine their practices from a close reading of the *Tanakh* alone. Among other issues, Karaism rejects the rabbinic separation of milk and meat, the festival of Hanukkah (because it is not biblical), *tefillin*, the rabbinic calendar, and rabbinic practices of divorce. It also follows patrilineal descent. Karaism grew considerably from the tenth to the eleventh centuries and its practitioners developed careful commentaries on and grammatical studies of the *Tanakh*. There are approximately 40,000 Karaites in the world today, primarily in the State of Israel.

Religious Variation in Judaism: Modern and Contemporary

Reform Judaism

A nineteenth-century product of the eighteenth-century German Enlightenment, Reform Judaism emphasizes the primacy of personal religious experience, and its core principles support individual freedom and decision-making. Reform prioritizes Judaism's ethical teachings over ritual and does not regard traditional *halakhah* as binding. In its earliest form, it added organ music to its worship services, abandoned skullcaps and the prayer shawl (*tallit*), and shifted much of the worship service from Hebrew to the vernacular, either German or English. Contemporary Reform congregations have shifted to guitars and other contemporary instruments; skullcaps and prayer shawls are now optional; and the liturgy has more Hebrew. Reform synagogues typically follow the traditional liturgical calendar and observe all the standard major holidays and life cycle events, but usually in an abbreviated form. The 2013 Pew Report showed that approximately 35% of American Jews were affiliated with the Reform movement; it is the largest Jewish denomination in the United States.

The Reform movement led the American denominations in welcoming its members' non-Jewish partners into synagogue life. Many Reform rabbis perform intermarriages between Jews and non-Jews, and the Pew statistics indicate that half of married Reform Jews have non-Jewish spouses.

Reform was the first denomination to ordain women as rabbis, and in 2019 approximately half of Reform rabbinical students were female. The Religious Action Center of Reform Judaism is committed to broad issues of social justice and civic equity. From its inception through the mid-1940s, the Reform movement was ambivalent about Zionism. It promoted instead the understanding that Jews are members of a religion, not a national or cultural group, and that they therefore merit full acceptance as citizens of the country in which they live. Since the Holocaust, Reform has become committed to the State of Israel. Reform has a presence in Israel, both in a Jerusalem branch of its seminary, Hebrew Union College—Jewish Institute of Religion, and in a number of synagogues. The Chief Rabbinate of Israel does not recognize Reform as a legitimate form of Judaism.

Orthodox Judaism

Orthodox Judaism is not a denomination; unlike the Reform and Conservative movements, it has no single central organization. Rather, "Orthodox" is a modern, broad designation that includes a number of diverse Judaic communities committed to *halakhah*. Orthodox Judaism exists along a continuum that ranges from relative engagement with the contemporary secular world (the Modern Orthodox) to relative seclusion from it (the *Haredim*, ("those who tremble before God").

Modern Orthodox Judaism

This sector of Orthodoxy is fully committed to the observance of *halakhah* and to traditional study of Torah, but it also draws on secular knowledge and learning. Graduates of Orthodox high schools in the United States typically pursue higher education and engage in the full range of contemporary careers. Modern Orthodoxy also has taken steps to offer Talmud study to women. The sector tends to regard the establishment of the State of Israel as part of God's plan for the redemption of the Jewish people, and many high school graduates spend a "gap" year there. Recent studies suggest that Modern Orthodoxy constitutes less than one-third of the Orthodox sector in the United States. It is represented institutionally by the Union of Orthodox Jewish Congregations of America and, in the world of higher education, by Yeshiva University, which houses the seminary at which many modern Orthodox rabbis are ordained.

Haredi Judaism

Haredi Judaism—sometimes called Ultra-Orthodox Judaism—is wary of secular Western culture, and *Haredi* Jews tend to live in closed communities. With some variation, *Haredi* men typically wear black coats, fedoras or fur hats, the clothing worn by eighteenth-century Polish nobility. *Haredi* women dress modestly and cover their hair, either by wearing a wig or a scarf called a *tichel*. In varying degrees, Modern Orthodox women also may follow these practices. *Haredi* groups are divided on the legitimacy of the State of Israel. Some see the founding of the State as an improper attempt to force God's hand in ending the Jewish people's exile. In their view, only God can determine when and how the Jews will be ingathered into the promised land, and they therefore do not recognize the State. But other *Haredi* groups participate in the Israeli government. Compared to other groups within Judaism, including secular Israelis, *Haredim* typically have large families, and they are a growing proportion of the population of Israel and the Orthodox community in the United States.

Hasidism

Hasidism ("piety") is a segment of *Haredi* Judaism. Its founding is attributed to the charismatic mystic Rabbi Israel ben Eliezer (1698–1760), aka the *Baal Shem Tov* ("Master of the Good Name"), aka *Besht*. Hasidism advances an experiential vision of Judaism that emphasizes the power of joy, intensity, and prayer, often, particularly in Hasidism's early years, instead of rabbinic study. On the belief that God is everywhere, including the material world, Hasidism holds that, with the proper intention, the performance of *mitzvot* and even the ordinary acts of everyday life can bring individuals closer to God's immanent presence. Hasidism contains practices to help individuals perceive a divine spark even in their inappropriate thoughts and thus redirect those thoughts toward God. Uniquely, Hasidic groups are centered around a "court" of a spiritual leader known in Hebrew as a *tzaddik* ("righteous one") and more generally referred to as *rebbe*, a Yiddish form of rabbi. Each Hasidic *rebbe* is an independent authority who, his followers believe, is able to mediate their relationship with God and support their lives. Hasidic communities speak Yiddish and have developed yeshivas and community support institutions. They generally engage in little secular, Western education.

Hasidism became a mass movement in early modern Eastern Europe. A counter-movement of Orthodox Jews (*mitnagdim*, "opponents") was committed to the centrality of yeshiva Torah study and resisted the idea of the *tzaddik*. By the mid-nineteenth century the division between the two had diminished. Most of Hasidic Jewry was murdered by the Nazis during the Holocaust. The communities that survived have experienced remarkable growth in both the United States and Israel.

Perhaps the best-known contemporary Hasidic group is *Chabad-Lubavitch Hasidism*, which has developed a successful global outreach program and is visible on many university campuses. *Chabad's* institutions welcome Jews of all denominations, and its representatives encourage less observant Jews to perform *mitzvot*—such as donning *tefillin* or lighting Sabbath candles—and thus hasten redemption. Its website attracts large numbers.

Contemporary films such as *One of Us* and *Menashe*, and the television series *Shtisel*, reflect broad interest in and curiosity about the life of *Haredi* and Hasidic communities.

Conservative Judaism

Conservative Judaism—whose branch in Israel is called *Masorti* ("traditional")—occupies a middle ground between Reform and Orthodoxy. It is committed to *halakhah* but is prepared to modify it on the basis of both the community's historic experience and contemporary needs. The movement's Committee on Jewish Law and Standards determines positions on halakhic questions and allows individual Conservative rabbis to decide what is most appropriate for their community. For instance, Conservative Judaism endorses congregants' driving to synagogue and using electricity on *Shabbat*. It judges the former to be consistent with contemporary demographic and social realities, and, since electricity did not exist when *halakhah* was first formulated, permitting its Sabbath use is an appropriate, scientific rethinking of what is or is not forbidden under the category of work.

Conservative Judaism represents 18% of American Jews (11% of American Jews under age 30). Its rabbinical school is the Jewish Theological Seminary. Most Conservative synagogues follow the traditional liturgy, and many employ instrumental

FIGURE 20 *A modern Conservative synagogue. Beth Sholom Congregation, Elkins Park, PA,* © *Karla Rosenberg / Alamy Stock Photo.*

music on Friday evenings, even if not during worship on Saturday. Although most Conservative rabbis do not conduct intermarriages, the movement welcomes non-Jewish spouses as members of its synagogues and increasingly has worked to address the social, spiritual, and Jewish educational needs of interfaith families. The Conservative movement accepts women and gays for ordination as rabbis and cantors and endorses a modified form of a Jewish wedding for same-sex couples. The Israel Chief Rabbinate does not recognize Conservative conversions or marriages.

Reconstructing Judaism

Reconstructionist Judaism is an American Naturalist Judaism based on the thought of Rabbi Mordechai Kaplan (1881–1982). It understands Judaism to be an evolving religious civilization that encompasses religion and peoplehood. It has a naturalistic conception of God as an intrinsic power or energy that generates good in the world and enables people to realize "the image of God." For that reason, Reconstructionism holds that historically Judaism interacted with other civilizations and thus expresses respect for all nations and peoples. In line with this thinking, it sidelines traditional claims of any special "chosen" status of the Jewish people. Reconstructionism understands *halakhah* as an inherited communal practice rather than a command from God, and it therefore encourages its participants to find appropriate ways to reinvigorate *halakhah* according to the needs of the age, thus making it possible meaningfully to integrate it into their lives.

Reconstructionism is inclusive and egalitarian in all respects, and Kaplan himself invented the ceremony of *Bat Mitzvah* for his daughter, Judith, in 1922. The *Bar Mitzvah* had been restricted to boys. The movement is positive about the State of Israel, and it allows discrete congregations to make their own decisions about intermarriage. The movement's focus is less on theology than on building and sustaining community through concrete activities that reflect the members' goals and aspirations. Reconstructionism is the smallest of the four major Jewish denominations, perhaps only 1–2% of Jewish adults.

Humanistic Judaism and Jewish Renewal

Humanistic Judaism is a non-theistic form of Judaism that fuses rationality and secular humanism with a commitment to the Jewish people and Jewish community. Jewish Renewal is a recent trans-denominational movement that uses *kabbalah*, music, meditation, and New Age spirituality to reinvigorate the Judaic religious experience. Each of these has a membership of fewer than 1% of American Jews.

Jewish Cultural Variation

Judaism is a global religion, practiced everywhere Jews have lived: Western and Eastern Europe, North Africa, the Middle East, and India and central Asia. In adapting and in some ways assimilating to these diverse regions and environments, Jews developed distinctive subcultures, Jewish languages, and religious and cultural practices. As noted earlier, the three largest of these groups are *Ashkenazi*, *Sephardi*, and *Mizrahi* Jews.

Ashkenazi Jews

Ashkenazi ("German") Jews descend from Jewish communities originally established along the Rhine River and in Northern France after the Roman period. In response to various expulsions and the violence of the Crusades, Jews gradually moved from Western to Eastern Europe, primarily Poland, Lithuania, and Ukraine. From the mid-seventeenth century to the Second World War, Jews in Eastern Europe lived mainly in relatively self-contained cultural and religious communities called *shtetls* (market towns). Beginning in the nineteenth century, many moved to East European cities or migrated to Western Europe or the United States. Ultimately, *shtetl* life was destroyed in the Holocaust.

Ashkenazi Jews created Yiddish, a European Jewish language written with Hebrew letters that combines medieval high German with elements of Hebrew, Aramaic, and Slavic languages. Over 80% of the world's Yiddish speakers were murdered in the Holocaust. Once considered a dying language, Yiddish has nearly one million contemporary speakers, primarily in Orthodox communities, and is undergoing a revival in drama and literature. In addition, *Ashkenazi* customs include, for example, distinctive melodies for chanting the synagogue liturgy and reciting the Torah, and not eating legumes during Passover. Roughly 63% of Jews worldwide and over six million of the seven million Jews in the United States are of *Ashkenazi* heritage. Since Zionism was primarily a European phenomenon, it was dominated for the better part of the twentieth century by *Ashkenazi* Jews.

Sephardi Jews

The book of Obadiah (1.20) predicted that when the Jews return to the promised land "the exiles from Jerusalem, who are in *Sepharad*, will possess the towns of the Negev." The location of Obadiah's *Sepharad* is uncertain, but since Roman times Jews have used the term to refer to the Iberian Peninsula, and descendants of Jews from Spain and Portugal are known as *Sephardim*. In the seventh century CE, some Visigoth rulers proscribed Judaism and forced Jews to convert to Christianity. The Muslim conquest of Spain in 711 inaugurated a period of cultural interaction between Judaism and Islam, sometimes called the "Golden Age" of Spanish Jewry. Judaism under Islamic rule was relatively tolerated, and Jewish intellectuals engaged in science, literature, and philosophy. They produced important works of Jewish philosophy, poetry, and religious thought.

The Christian appropriation of Spain began in the eleventh century. In 1391 there were extensive pogroms against Jews in Spain, and in the aftermath perhaps as many as 200,000 Spanish Jews converted to Roman Catholicism. These forced converts were called *conversos* in Spanish, *'anusim* ("forced ones") in Hebrew. Some lived as crypto-Jews, who were publicly Christian but practiced Judaism secretly in private. In 1478, after the Christian "reconquest" of all of Spain, King Ferdinand and Queen Isabella instituted the Spanish Inquisition, which aimed to remove heresy from the Church and focused on Jewish and Muslim converts to Christianity, who were suspected of "backsliding." In 1492, the royals issued the Alhambra Decree, otherwise known as the Edict of Expulsion, which gave Jews four months to avoid execution either by publicly converting to Christianity or leaving Spain. Large numbers converted, and between 100,000 and 200,000 Jews fled the region, most settling in North Africa and Turkey, under the Ottoman Empire. Others settled in Italy, Brazil, Mexico, and Curacao. In 1497 there was a subsequent forced conversion in, and expulsion from, Portugal. There was a Muslim expulsion in 1502.

Sephardi Jews developed Ladino, which combines medieval Spanish, Hebrew, Aramaic, and local languages. Ladino is written with either Hebrew or Latin letters. Sephardic Jews also have distinctive melodies for the liturgy and recitation of the Torah and other unique ritual and religious practices.

In 2015 the government of Spain invited "descendants of those expelled from Spain in the fifteenth century" to become naturalized citizens if they could prove their "Sephardic status" and a "special connection" to Spain. In the same year, the Portuguese government enacted a similar law. As of 2019, approximately 127,000 individuals had applied for naturalized citizenship in Spain and over 30,000 in Portugal. It is estimated that a significant number of residents of Latin America may be descendants of *'anusim*.

Mizrahi Jews

Mizrahi ("Eastern") Jews plausibly claim descent from the Jews who were taken into exile in Babylonia (contemporary Iraq) after the destruction of Solomon's Temple. The term emerged in the early years of the founding of the State of Israel and applies generally to the Jewish populations in the Muslim and Arabic-speaking countries of the Middle East and North Africa. It also includes Persian Jews and Jews from central Asia. *Mizrahi* Jewish culture developed primarily under Islam. Because of their overlapping histories, *Mizrahi* Jews follow *Sephardi* religious practice. There was anti-Jewish violence in the 1940s in Iraq, Egypt, Libya, Syria, and Yemen. Between 850,000 and 900,000 *Mizrahi* Jews emigrated to Israel from those nations and from Algeria, Iran, Iraq, Lebanon, Morocco, Tunisia, and Turkey as well. *Mizrahi* Jews, many of whom are people of color, constitute about half of Israel's citizens.

Although cultural, educational, religious, and class differences have strained relations between the *Mizrahi* and *Ashkenazi* sectors, *Mizrahi* Jews have become increasingly influential in Israeli society. *Mizrahi* music and musicians are extremely popular in Israel. In 2016, Israel's Ministry of Education announced that university and school curricula would now include *Mizrahi* and *Sephardi* history and culture.

Christianity

As has been discussed earlier in this book, Western Christianity existed as one Church, namely the Roman Catholic, until the 1500s. However, given the geographic expansion and cultural diversity of Christianity, even when Christianity appeared as one unified Church, diversity and dissent has always been a part of this religion, even in the first churches that were established by the Apostle Paul. We have seen this, for example, in the fourth-century debates on the nature of Jesus which led to the establishment of the Trinity. After the Reformation, Western Christianity became institutionally divided and from that point on we speak of churches within Christianity. Since that point, it is division, not unity, which has marked Christianity. This is found in the growth of

FIGURE 21 *Traditional Protestant Church, Seminario Evangélico de Matanzas, Cuba,* © *Michelle A. Gonzalez.*

denominations and also independent churches that claim a Christian identity but do not have any other affiliations. Today, when we speak of different types of churches within Christianity we are talking about thousands of different types of Christian institutions and expressions, from the local non-denominational church to the global Anglican Church. This section on Christianity will focus on those moments of unity in tension throughout Christian history versus providing a denominational history, which is too lengthy for this project.

Ecclesiologies

In spite of their affiliation or independence, contemporary Christian understandings of Church and community are always grounded in the New Testament witness of the first Christians as well as the historical events and theological developments that shaped the historical church. However, contemporary Christians interpret the history and the New Testament witness through the eyes of the modern world. While within Roman Catholicism the notion of tradition is key, all Christian churches have traditions and figures with authority that shape their understandings of Christianity, how it is taught and lived. The notion of a Christian tradition is grounded in the first twelve apostles and the teachings found in the Christian Scriptures. Traditions are handed down and transmitted; they are active and living. What was considered an important part of the Christian tradition in one period can be devalued in the next era. Like all dimensions of religion, tradition is shaped by its social and historical context.

While knowledge of the diverse ways that Christian churches have defined themselves historically informs contemporary understandings of the Church, overwhelmingly scholars today begin with the contemporary world and the manner in which the issues raised by this context shape ecclesial self-understandings. Within the study of Christianity, the field that directly addresses the nature of the church is called ecclesiology. The word *ecclesia* refers to an assembly, community, or congregation of people. In Romans 6.5 the *ecclesia* is all of the faithful, "For if we have been united with him in a death like his, we will certainly be united with him in a resurrection like his." This sense of *ecclesia* extends beyond this world into the afterlife. In a similar vein Galatians 1.13 describes the "church of God." In Matthew 16.18 Jesus proclaims "I will build my church." This passage, among others, will be used to more narrowly associate *ecclesia* throughout the history of Christianity with Christian institutions versus a broad association of it with the faithful. It is important to highlight, however, that contrary to its usage today, *ecclesia* in the Christian Scriptures did not refer to a physical place or building. Questions about the nature of the Church were not an issue for early Christians because they lived in scattered communities, often in hiding. It is only as the Church entered into the public sphere and expanded globally that the question of the role of the Church came to the forefront. Whether we consider early debates on the nature of the Trinity to the Reformation or contemporary debates on the role of women in Christian leadership, Christians reinterpret the nature of the role of churches in society much in the same way they constantly reinterpret Jesus.

The Church in the World

The Donatist controversy of the fourth century illustrates how ecclesial debates inform Christian monotheism. The controversy emerged as a result of the persecution of Christians under the Roman emperor Diocletian. Christians were forced to burn Christian books, and those who did were known as *traditores* (traitors) by those Christians who refused to do so. One of these "traitors" was later consecrated a bishop. A faction of Christians challenged the bishop's authority based on what they interpreted as a betrayal of his faith. The group that opposed the consecration of the bishop challenged the purity of the Church under his leadership. They separated and formed their own church. They believed that since the bishop had betrayed his Christian faith by burning the books, any sacraments performed in his church would not be legitimate. The sacredness of the sacraments was interpreted as based on the holiness of the clergyman that administered them. One of its initial leaders was a bishop named Donatus Magnus, and the schismatic movement took his name. The breakaway church grew in numbers.

In response, Church Father Augustine of Hippo, who you may remember from our discussion of original sin, argued that all humans are sinful and that the holiness of the Church comes from Christ, not its members. This is an important point to emphasize in discussing Christian communities. Ultimately for Christians, though they vary on how much they highlight this point, churches are churches of sinners. The holiness of the Church comes from outside of it, from God, not from its members. If the holiness of a church depended on its members then that could lead one to diminish the importance of God. Christians cannot achieve holiness without the divine. Another point that is important to highlight within Augustine's response to this controversy is that he held that a schism among Christians is far worse than handing over books in the face of persecution. In other words, division among Christians is a much greater betrayal of one's faith than the sinful act of burning Christian texts. As is clear from the history of Christianity, Augustine's emphasis on the unity of the Church is one that will not endure.

As with Augustine's emphasis on the holiness of the church being not dependent on its membership, Martin Luther argued during the Reformation that the identity of the church is rooted in the preaching of the gospel, not the clergy. In other words, the manner in which the Good News of Jesus is proclaimed, and not the nature of the leadership, is what defines Christian communal identity. John Calvin, also a European Protestant Reformer, claimed that there is both a visible church and an invisible church. The visible church is the community of believers. The invisible church is the assembly of the elect that will only be known by God. The invisible church is what the visible church will become at the end of time. What all these Christian leaders share is a sense that the holiness of the Church resides in its witnessing of Christ, not in its membership. Christ unifies all Christians, and the Church as witness is the exclusive bearer of Christian teachings. Through the community and collectivity of believers, the Church is understood as bringing Christians together in order to grow in their faith and love of God.

A fairly modern debate is the question of the role of Christian churches in the broader society. Does the Church have a role in the broader society, and what is the extent of the role? Should Christians be involved in what are often described as secular affairs? Should churches be worried about saving lives or just focus on saving souls? Does the witness of Christian faith extend to everyday affairs? The question of religious pluralism is one of these issues. Some Christians embrace what is often referred to as particularism, the belief that revelation can only be understood in light of Jesus Christ or even exclusively through Jesus Christ. Those who embrace inclusivism argue that non-Christian religions contain God's grace but may or may not—depending on varied perspectives—have salvific potential. Those who embrace pluralism believe that each religion is distinctive and equally valid. For Christians the question becomes whether the One God is present and active outside of the mediation of the Church. For some this is the case, but in varying ways. For others the church becomes the exclusive mediation of God. To add even another level of exclusivity, for some churches it is only their church, and not other branches of Christianity, that has the ability to mediate God's grace.

Corinth

Christians have never had a unified understanding of both what it means to be Christian and the appropriate expression of Christian faith. Paul's first letter to the church in Corinth reveals that these issues plagued the Church even in New Testament times. Reading his letter one learns of the myriad of problems among the Corinthian Christians that included claims of spiritual superiority over one another, suing one another in public courts, abusing the communal meal, and sexual misbehavior. Paul wrote to the community critiquing these behaviors and demanding higher ethical and moral standards. Paul, along with fellow apostles Timothy and Silvanus, traveled to Corinth and began to preach the gospel after leaving Thessalonia. Luke's account of Paul's missionary tactics, found in the Acts of the Apostles, differs from Paul's account: Luke indicates that Paul began his ministry among local Jews and turned to the Gentiles only after he found that the Jews would not accept his teachings. Paul, however, insists that he was always the apostle to the Gentiles; he says that he arrived in Corinth and preached to Gentiles about the One God and God's son, Jesus. These different accounts also remind us of the diversity of interpretations that has accompanied Christianity from its earliest years.

Most of the Corinthian converts were from the lower economic classes, but at least some of them must have been wealthy and educated. This economic diversity helps explain some of the problems in this community: the wealthy members arrived at the communal meal before the others (because they didn't have to work); by the time the working class members arrived, the food and drink had been consumed. Another problem that may be traced back to the differing socioeconomic levels of the Christians at Corinth is the question of eating meat offered to idols. Those educated Christians recognized that the worship of pagan gods was a superstition and, thus, eating the sacrificial meat posed no theological problem for them. The less educated Christians among them, however, saw this as dangerous, perhaps because they believed that eating the meat was tantamount to idolatry. Paul writes in the letter that his primary message to the Corinthians was "Christ crucified."

Many of the difficulties in the Corinthian community can be traced to a fundamental theological misunderstanding of the import of Jesus' death and resurrection. The Corinthians believed that they had died and risen with Christ and therefore already enjoyed the full benefits of salvation. This led some to lead a more hedonistic life. Paul, on the other hand, insisted that salvation was not yet accomplished; it would occur when Jesus returned. Paul tells the Corinthians that they "are being saved" (1 Corinthians 15.2). Rather than enjoying their salvation, Paul believed that this world continued to be ruled by evil forces, and life would be full of pain and struggles until Jesus' return. Paul "proved" his point by reminding the Corinthians of his teachings about Jesus' resurrection. Paul taught that Jesus' resurrected body was a glorified spiritual body. His was a bodily resurrection and so, too, will theirs be. Jesus' resurrection, moreover, was the first fruit of the resurrection. There is going to be a future resurrection of the dead, and that is when Christians will enjoy their salvation. According to Paul, the community's problems were the consequence of the Corinthians' mistaken belief that they had already been exalted. They failed to take seriously the power of evil; their behavior caused divisions in the Church and led to a lack of concern for other members. They were becoming morally lax in their certainty that they had already been saved,

Unity Amidst Diversity

What appears to be a minor dispute in one Christian community actually reveals that the notion of a unified and homogenous Christianity is exaggerated. Christians have always struggled to maintain a global and unified sense of what it means to be Christian because of local contours that shape Christian life and theological interpretations based on culture, history, and social location. The Council of Nicaea showed that Christians were even divided on how to understand the nature of God and Jesus Christ. During the latter half of the Patristic period (100–451), once Christians ceased to be persecuted, Christian leaders struggled to build consensus among divergent religious groups. This entailed tensions and debates among Christian churches. The Middle Ages (1050–1500) are marked by increasing tensions between Western and Eastern churches, which led to their break in 1054. We have already seen the later split in Western Christianity during the Protestant Reformation. The contemporary diversity among Christians today is not a new reality. Christians have always struggled to maintain a unity not in spite of but because of the diversity among them. This is even more pronounced today, particularly in the division between Catholics and Protestants. Too often a Catholic will claim that she or he is Catholic and not Christian, for Christian implies Protestant. On the flip side Protestant Christians will claim they are Christian and place Catholics in a different category, thus excluding them from their definition of authentic Christian identity.

In contemporary scholarship on Christian communities and churches there is increasing recognition that too often in the study of Christianity there is an unhealthy emphasis on Euro-American communities in North American and European churches. Scholars of Christianity overwhelmingly emerge from these regions and backgrounds and their insights are shaped by their context. This gives a false impression of the contemporary globalized Church that finds its centers more in Latin America and Africa than in Europe, and in the United States more likely among Latino/as than Euro-Americans. Christianity is often erroneously reduced to a European religion in its past as well, ignoring the vital role of, for example, North African thinkers and leaders in shaping Christian history and teachings. This is also translated for decades into a very narrow understanding of the culture of Christian communities and worship. Today, however, the unity within diversity that is Christianity is much more readily acknowledged and studied.

Most often today when you hear the word "church" you think about a building or structure. However, as mentioned above, the first uses of the word *ecclesia* referred to the community or assembly of believers. The first followers of Jesus did not build churches. We know from the Acts of the Apostles that the first Christians regularly broke bread together in honor of the Last Supper and that they shared common property and possessions. "Every day they continued to meet together in the temple courts. They broke bread in their homes and ate together with glad and sincere hearts" (Acts 2.46). They gathered in public spaces, such as the Temple and synagogues, or in people's homes. In the third century we begin to see the acquisition of buildings or construction of spaces intentionally for Christian worship. In the Middle Ages we see an explosion of constructions throughout Western Europe of what many classically think of when the word "church" is used. Today, in many ways, the pendulum has swung the other way. While we still have churches, there are also congregations that do not have a physical space in a traditional sense. Churches can be found in strip malls and store fronts or in rented hotel conference rooms and movie theaters, and they have also returned to people's private homes. There are even churches today that exist exclusively as online communities. This diversity in terms of space and structure mirrors the diversity of the religion as a whole.

Diversity within Christianity is not without boundaries, however. This is clearly evident in debates about orthodoxy (right thinking/opinion) and heresy (unorthodoxy or blasphemy). Overwhelmingly, minority opinions within the history of Christianity are deemed heretical and are suppressed by Christian authorities. Because the first Christians were scattered and isolated, what united them was not holding the exact same doctrinal teachings, but rather the fact that they worshipped Jesus. With the growing centralization of authority within the Church in Rome and the emerging papacy, clearer lines began to be drawn defining authenticity of Christian belief and practices. By the eleventh century the title "pope" is used exclusively for the Bishop of Rome, though it had previously been used to refer to all bishops. The Pope is the successor of Peter, who is given a privileged place among the twelve apostles—Jesus proclaims:

And I tell you that you are Peter, and on this rock I will build my church, and the gates of Hades will not overcome it. I will give you the keys of the kingdom of heaven; whatever you bind on earth will be bound in heaven, and whatever you loose on earth will be loosed in heaven.

MATTHEW 16.18–19

The Reformers not only challenged the hierarchical authority of the papacy but also accused the Catholic Church of failing to uphold the doctrine of grace. Luther's doctrine of justification argued that the precondition of Christian salvation is a gift of grace not human works. In other words, salvation is not something that can be earned through human action and must always be a gift of God's grace and love. The Protestant teaching of justification by faith alone emphasizes that we receive God's grace and forgiveness through faith alone, not through any actions on our part. While this distinction between Protestants and Catholics is often caricatured as an extreme divide, in reality both Catholics and Protestant value, albeit at different levels, faith and works.

The unity, or perhaps more appropriately, the disunity of the Church is an issue that plagues Christians. The Reformers argued that due to corruption the Catholic Church had ceased to be the authentic Church and thus required renewal. While the notion of one Church is found in Christian creeds, institutionally this is far from reality. The ecumenical movement in modern Christianity, which promotes unity among Christian churches, strives to build bridges between and among churches in varying degrees, though many have accepted the reality of diverse institutional churches that are unified through the saving work of Christ. While Christians continue to build bridges between them and acknowledge that what makes them Christian is far more distinctive than what divides them, Christian churches have not made any grand gestures in terms of dismantling their particular denominations. The Christian community remains divided, in spite of historical and contemporary pronouncements regarding the scandal of division within the religion.

Islam

The Qur'an makes clear to Muslims that they hold the final and seal of all revealed Scriptures. They are warned that there will be no further prophets after Muhammad, and this means that they have only the perfected Qur'an to guide them. It was this revelation that created the early Muslim community—the *ummah*. In a context of tribal groups and affiliations, the concept of *ummah* brought together different parts of society. The distinction was being made of those who submitted fully to the oneness of God and those who did not, and so when Muhammad was invited to mediate between warring factions in Medina, he put forward a peaceful constitution that also included the Jews and Christians in the concept of the *ummah*. There is much discussion about when the concept was widened and then narrowed, but in current times it would generally be used for a global community of Muslims. This, of course, differs even at an intrafaith level, where some Muslims will reject the Muslimness of others. In order to understand this further, we must look at the differing sectarian divisions that occurred in Islamic traditions.

The notion of an *ummah* was easier to identify with the early converts to Islam but the community clearly became *communities* very quickly. The division of the Shi'a (who believed that succession after Muhammad should remain in his bloodline) and Sunni (who believed that succession should come from community election) are the most commonly understood denominations. Sunnis make up around 90 percent of all Muslims, and they are also extremely diverse in their understanding of Islam. After the death of Muhammad, another breakaway denomination emerged in opposition to the Shi'a and Sunni. The *Khawarij* (meaning "to leave") argued against both the Shi'a and Sunni position on succession and held that the most noble should lead the community. They took a more extreme view of upholding this and categorized anyone against their position as non-Muslim. Although with a different ideology, they still exist to this day in Oman and Algeria but are known as Ibadis.

The central difference between the Shi'a and Sunni communities is leadership, namely the authority of the *imama*, the rightful successors of Muhammad who are able to teach and understand doctrine. The differences are more theological than political. These different Muslim communities disagreed on matters of faith but remained united in their submission and belief in One God. The first Shi'i imam was Ali, who was the prophet Muhammad's cousin and son-in-law. Shi'as believe that he had the rightful claim to the caliphate after Muhammad's death. However, he had to wait around twenty-four years after Muhammad's death to be appointed. Ali was appointed in difficult political turmoil after the assassination of Uthman, the third caliph. Muslims at the time accused him of not doing enough to find the killers of Uthman, and he faced opposition from Muhammad's wife Aisha, who led a battle against his army in November 656 CE. This battle further cemented the Shi'a and Sunni division. Ali was assassinated by members of the *Khawarij*. After Ali's death, his sons, Hasan and Husayn became the next imams of the Shi'a communities. Hasan was challenged politically by the caliph at the time, Mu'awiya, but he gave up his claim to the caliphate in Kufa in 661 CE and retired to Medina. Hasan died around 670 CE. His brother, Husayn in 680 CE was convicted of confronting the caliph Yazid on the plains of *Karbala*. It was here that he was outnumbered and killed. The date remains memorable, 10th Muharram 680 CE. This day is commemorated by Shi'as who seek penitents for those in Kufa who did not help save him. The ritual of self-flagellation is connected with this event, as Shi'as remember their "prince of martyrs."

The Shi'a communities emerged more boldly after the events of *Karbala*. The *Zaydis*, also known as the Fivers, emerged in the eighth century. They believed that *Zayd ibn Ali* (695–740 CE), the great-great-grandson of Muhammad, was the rightful imam after Hasan and Hussain. They differed from other Shi'as on the infallibility of the Imamat emerging from father to son from Muhammad to the entire family of Ali. They held similar theological views as the *Mu'tazila* (understood as a rationalist school of theology during the eighth to tenth centuries) but differed on the *Imamat*.

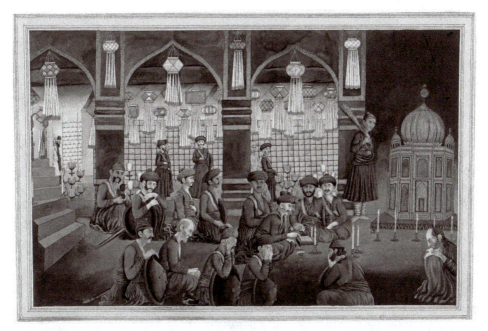

FIGURE 22 *Shi'a Muslims mourning for 'Ashura at a Ta'ziya model of Imam Husayn's tomb, Lucknow, India, c. 1800. Folio, colors on paper. Folio: 28.3 x 43.2 cm. Chester Beatty (CBL In 69.18), © The Trustees of the Chester Beatty Library, Dublin.*

The *Isma'ili* Shi'a, also known as the Seveners, emerged in around 765 CE. The Shi'a communities split after the death of the sixth imam, Ja'far al-Sadiq (d. 765). The Isma'ilis accepted Muhammad Ibn Ism'ail (d. 775) as their seventh imam, whereas the *Ithna Ashariya* (Twelvers) accepted Musa Ibn Ja'far (744–799). The Fatamid dynasty was associated with the Isma'ilis from 910 to 1171 CE. The Isma'ilis further split during the time of the eighth caliph of the Fatamid dynasty, *al-Mustansir Billah* (1029–1094 CE). The largest branch of Isma'ilis are the Nizar Isma'ilis, who hold Aga Khans, direct descendants of Muhammad, as their religious and spiritual leaders.

The current Aga Khan, Prince Shah Karim al-Hussaini (b. 1936), is said to be their forty-ninth and has been the imam since 1957. He leads a global community of Isma'ilis, around 25 million people. Isma'ili doctrines are kept secret, as they believe that some things are known and some things kept hidden, esoteric, and only known to the imam. This means that there is existentially a unity of meaning, but exoterically there is a plurality of meanings. They worship in what is known as *jam'atkhana* (an assembly house) and also worship on a Friday. Alongside their belief in the Qur'an, sunna, and Hadith, they include a collection of poems and songs known as *ginans* (wisdom). These are colorful and mystical tales and stories of ethical and moral instruction. The other branches of the Isma'ili communities are the Druze and Bohras. The *Hashishiyyun* (the assassins) split from the Nizari Isma'ilis in 1094 CE and are often depicted as an extreme denomination who preached an esoteric version of Shi'ism and carried out high-profile public killings as they aimed to uphold good and justice.

The Ithna Ashari Shi'as (Twelvers) are the largest Shi'ite denomination. They believe in twelve divinely ordained imams. They are the political and religious successors to Muhammad. However, the twelfth imam is in occultation (hidden/absence), and this is where they differ from the Shi'a Zaydis and Shi'a Nizaris. A few other Shi'a denominations are worthy of note. The *Alawis* (also known as *Nusayris*) compose a syncretic Shi'a denomination whose name originates with Ali (the first caliph/imam), and they revere him to the point of deification. Their Islamic beliefs are mixed with gnostic and Christian theological elements. They emerged in the ninth century under the leadership of Ibn Nusayr (d. 873), a disciple of the tenth imam in the Twelver tradition, Ali al-Hadi (828–868 CE) but he differed with him on matters of authority. The *Alevis* are also a syncretic Shi'a denomination who are largely found in current-day Turkey. Their beliefs are in line with Shi'a beliefs, but they hold more heterodox views, in that they permit the drinking of alcohol, consider dancing a kind of spiritual submission to God, and practice shamanism. Much of these teachings came from *Haji Bektash Wali*, who was a Muslim mystic of the thirteenth century and claimed to be a direct descendant of the seventh imam, Musa Kazim. *Ahmadis* originate with Mirza Ghulam Ahmed, who was born in 1835 in British India in the Punjab region. Ahmed presented himself as the *Mahdi* (the Messiah) and *Mujaddid* (renewer of the faith). Ahmadis believe that Jesus died, which differs from Sunni thinking, which holds that Jesus is the Messiah, did not die, and would return to earth during the end of times. The Twelver Shi'as believe that the twelfth imam is the Messiah and will return alongside Jesus before the end of times.

All Islamic denominations accept the centrality of God's oneness—this has never differed but what has differed are theologies (*kalam*, meaning speech) or interpretations of this oneness. The main reason for this is that theological ideas had played a huge impact on the political, economic, and social life of Muslims. These ideas have played a role in how caliphs, muftis, and qadis would administer Islam. For example, if God allows good and evil, does God have an evil aspect? This question has serious implications not for the existence of God but for how one understands submission to God—how one upholds good and not bad. Here is one such example and its implications: The created-or-uncreated Qur'an debate was between the *Mu'tazila* schools of thought (around the eighth and ninth centuries), who argued that the Qur'an was separate from God, created and fixed in time and place, and the *al-Ashari* schools of thought (around ninth and tenth centuries), who considered the Qur'an to be coeternal with God and therefore "uncreated." The Sunni Caliph *al-Ma'mun* (787–833 CE) decreed that the created Qur'an doctrine be upheld at all levels, and he instituted what was known as the *mihna* (a test or inquisition) to make sure that everyone complied. It was opposed by one of the key figures of Islamic law, Ahmad Ibn Hanbal (780–855), who opposed this type of reasoning. He was imprisoned and continually refused to uphold the doctrine. A later caliph, al-Mutawakkil, abolished this doctrine in 850. This scenario showcases one of the first theological differences among Muslims, and the debate affected all denominations in

Islam. Denominational diversity is not as simple as Shi'a and Sunni—the inner differences are immense and just as diverse.

Sufism is the mystical path to God in Islam. The term is one that many have tried and failed to define, but at the very essence it is a path that attempts to strengthen the direct and personal relationship with God. *Suf* in Arabic basically means "wool." It is said that the early Sufis would cloak themselves in only wool as they attempted to strengthen their relationship with God and without distraction. Their key concern is to give up material attachments and to live a life of deep spirituality. *Tasawwuf* is the mystical practice that makes one a Sufi. Many different commentators and Sufi orders have tried to stipulate what needs to be done in order to be on the Sufi path, but there is no one way to walk the Sufi path, *Tariqa*. Sufis give us a more deep insight into the diversity of Islamic thought and practice. Sufis emerged to counter the more law-driven, formalistic methods that some Muslims were advocating that were mixed with politics. The Sufis attempted to recover what they think of as core, simple acts and thoughts of submission to God. A few of the most inspirational Qur'anic quotes for Sufis read:

> God is the Light of the heavens and the earth. The Parable of His Light is the niche, wherein is a lamp. The lamp is in a glass. The glass is as a shining star kindled from a blessed olive tree, neither of the East nor the West. Its oil would well-nigh shine forth, even if no fire had touched it. Light upon light. God guides unto His Light whomsoever He will, and God sets forth parables for mankind, and God is knower of all things.
>
> Q24:35

> We did indeed create man, and We know that his soul whispers to him; and We are nearer to him than his jugular vein.
>
> Q50:16

It was such verses that led Sufis to renounce worldly connections: for example, long periods of fasting and celibacy. There is much discussion on gender and Sufism. Although the ideals or philosophy of Sufism are egalitarian, it was still not able to buck patriarchy. One of the most famous Sufi women is *Rabia al-Adawiyya* (often called Rabia of Basra), who lived from 718 to 801. Born into a poor family, she was said to have been a slave freed because her master realized her mystical qualities. She advocated total commitment to and love of God and argued that marriage meant nothing to her. At an early age she left for the wilderness and became an ascetic in the desert. Tradition holds that Rabia was seen running through the street with a bucket of water in one hand and a pot of fire in the other. When asked why she was doing this, she responded, "I want to put out the fires of hell and burn down the rewards of paradise. They block the way to God. I do not want to worship because of the fear of punishment or the promise of reward but only for the love of God." In another tradition,

FIGURE 23 *Sufi dervishes dancing the* sama *ritual, from* Nafahat al-uns *(Breaths of Fellowship), by 'Abd al-Rahman Jami (d. 1492), Turkey, dated 1003H, 1595. Folio, ink, colors and gold on paper. Folio: 30.6 x 18.4 cm. Chester Beatty (CBL T 474.248), © The Trustees of the Chester Beatty Library, Dublin.*

she stated, "O God, if I worship you for the fear of hell, burn me in hell and if I worship you for paradise, exclude me from paradise. But if I worship you for your own sake, grudge me not your everlasting beauty."

When one seeks to understand internal diversity in the Muslim community, we often see this being reduced to Shi'a, Sunni or Sufi. This is not the complete story of internal Muslim communities. Muslims are united on the core tenets of belief, namely One God and Muhammad, but the lived practices lead to a wide variety of communities taking shape. A way to understand this diversity is to think about mosques. Mosques were established as a focal point for the Muslim community when Islam emerged. It was a place of worship but also a place strengthening all sorts of communal affairs. In any city today we find a variety of mosques. They bring together Muslims who understand Islam differently. The imam at the pulpit on a Friday speaks to the gathered congregation. Some may agree with what he (or she) is saying and some may not. Mosques are now emerging which allow women to be imams. Some Muslims disagree with this and attend mosques led by a man. This extremely local diversity challenges further the assumptions of what the Muslim community looks like.

It is difficult to define and outline what the ummah looks like. It should be understood in the most general sense of a complex unit. The billion or so Muslims globally are very different and make up different communities globally. Mosques are not set up as churches or synagogues so this makes it difficult to compare their role in defining community. This is not to say that community is not important in Islamic societies. Islam builds on the understanding that connection with others can help strengthen belief and practice.

Muslims globally pray in Arabic, even where they may not be able to communicate with each other. Arabic connects them in community to the Qur'an, to God. This also leads to differences in the community. Learning and understanding Arabic has become a widespread issue amongst Muslims who want to get close to the Qur'an but it has inevitably led to some Arabic-speaking Muslims thinking they are, in some way, superior to those Muslims who merely recite the Qur'an without understanding the language. Language is important for communication and community. Arabic has then become a vehicle to unite Muslim focus on the Qur'an but it also allows us to see differences amongst Muslims.

The ummah is a mixture of agreements and disagreements on different matters but they are united in the belief of One God and acceptance of Muhammad as the last and final messenger of God.

Afterthought: Peoplehood and Community

Monotheism is not monolithic. Because there is only One God in the cosmos, and because human beings are created with free will, it is inevitable that they will disagree about the nature of God and what God expects. This book has traced some of the major different understandings among Judaism, Christianity, and Islam. This chapter addresses the variations within the traditions and attempts to identify the sources and reasons for the differences.

In Judaism, communal variation is both religious and cultural. The Samaritans' claim to be a distinct group that possesses the correct Torah and practices the authentic religion of the land of Israel from before the time of the Babylonian exile represents both those realms. Perhaps in contrast, the Karaites were Jews who rejected rabbinic authority and appealed only to Scripture. In so doing, Karaism presaged Reformation Christianity and exposed the unavoidable tension between Scripture and tradition in monotheism's structure.

Judaism's other religious variations are adaptations of a religious minority to shifting political and cultural conditions. They represent the strategies of a religion that, unlike Christianity and Islam, grew up abroad rather than at home. The differences among *Ashekanzi*, *Sephardi*, and *Mizrahi* Jewish communities are primarily cultural and reflect a kind of dual identity, both Jewish and cultural.

Unlike Judaism, Christianity and Islam ran and dominated the nations and cultures in which they developed. Their internal differences, therefore, reflect the character of their religious structures more than Judaism's variations do.

Diversity within Christianity and Islam is primarily theological. Since Christianity is a religion of consent, differences of belief have communal consequences. It is difficult to worship with others unless all parties agree on to whom, and the way, the worship is directed. This is the reason that creeds play an important role in Christian community and Christian worship. The Reformation is perhaps the most consequential religious division within Christianity, and the Reformers' emphasis on the authority of Scripture reinforces a distinctive trait of the monotheistic heritage. The same is true of different Muslim communities, which have all differed on understandings of faith.

Study Questions: Peoplehood and Community

Discuss the relationship among Scripture, peoplehood, and community in the three traditions.

What are key factors that provoke and promote communal and religious diversity within each religion?

How do the three religions understand religious leadership and/or authority?

Is it possible for an entire religious community to make a mistake on an issue? Think of a historical and contemporary issue that exemplifies this.

8

Gender, Sexuality, and Marriage

This chapter examines a pressing conundrum for these religions: questions and debates surrounding gender, sexuality, and marriage. We have chosen to focus on this issue exclusively because it affects Jews, Christians, and Muslims across the globe. Also, contrary to popular belief, issues of gender impact all humans, not just women. In addition, our emphasis on marriage and sexuality gets at the core of how these religions influence not only how people live their everyday lives, but how religions shape their lifelong decisions and commitments and understandings of community and relationships. This chapter emphasizes points of tension and growth and considers the diverse views on these themes within each tradition.

Judaism

In Judaism men have had the primary responsibility to study Torah and determine and lead correct halakhic practice. Since the 1970s, the work of Jewish feminists has shifted and expanded that focus in all Judaism's denominations across the globe, so that contemporary Judaic thinking and practice in the areas of gender, marriage, and sexuality exist along a continuum from androcentric to egalitarian.

Marriage

Rabbinic teaching acclaims marriage, values heterosexual sex, and opposes celibacy. It also advocates sexual activity within marriage not solely for procreation but also for its intimacy and enjoyment, which enhance the marital relationship. Sexual behavior within marriage is conditioned on consent, and *halakhah* prohibits marital rape. Kabbalah understands marital intercourse, particularly on the Sabbath, to represent the integration of the masculine and feminine aspects of God's nature, the perfection of creation.

Halakhah defines marriage as a contract between a man and a woman that is created in three steps: engagement (*Shiddukhim*), betrothal (*'Erusin* or *Kiddushin*), and consummation (*Nissu'in*). The engagement expresses the intention that the marriage will take place in the future. In the betrothal, the parties sign a halakhically binding marriage contract (*Ketubah*), which is written in Aramaic. It specifies the husband's obligations to his wife, which include food and clothing, conjugal rights, and financial support in the case of divorce or the husband's death. Part of its purpose is to protect the wife from an irresponsible or unfit husband. The woman can reject the proposal but must do so verbally. Contemporary Jewish denominations have devised modifications to the traditional *Ketubah* that stress love, mutual respect, responsibility, and commitment. In Reform Judaism, the *Ketubah* is optional. *Ketubot* are valued objects of contemporary ceremonial art, which families display in their homes.

The marriage ceremony takes place under a temporary canopy (*chuppah*), conventionally understood to represent the couple's new home. After blessings over wine and betrothal are said, the couple sips from a cup of wine. The groom gives the bride a ring and recites a formula that declares her "sanctified" to him "according to the law of Moses and Israel," and the *Ketubah* is read aloud. The consummation (*Nissu'in*) completes the marriage with the recitation of a special set of seven benedictions that celebrate God's joining male and female and invoke the image of Adam and Eve. The couple drinks from a cup of wine again. At the ceremony's end, the groom (and now some brides as well) breaks a glass by stepping on it, an act traditionally understood to recall the destruction of the Temple. In the *Ashkenazi* tradition, the bride and groom spend a short period of time alone together (*yichud*), at which point the marriage is regarded as effectuated.

FIGURE 24 *A bride and groom breaking a glass as part of a Reform wedding ceremony in Israel,* © *Nir Alon / Alamy Stock Photo.*

Ritual Purity in Marriage

Because the Torah classifies women as ritually impure during menstruation (See Chapter 2), *halakhah* obliges married couples to avoid sexual contact during the woman's menstrual period. Rabbinic Judaism extended the time of impurity—and thus of separation—to one week after menstruation ceases. The wife then immerses in the *miqveh*, and the couple can resume marital relations. Menstrual impurity is a Torah regulation still practiced in Judaism, primarily among the Orthodox.

Some contemporary Jewish feminist responses to menstrual separation have proposed abandoning the practice entirely. Others have reclaimed the ritual and suggested dropping the rabbinic additional week and introducing the married couple's joint immersion in the *miqveh* to celebrate life's rhythms. Boston's innovative *Mayyim Hayyim* ("living waters"), for instance, invites Jews to use the ritual of the *miqveh* for a range of purposes, including life milestones and healing.

Divorce

The contractual nature of Jewish marriage shapes the practice of divorce, which, though not encouraged, is permitted. Just as the man alone acts to create the *Ketubah*, so, according to *halakhah*, only the husband can initiate the divorce. In general, the wife's consent for the divorce is required. Although *halakhah* permits the husband to initiate divorce for any reason, justifications may include apostasy, sterility, refusal of sexual relations, criminal behavior, and interpersonal physical incompatibility. To effect the divorce, the husband, of his own free will, must give a special document (*get*) to the wife before two witnesses; a rabbinic court (*Bet Din*) then officially ends the marriage. Each *get* is written on an individual basis by a trained scribe. Outside the State of Israel, the transmission of the *get* presupposes a civil divorce. In some cases—for instance, physical violence—the wife can initiate divorce and petition the *Bet Din* to compel it. But even then, the husband must still transmit the *get*. If he refuses to do so or cannot be found, the woman acquires the status of an *agunah* ("chained woman") and may not remarry because she is not divorced.

Various solutions to the halakhic requirement that the husband must transmit the *get* have been proposed. Some rabbinic authorities have advanced the idea of annulling failed marriages on the grounds that the *Ketubah*, which is a contract, was flawed. Others have suggested including a prenuptial clause in the *Ketubah* to facilitate a halakhic divorce. In the State of Israel, where the Chief Rabbinate's adherence to halakhic practice in divorce has increased the number of *agunot*, the Center for Women's Justice has devised a prenuptial "Agreement for a Just and Fair Marriage." In it, the couple agrees to empower Israel's civil—as opposed to religious—courts to adjudicate the terms of separation. In principle, an Israeli court can imprison a resistant husband if he refuses to follow a rabbinic court's directive to transmit the *get*; this step requires, among other things, that the husband, who may have left the country, be found.

Conservative and Orthodox Judaism require a *get*. Reconstructionist Judaism offers egalitarian divorce. The Reform movement accepts a civil divorce as determinative and does not require a Jewish divorce or *get*.

Religious Responsibilities

Rabbinic Judaism (Mishnah *Kiddushin* 1:7) releases women from performing the "positive" commandments ("Thou shalt" . . .) that apply at a fixed time, but it obligates them, along with men, to fulfill all the "negative" commandments ("Thou shalt not" . . .). This distinction exempts—and thus, practically speaking, may exclude— women from routine religious activities, such as daily worship, participation in a prayer quorum (*minyan*), leading prayer as a representative of the community, reciting the *Kaddish*, offering the blessings surrounding the recitation of the Torah. With a few notable exceptions, rabbinic literature describes no role for women in the study of Oral Torah. In most Orthodox congregations, men lead the worship, and women sit separately, typically either in a balcony or behind a divider.

Judaism historically has focused women's responsibilities on the home and family, i.e., preparing food (keeping kosher), raising children, and supporting their husbands. Indeed, the three commandments *halakhah* deems specific to women—lighting candles on the Sabbath and holidays, performing *hafrashat challah*, and maintaining the practices of menstrual purity—are all home-centered.

Jewish Feminism

Although it is often supposed that the *Tanakh* presents a gendered hierarchy, Professor Carol Meyers shows that the *Tanakh* supplies evidence—reinforced by anthropological data—that in ancient Israel, as in other agrarian societies, women and men had paired responsibilities. She suggests that changing conditions in the ancient world—such as urbanization, new technologies for baking and weaving, increased governmental and priestly control, and philosophical dualism, among others—reduced the importance of the household economy and limited the range of women's responsibilities. Over time, she suggests, these conditions created a context for the androcentrism that came to define much of the monotheistic tradition.

The *Tanakh* does provide examples of independent women of consequence. The matriarchs Sarah and Rebecca determine the line of Abraham's descent; Tzipporah saves Moses from God's wrath; Deborah is a fighting prophetess; Ruth exemplifies loyalty; and Esther exhibits courage on behalf of her people. In the apocryphal book of Judith, a Jewish heroine slays her people's enemy, and Greek and Latin inscriptions suggest that women played leadership roles in some ancient synagogues. In the medieval and early modern periods, particularly in Europe, while managing the affairs of their homes, Jewish women engaged in commercial activities, often in support of their husband's business or their own. In medieval Germany and France some Jewish women received rabbinic permission to perform the "positive" religious commandments.

Though important, these and comparable cases did not fundamentally change Judaism's androcentric structure. Modern Jewish feminism did.

Beginning in the 1970s, Jewish women inspired by the feminist movement challenged Judaism's inherited gender structure and provoked change. In 1972 a feminist study group called *Ezrat Nashim*—a term that means "with the help of women" but that also, ironically, was the name of the women's section in the Jerusalem Temple—demanded gender equity in Conservative Judaism. Early members of *Ezrat Nashim* included Judith Plaskow, whose pioneering work, *Standing Again at Sinai*, called for Torah, midrash, and Jewish liturgy to become inclusive and fully incorporate women's voices and experiences. Another participant was Arlene Agus, who was instrumental in reclaiming and reviving *Rosh Chodesh*, the traditional holiday of the new month, on which Talmudic rabbis said women were exempt from work. Among other contributions, she also acted forcefully to free *agunot* and created a range of egalitarian ceremonies and liturgies.

Jewish feminism also has changed the face of Judaic religious participation and leadership.

Although the Rabbinical Council of America, the main modern Orthodox rabbinical group, prohibits the ordination or hiring of women rabbis, on the issue of gender equity Orthodoxy is changing. In 2009, Rabbi Avi Weiss instituted a new academy, *Yeshivat Maharat*, to prepare women to be spiritual, halakhic, and Torah leaders. One of its graduates, Rabbah Sarah Hurwitz, is its dean. The 2017 Nishma Research Profile of Modern American Orthodox Jews showed support for increased women's participation in religious and synagogue leadership roles. The survey also showed support for women to study Torah on a level equal to that of men, co-educational classes, to recite *Kaddish* without men, and to deliver sermons from the *bimah*. In January 2020, over 3,000 mostly Orthodox women celebrated thirty women completing their study of the entire Talmud through the *Daf Yomi* program. The Jerusalem event was sponsored by *Hadran*, an organization whose purpose is to extend Talmud study—taught by women—to women at all levels.

Gender equity among religious professionals is now standard in the non-Orthodox denominations. In 1972, the Reform movement ordained the first American female rabbi, Sally Priesand. Reconstructionist and Conservative female rabbis were ordained respectively in 1974 and 1985. The Reform movement and some Conservative congregations have expanded the introductory blessing of the 'Amidah prayer to include Israel's matriarchs:

> Blessed are You, Lord, our God and God of our fathers and mothers, the God of Abraham, the God of Isaac, the God of Jacob, the God of Sarah, the God of Rebecca, the God of Rachel, and the God of Leah.

Jewish feminism has created gender-neutral alternatives in the liturgy, which traditionally refers to God as male, and has inspired such practices as women's prayer groups, healing services (often involving the *miqveh*), and guidance on care for the sick. It has generated fresh and inclusive understandings of God and Torah and created unprecedented Judaic educational opportunities for girls and women. Jewish feminism has been a vital and effective force is adapting Judaism to a changing world.

Gender in Israeli Judaism

The first female rabbi in Israel, Naamah Kelman, was ordained by Reform Judaism in 1992.

In the State of Israel, there are opportunities within Orthodox Judaism for women to receive halakhic training. The *Beit Midrash Har'el* ordains both women and men. The Susi Bradfield Women's Institute for Halakhic Leadership, which is part of the Orthodox educational network Ohr Torah Stone, offers women the same rabbinic curriculum as men in the areas of marriage and divorce, mourning, the Sabbath, family purity, and *kashrut*. Graduates receive a *Heter Hora'ah* ("License to Teach") which entitles them to issue halakhic opinions. Since 2002, *Kehillat Shira Hadasha*, a synagogue in Jerusalem, has developed an egalitarian mode of traditional worship intended to meet the needs of contemporary Orthodox women and men by creating a leadership role for women in the synagogue. *Nishmat*, the Jeanie Schottenstein Center for Advanced Torah Study for Women, prepares and certifies Orthodox women to advise other women in matters of women's health and family purity. *Matan*, The Women's Institute for Torah Studies, provides advanced halakhic education.

Full gender equity in Israeli Judaism continues to develop. Worship at the Western Wall of the Jerusalem Temple (the *Kotel*), for instance, is segregated by gender, and women are restricted to the smaller women's section. Since 1988, a group known as the "Women of the Wall" has promoted women's right to engage in communal prayer at the Wall, where they congregate to pray on *Rosh Chodesh*. These prayer services have encountered hostility from both male and female religious traditionalists. After multiple court cases—and despite ongoing opposition and obstruction from other groups and the *Kotel*'s administration, the Western Wall Heritage Foundation—women now pray at the *Kotel*, wear prayer shawls and *tefillin*, recite the *Kaddish* and other blessings, and read from the Torah (which sometimes means clandestinely bringing in small scrolls.) In response to *Haredi* disruption of prayers on their thirtieth anniversary, March 8, 2019, they demanded a government inquiry.

An effort to establish *Ezrat Yisrael* ("Help of Israel"), an egalitarian prayer site south of the main Western Wall plaza, at Robinson's Arch, as a permanent place of Jewish worship for all denominations and genders, remains uncertain.

LGBTQ

Halakhah holds that there are only two genders, male and female. It recognizes intersex persons, treats them with respect as God's creatures, and discusses how to integrate them into the halakhic system of gender classification, marriage, and religious responsibility.

FIGURE 25 *A member of the "Women of the Wall" reads Torah at* Ezrat Yisrael *on their group's 30th anniversary, which also was* Rosh Chodesh *and International Women's Day. Israel's Masorti Movement manages the site. The women moved their service there because hostile demonstrations interrupted their worship at the main Western Wall plaza,* © GALI TIBBON/AFP *via Getty Images.*

As a matter of principle, and within the framework of congregational autonomy, the Reform, Conservative, and Reconstructionist movements all welcome LGBTQ persons into their congregations, support marriage equality, and ordain LGBTQ persons as rabbis and cantors. In Conservative Judaism, same-sex marriage must be between Jews. Reconstructionism was the first to admit LGBTQ rabbinical students, and the Reform seminary, Hebrew Union College-Jewish Institute of Religion, developed the Institute for Judaism, Sexual Orientation, and Gender Identity to educate its students about LGBTQ issues.

Since the Torah prohibits male intercourse (Leviticus 20.13), *halakhah* opposes male homosexuality. Halakhic tradition does not classify lesbians' relations as intercourse and applies less stringent judgment to them than to male homosexuals. While the issue of LGBTQ acceptance is controversial in Orthodox Judaism, the 2017 Nishma survey of the Orthodox community showed increased acceptance of LGBTQ Jews. In 2018, responding to a letter from the Israeli Orthodox establishment critical of the LGBTQ community, seventy-five Orthodox rabbis and educators from Israel and abroad—invoking the commandments (Leviticus 19.18, 16) to love your neighbor and not stand idly while your neighbor is harmed—wrote in support of the LGBTQ community.

In the United States, multiple organizations serve the LGBTQ Jewish population. For example, *Beth Chayim Chadashim* in Los Angeles, founded in 1972, is the world's first LGBTQ synagogue, and New York's Congregation *Beit Simchat Torah* is the nation's largest. Among other services, *Beit Simchat Torah* houses the Jewish Queer Youth's Drop-In Center, a resource facility for Orthodox LGBTQ youth aged 13–23. Abby Stein, the transgender female activist and former ordained rabbi, who left the Hasidic community, founded the first support group for Orthodox trans people. There is also SVARA, "a traditionally radical yeshiva dedicated to the serious study of Talmud through the lens of queer experiences," and Eshel, an Orthodox support organization for LGBTQ Jews in the United States and Canada. In the State of Israel, there is *Bat Kol*, which supports Orthodox lesbians, and *Havruta*, an Orthodox LGBTQ organization. A 2019 survey found that 78% of Israeli citizens—93% of secular Israelis, 54% of Zionist Orthodox Israelis—support gay marriage or same-sex relationships.

Christianity

One dimension of humanity's historical particularity that has been the subject of debate within Christianity since its inception has been the question of gender and the relationship between gender and biological sex. For centuries Christian thinkers have debated: What does it mean to be created male and female and how should the relationship between the two sexes be defined by Christian theology? Far from being a recent concern raised by contemporary theologians, this is a fundamental question in the history of theology and philosophy.

Feminist Theology

Building on the insights of feminist activists that defined the women's movement in the 1960s and 70s, feminist theologians apply a critical approach to the manner in which women have been marginalized within Christianity. At the core of their work is highlighting the invisibility of women within religious history and the ways in which women have been written out of the history of Christianity. Feminist theologians emphasize that gender identity is a social construction and cannot be equated with biological destiny, meaning that gender identities are socially acquired roles for men and women. They also highlight how patriarchy, literally translated as the rule of the father, shapes Christianity in such a way that social, political and religious relations are constructed to validate male sovereignty. However, feminist theologians argue, this patriarchal understanding of Christianity is a distortion of the authentic Christian message.

Feminist theologians work in both academic settings and also at the grassroots level in churches and faith-based organizations. They are hesitant to give unequivocal normativity to the Christian tradition, Scriptures, and theology due to its androcentric foundation. Therefore, women's experiences and struggles for liberation often become the central commitment and norm in their interpretation of Christianity. Fundamental to these theologians' work is recovering women's contributions to the history of Christianity and the ways in which Christian structures have excluded women or rendered them second-class citizens within the religion. Through privileging gender as a primary analytic category, feminist theologians seek to highlight the ideologies operating in historical and current understandings of Christian tradition. Using their critical methodology feminist theologians uncover the patriarchal impulses that have shaped Christianity and offer an alternative vision grounded in feminist interpretations of the Christian tradition. Their understanding of Christianity, they argue, is more authentic, for it embraces an egalitarian vision of humanity as created in the image of God.

God-talk

One of the strongest indicators of how androcentrism has come to dominate our views on the One God is found in our language about God. The One God that is described throughout this book in Judaism, Christianity, and Islam is overwhelmingly or exclusively described as male. The masculinity of God is normative and unchallenged. To fully embrace men and women as equal bearers of the image of God, Christians must become comfortable with male and female symbols and language about God sharing equal value. This is an extremely difficult task for Christians, for male images of God are the norm within the religion. In addition, within broader society, popular culture, and the history of art one finds overwhelmingly male imagery of God. The fact that the very notion of calling God "She" is seen as shocking, ridiculous, and offensive to many demonstrates how engrained masculinity is in the nature of God. Imaging God exclusively as male raises masculinity to an idol. While none of our language, symbols, and names for God can be taken literally, exclusively imaging of God as male leads to the conclusion that God is literally a man. In addition, to draw exclusively from male imagery, feminists contend, limits the very nature of God. The attributes of God become those that are exclusively associated with heterosexual men. Exclusive male God language supports structures that subordinate women for it implies that the male is more representative of the sacred than the female.

In addition to idolizing the male, exclusive male God language only contributes to women's own alienation from the sacred. It is more difficult to see oneself as created in God's image if that God is limited to men. One could also add to this analysis that if God is imaged exclusively representing one racial or ethnic group, this is also idolatry. Imaging the divine as one social group or gender distances those who are excluded from those images from their creation in the *imago Dei*. It is a lot easier to say and believe that women do not share the divine image equally when only male images of the divine are normative. This incorporation of female images, however, should not be construed as an essentialized feminine that complements the already established masculine. Instead, both male and female images of God, with all the limitations they contain based on their human origin, must equally express the fullness of God's nature. Patriarchal images of God have implications for how we understand not only humanity, but also the rest of creation. Within Christianity all language surrounding God is limited by our very humanity and is always understood as symbolic.

Christian understandings of the image of God are intimately linked to Jesus Christ. Jesus is often used to legitimize the claim that God is male. However, as highlighted in our discussion of the Trinity, Jesus' divinity is not in any way limited by his historical humanity. Too often however, it is Jesus' maleness that becomes normative within patriarchal theological claims, limiting women's ability to reflect God and arguing that men reflect God's image more appropriately. Feminist theologians, like liberation theologians situate Jesus' liberating message in his concrete outreach to and inclusion of the marginalized. Grounded in this liberating understanding of Jesus is an image of Christ that we are challenged to reflect in our spirituality and actions. Feminist theologians argue that the egalitarian understanding of the human at the center of Jesus' message is one that undermines the gender hierarchies that developed within Christianity. This is reinforced by the creation account in the book of Genesis, which claims that gender hierarchy is a product of human sin and not the way in which God intended humanity to exist.

Tradition

Christian language surrounding God's nature is a key theme within feminist theology. Another is the role of tradition and the manner in which the Christian tradition has been so saturated with patriarchy that a hierarchical understanding of men and women is normative for the majority of Christians. This claim leads some feminist scholars to wonder if the Christian tradition can be "redeemed" from the sin of sexism. Another perspective argues that it should be the very work of feminist scholars to uncover the authentic Christian tradition and liberate it from the web of patriarchy. Feminist scholars remind us that Scripture and tradition have always been defined by and created by men. They also remind us that all religious traditions are not created in a power vacuum and are subject to the dynamics of power relations. This is clearly seen even beyond the realm of gender through the study of the divisions, schisms, and struggles that have characterized Christianity throughout its history. Similarly, many feminist scholars argue that we must look at some countercultural movements within the Christian tradition as sources for re-envisioning our understanding of Christianity today.

Women's Access to Ordination and Ritual Life

A key issue within twentieth century Christian feminism that continues even today is the exclusion of women from religious leadership within Christian churches and the priesthood. Contrary to the institutional exclusion of women from Christian leadership there existed in the Jesus movement an alternative. The Gospels attest, for example, to Mary Magdalene's importance as one of Jesus' closest followers. Two Gospels tell us Jesus appeared first to her and not to his twelve male apostles. Similarly, we know that within Paul's missionary movement women served as deaconesses. In Romans

16, for example, he describes sister Phoebe as a deacon. While some Christian churches have begun to ordain women, such as the Anglican Church, many women leaders in these churches highlight they are often treated as second class citizens. Within the Roman Catholic Church, the issue of women's ordination remains a hotly contested and vibrant issue. Catholic leadership has consistently argued that Jesus' maleness is normative and, as Jesus' representatives here on earth, the Roman Catholic clergy must remain exclusively male. Many evangelical Protestants turn to the writings of Paul to legitimize exclusive male church leadership, for example 1 Timothy 2.11–13: "A woman should learn in quietness and full submission. I do not permit a woman to teach or to assume authority over a man; she must be quiet. For Adam was formed first, then Eve." Here we find the justification of women's subordination situated in the Genesis 2–3 accounts. However as discussed earlier in this book,

FIGURE 26 *Vatican,* © *Byron Maldonado*

Genesis, and Timothy, must be read in light of their historical and cultural context and intended audience. This is the case for all of the Christian Scriptures.

Linked to women's historical exclusion from church leadership is women's ability to participate fully in the religious life of Christianity. Even with the advances made due to the women's ordination movement, a movement that struggled for women's full inclusion in Christian leadership and rituals, women continue to be excluded from higher leadership positions in Christian institutions. Ordination, inclusion into the order of the priesthood (and later the diaconate), is different from consecration, which is when men and women join a religious order as a monk or nun. The manner in which women are allowed to access leadership positions varies dramatically not only by denominational affiliation but also by geographic location. While women are not separated from men during Christian worship, many point out that the true separation is found in women's lack of access to the altar throughout the majority of Christian history. This continues to be an unresolved issue in Christianity today.

Marriage

Within Christianity heterosexual marriage is ordained by God and a sacred institution. For Protestants, marriage is a sacred union. Among Protestant denominations, however, there is diversity surrounding the nature of that union. More conservative Protestants, for example, see marriage as a covenant between the married couple and God. Therefore, you find varying opinions among Protestants regarding the appropriateness and preconditions for divorce. Within the Roman Catholic Church marriage is a sacrament. As a sacrament, a ritual that conveys God's grace, marriage is a lifelong divine institution that cannot be undone by us. Therefore the Roman Catholic Church does not recognize civil divorce. The only manner to dissolve a Roman Catholic marriage is through an annulment. An annulment, which can only be granted by a Church tribunal, declares that what was thought to be a valid sacramental marriage is invalidated and thus the sacrament of marriage never occurred. The civil nature of the union is not questioned, instead an annulment claims that the marriage was not valid according to Church law. While there is some diversity in perspectives among Christians, the major Protestant Churches and Roman Catholic Church permit interfaith marriages.

Overwhelmingly today Christians globally continue to define marriage exclusively as heterosexual marriage. This is based, in many cases, on a theology of gender complementarity that emphasizes an understanding of humanity where the female complements the male. Gender complementarity is a "distinct but equal" understanding of humanity where women are defined as complementing men and those attributes associated with men are of central value, too often leaving women in the margins. This bipolar anthropology essentializes sexual identity and social roles. What is deemed feminine is the male projection of attributes that are excluded from the construction of masculine identity. Gender complementarity denies the fullness of the individual human and his or her nature by characterizing certain attributes based on biological sex. Too often, the dualisms found within the complementarity model are grounded in an outdated, essentialist biology. This is seen, for example, in the labeling of women as passive and men as active. Too often, this model reduces women to motherhood. This should not be surprising, for many Christian justifications for exclusively heterosexual marriage cite procreation as a key aspect of a sacred marriage.

In spite of the normative heterosexual understanding of marriage within Christianity, there are ecclesial movements, churches, and denominations that are challenging these heterosexist assumptions. The Universal Fellowship of Metropolitan Community Churches is a Protestant denomination with churches across the globe that has outreach to the LGBTQ community. Jesuit priest and author James Martin has argued that the Roman Catholics must stand in solidarity with the LGBTQ community through respect, compassion, acceptance and support. And though Pope Francis famously called Catholics to not judge someone who is homosexual, the Catechism of the Catholic Church and more recent statements by the Pope characterize homosexuality as a choice that can be treated psychologically. In other words, there is not one definitive stance regarding LGBTQ issues within Christianity. Not only is there great variance between churches; in certain denominations there are significant disagreements between geographic regions. This is seen, for example, in the 2020 proposal for the Methodist Church to split into two churches based on differing views on homosexuality. Some argue that this will be a definitive issue in the future not only for Christian denominations and their stances, but for the very future of Christianity itself, for Christian views on homosexuality are often cited as the primary reason young adult Christians are leaving the religion.

Women in Christianity Today

The role of women in Christianity remains contested. Due to the work of feminist theologians and their allies, the entire history of the role of women in the religion has been revised in the past forty years. Women have been retrieved and recuperated in this process. Nowhere is this better seen than in the recovery of Mary Magdalene. For centuries Mary Magdalene has been depicted as a whore in the history of Christianity. She was incorrectly associated with the repentant woman in the Gospel of Luke, chapter 7, and the prostitute saved from stoning by Jesus. She was, in fact, an influential follower of Jesus who was present at the foot of the cross when Jesus was crucified, at his burial, and at his resurrection. Feminist scholars have recuperated the figure of Mary Magdalene, considered a saint in various Christian denominations.

One area that deserves emphasis is the role of the body within Christianity, which has a very ambiguous and sometimes distorted relationship with human bodies. Too often, bodies are seen as an impediment to our relationship with the sacred. Bodies are something that must be controlled and regulated in order to cultivate the spiritual life. Our bodily desires are often depicted as disordered and overwhelming. This is clearly seen in the religious practice of fasting, one of the few rituals that crosses multiple religious traditions, cultures, and geographic locations. Depriving the body of food becomes a spiritual practice whose intention is to redirect the mind from the material world, from the bodily world.

Within the Christian tradition, one finds a very complex relationship with human bodies. On the one hand our bodies are created by God. In the book of Genesis God creates human bodies and deems them good. On the other hand, however, bodily desires such as sex and hunger are seen as dangerous and sinful. Augustine of Hippo famously described the human plight as one dominated by concupiscence—disordered, insatiable desire that prevents us from focusing on our true destiny of union with God. Our bodies must be regulated and controlled or we will fall into a life of sin. This is especially relevant in a discussion of gender, for throughout the history of Christianity women have been associated with the human body, while men have been associated with the rational mind. Women are thus reduced to bodily desires and impulses while men are associated with the spiritual and rational. Because of her association with bodiliness woman is often interpreted within the Christian tradition as reflecting the image of God in a flawed or lesser manner. The body is also often interpreted as that which impedes us from true union with God or reaching our full potentiality as faithful Christians.

The role of women continues to be a contested and debated subject within Christianity and there is not one monolithic stance. To claim that all Christians view women in a certain way is misleading. Similarly, this is a very dynamic topic where shifts in perspective happen constantly. This is a fundamental issue within the religion, and how Christianity addresses the role of women within it will be a pressing topic for the future of the religion.

Islam

Gender and sexuality questions are some of the key critical issues facing Muslims globally. The topic is crucial both within the world of Islam and outside. Rigid notions of gender and sexuality are being challenged among contemporary Muslims. One size does not fit all, and there are Muslim men and women who thrive in the rigidity of neat gender roles. However, challenging these roles has largely been led by Muslim feminists who started a debate about gender, rooted in the Qur'an. Muslim feminists brought light to the fact that where a rigid way of being can be constructed, the opposite can also be done: if a system can be constructed to support women as homemakers, the same could happen for women outside the home.

Many outsider understandings of Islam seem to begin and end with what Muslim women are wearing. Insider perspectives on the topic vary, with the roots of the variance lying with general statements in the Qur'an about men and women dressing modestly. The idea of modest dress is connected to the fall of Adam and Eve, and it is only after their disobedience that they become aware of their nakedness. In their embarrassment for failing to follow God's one and only command to stay away from a forbidden tree, they become aware of their modesty and find things to cover up with. In a way, that pure state of nakedness was lost when Adam and Eve failed in their submission to God. Discussions about types of clothing are therefore prevalent in

Muslim societies. Muslim women's veils vary from place to place, but more importantly from woman to woman. Some cover their hair and their faces, and some do not cover their hair at all. Let us look at one such passage from the Qur'an:

> The believing men and believing women are allies of one another. They enjoin what is right and forbid what is wrong and establish prayer and give *zakah* and obey Allah and His Messenger. Those—Allah will have mercy upon them. Indeed, Allah is Exalted in Might and Wise. Allah has promised the believing men and believing women gardens beneath which rivers flow, wherein they abide eternally, and pleasant dwellings in gardens of perpetual residence; but approval from Allah is greater. It is that which is the great attainment.
>
> Q9:72–73

Qur'anic passages such as this offer general parameters of ethics—they are sharpened by commentaries. They are almost always not clear but are made clearer through commentators, almost always men. Commentary from the outside on matters of dress, especially Muslim women's dress, is often far from these deeper theological concerns: they are often used for political purposes, to strengthen stereotypes not just about Muslim women wearing them but about Islam as a religion as a whole. One thing is clear: Muslim women's choice and reasons for wearing or not wearing specific items of clothing are diverse. These varied voices should be sought out as opposed to thinking that all Muslim women are the same.

There have also been discussions about what men do to their bodies. In places such as Iran, men are often policed for the types of hairstyles that are deemed Islamic or un-Islamic. Some Muslims also frown upon body piercings and tattoos. Then there are mendicant Muslims in India and Pakistan; some wear women's clothing and jewelry and believe they are the brides of God. There is no single standard for what Muslim men and women are wearing in the world today, and it is not possible to determine religiosity from outward presentation. Belief is a matter of the heart, and this has allowed for many different expressions of the Islamic faith. Religious expressions in Muslim communities globally are now making clear statements about diversity.

Historically, Islamic thought about gender generally focuses on heterosexuality. Muslims globally are seeking diverse models of gender and sexuality rooted in historical Islamic traditions. These models, which are now more openly discussed and acted on, could come under the framework of queer identities and relationships—those Muslims who do not fit the regular heterosexual boxes. Can this be supported by the Qur'an? And how do the emerging Muslim identities in the world support this? Here is one possible way. At the very core of Islamic traditions is the Qur'an. Its outworking and readings have been largely used to support the family unit through a husband and wife and children. Muslims in the past, especially during the nineteenth and twentieth centuries, accepted this because it separated them from this co-called Judeo-Christian West, which Muslims believed had corrupted the divine instruction about marriage and procreating. To refute this in the past was unfathomable, but today we see Muslims globally challenging the authorities that presented these rigid models of gender and sexuality. Some have done this by adopting a purely secular approach. They live their lives beyond these boundaries and accept that what they are doing is un-Islamic. This would support the Islam-versus-the-West psychology. But a new wave of Muslims is emerging who are not accepting particular forms of gender and sexuality at the center, and they do this through their interpretation of the Qur'an. Their argument is that the Qur'anic world is full of dysfunction and difference. There are some who are married, some who are not, some who have parents and some who do not. The divine world is full of queer creatures—jinn and angels, for example. If the most crucial and essential relationship in the Qur'anic world is the one between creation and God, then that relationship cannot be typified, which in turn allows for a variety of gender and sexual expressions. God created things in order for them to understand their first and central role: to obey God and submit only to God. In this way, we see the variety of living in the Qur'an as long as it returns back to strengthening submission to God. There is an ethical and moral side to this, too, but that comes from the strengthening of the relationship between human beings and God.

Although this may seem a logical and quite all-encompassing Qur'anic viewpoint, it has not gained widespread appeal. Why not? The Qur'an lives through the hands of those who hold it at any given time. The historical trajectory that has shaped Muslim identities gives us an understanding of why rigid notions of gender and sexuality have become so entrenched. The men who have read the Qur'an, commented on it, and legislated from it have interpreted it from their perspective, usually in reaction against the opening-up of such discussions among Jews and Christians. Quite recently, Muslim feminists have brought this into question by using the Qur'an itself to unread the rigidity which has heretofore been upheld. Globally, Muslims are asking these questions from a committed and faithful position: Was Eve really the homemaker? Was Adam really the breadwinner? How much of a domesticated life did they have in the Qur'an? How do Muslims make sense of the immaculate conception of Jesus? Why did he not marry? Was does it say about Jesus' Islamic masculinity? Was Joseph also to blame for falling in love, or lust, with his stepmother? Why did Joseph not get married? Why did the Queen of Sheba have such an elevated position in society? Or should we look to women prophets of Islam? How do we make sense of Muhammad's multiple marriages?

Today Muslims of all genders and sexual expressions are saying it out loud: that the Qur'an may have come from God, but its interpretation is human. Bearing in mind the flawed nature of human beings, we begin to understand the complexity of this process and why it also required the lived experiences of prophets to complement and explain submission further. The many interpretations of these prophetic stories have led to a variety of understandings of what it means to be human, but the most critical question has had to do with gender issues. The text cannot be taken out of its context, and the context has been and continues to be patriarchal and male-centered. This reality has allowed some to proclaim that clear understandings of what it means to be male and female can be read out of the text. The most generalized understanding has been that Eve is the perfect role model for women as homemakers, wives, mothers, and daughters and that Adam is the perfect role model for breadwinners, husbands, fathers, and sons. Of course the story could fit this conclusion but other dysfunctional family setups in the Qur'anic world allude to the fact that gender construction and even sexual activity is always secondary in relation to human beings' submission to God. Jesus is born without a biological father, Joseph falls in love with his stepmother, and Muhammad has multiple marriages. The experiences may differ, but every creation in the Qur'an submits to God and makes it central to their life.

The Qur'an presents us with many powerful faithful women. Their stories become the focal point for many Muslims attempting to understand gender and sexuality. Let us look at the story of one powerful woman in the Qur'an and how she is understood—Bilqis, the Queen of Sheba, who is also found in the Hebrew Bible. The story goes that a hoopoe bird sees that the land which the Queen of Sheba rules worships the sun. The bird returns to the prophet Soloman and tells him this.

> Indeed, I found [there] a woman ruling them, and she has been given of all things, and she has a great throne. I found her and her people prostrating to the sun instead of Allah, and Satan has made their deeds pleasing to them and averted them from [His] way, so they are not guided.
>
> Q27:23–24

Soloman then writes her a letter inviting her to submit to the one true God. The Queen seeks counsel from her advisors but her wisdom is far beyond theirs. The Queen then sends a gift to Soloman. Soloman responds by saying that God's gifts are greater than what has been presented to him and that the Queen needs to prepare to meet him in person—possibly a declaration of war. The Queen then visits Soloman. Her throne is moved to Soloman's palace and disguised. The Queen is asked if she recognizes the throne and she responds by saying that this miracle has led her to believe in the one true God. In another incident, she enters a room upon the invitation of Solomon. She thinks that the room is a lake and lifts up her skirt only to be told that it is not water but slabs of glass. The Queen once again states her belief in the one true God is strengthened.

> She was told, "Enter the palace." But when she saw it, she thought it was a body of water and uncovered her shins [to wade through]. He said, "Indeed, it is a palace [whose floor is] made smooth with glass." She said, ""My Lord, indeed I have wronged myself, and I submit with Solomon to Allah, Lord of the worlds."
>
> Q27:44

There are a number of different endings to this story in Islamic traditions. Some say she married Soloman, some say she returns as Queen and some say Soloman used to visit her a few days a month.

FIGURE 27 *Solomon and Bilqis enthroned, surrounded by the animals, angels, and de[m]*
1528–1529. Codex, colors and gold on paper. Folio: 30.7 x 19.2 cm, Chester Beatty (CB

This story, and others on women in the Qur'an, are important because of how they are read and understood and, most importantly, impact gender and sexuality in Muslim life. Some commentators have used this story to criticize and humiliate not just the Queen but women in general. These interpretations are done through androcentric (focused on men) lenses. They fail to highlight anything positive in the Queen's actions, especially as they relate to Soloman, who becomes the embodiment of maleness, of all men. Rather than highlighting the fact that the Queen was a remarkable and noble leader, she is understood as someone who was weak. This brings us back to how sacred Scripture is understood and how it shapes the way gender and sexuality is understood in Muslim societies. The Queen of Sheba, understood through a feminist lens, has inspired many Muslim women to strive to the highest office. Muslim women such as Benazir Bhutto of Pakistan, Megawati Sukarnoputri of Indonesia, Tansu Ciller of Turkey, Mame Madior Boye of Senegal, or Khaleda Zia and Sheikh Hasina of Bangladesh, amongst others, are just some positive examples of reading the story to understand political leadership and gender.

Does Islam liberate or subjugate women? This is a question that comes up time and time again. The question is a difficult one, often simplistically answered, but it depends on who is asked. Some may answer in a relational way: women in Scotland can wear what they like, but women in Saudi Arabia cannot. "Islam subjugates women": the shallowness of this answer is extremely damaging to cultural divides which continue to strengthen. If we were to take a fundamentalist approach, would we say that the Qur'an subjugates women? It depends on how it is read and interpreted. That the Qur'an can liberate or subjugate has made the Qur'an a text that has sustained itself for so long, but at a deeper level it is the ambiguous and doubtful idea of God and all that comes from God that allows these various views to be expressed. The power of God comes from the sacred struggle that believers have to take part in. That struggle is in trying to make sense of God through that divine text. The same answer comes when dealing with issues of sexuality. Does God really have a view on what is the best form of sexuality? If we are to return back to the dynamics of Adam, Eve, angels, and Satan, we begin to see quite clearly that there is a more pertinent command that they must submit to. Is the covenant between human beings and God broken through sexual practices? Yes, if the sexual practices become so important that they remove God's centrality to human life but, some Muslims may argue, affirmed if they are helping strengthen the covenant with God. Gender and sexuality are what make us human, and even Muhammad said that it was not good enough to isolate oneself from society and real life. Contemporary Muslims today are deliberating the idea that being human is less about the form of creation and what it does with its essential parts rather than its submission and obedience to God. Muslims who seek queer alternatives are arguing that such a deeper understanding of the purpose and order of the cosmos allows for an extension of limited gender and sexual categories, which can easily be extended to queer and transgender identities. Important to keep in mind that feminist questions and actions differ from location to location. There is ongoing debate on deconstructing Western feminism in relation to Islamic feminism—both are difficult to label with much overlap but what this debate brings attention to are the long histories and contextual realities through which we understand the West and East.

God is not male. It is vital to understand this tenet of Islam because it prevents men from being seen as at the center of the created order. The Qur'an complicates this by using male pronouns to speak of God, but it makes explicit that God should not be understood in human gender terms—that he was not born and does not reproduce as humans do. This gender-queer God presented in male pronouns has been a challenge to Muslims in the past and present. The ambiguity has allowed for any given context to effect the psychology of Islamic theology and elevate the position of men.

Some Muslim women are taking a more prominent role in leadership and authority.

Amina Wadud (b. 1952), an African American convert to Islam, led a mixed-sex prayer in March 2005. This prompted an international outcry among some Muslims who do not accept Muslim women leading prayers, but her action started a new wave of Muslim women taking on roles in spiritual leadership. It is now not uncommon to find Muslim women who are chaplains at universities in the United States. and it is also not uncommon to find Muslim women reciting the Qur'an publicly and posting recordings on social media. In the past, the public recitation of the Qur'an was done by men because it was said that a Muslim woman's voice could be more alluring, leading to sexual thoughts. Many Muslim women reject these patriarchal interpretations.

A recent development has also seen the emergence of "inclusive" mosques. These mosques advocate a platform allowing those of all denominations, genders, races, ethnicities, and sexualities to participate and even lead prayer. The Inclusive Mosque in London was established in 2012. The very vocal diversity of identities, especially in terms of gender and sexuality, in younger Muslims is often ignored and not talked about, so younger Muslims have felt that mosque leadership is out of touch on these matters.

Marriage continues to be of central significance in understanding contemporary Muslims. Immigrant parents understand marriage as a way of instilling values and traditions from "back home." This has certainly been the case for Pakistanis in Britain. It was not uncommon for British-born Muslims to get married to cousins or members from the same Pakistani caste. The most general view is that young, free, and single Westerners are having illicit sex, whereas good Muslim children should stay away from this through marriage. The contract of marriage was strengthened in Islamic law because it was a good way to set up society. Rigid notions of what men and women should be doing helped early jurists to create order in society, and this has gained traction even today in Muslim countries that emerged after colonialism. Just as understandings of modesty and women became associated with veiling and homes, notions of chastity and illicit sexual relations were to be upheld and corrected through marriage. Marriage was a contract that would allow men and women to have sex within an Islamic legal framework. This became the norm and continues to be seen as the socially acceptable option for Muslim men and women.

There is now a growing number of Muslims, both men and women, who are marrying outside of their religious community. This has been a challenging phenomenon for the first-generation Muslims who wanted their children to live the traditions in the same way that they did. But the change was inevitable as the new generation of Western Muslims grew up alongside outsiders. Same-sex marriage is now adopted as legal in many Western European countries. Muslim countries have not only resisted legislating on this but have gone as far as not even acknowledging that they have any LGBT citizens. Some advocate for a response formulated by Christians: "love the sinner and not the sin." Some have made it clear that Islam will never accept LGBT Muslims, but Muslims should cause no harm to those who identify as Muslim because the law of the land should be respected. The harm that such statements have caused LGBT Muslims has been immense, but such statements also help strengthen the Islam-versus-the-West divide.

Contemporary Muslims are making it clear that LGBT Muslims do exist and feel fully Muslim and Islamic. LGBT Muslim organizations are now visible globally. In the UK, Imaan is Europe's biggest charity supporting LGBT Muslims and was founded in 1999. The founding members came from different parts of the UK, including London and Glasgow.

Muslims are dealing more publicly with issues of sexuality like never before. It would be so much simpler to give a single view of Islam on gender and sexuality. These single stories might have been possible in the past but in times of Twitter and Instagram, it is just not possible. This is challenging to many who want to hold strongly to their ideal or traditional view. There is no easy answer to sexuality in terms of historical religious traditions. They were written at a time where "don't ask, don't tell" was not only the Islamic view on gender and sexuality but the lived reality.

Times have changed. People are now showing their vibrant colors and each is claiming their authority on traditional views.

Afterthought: Gender, Sexuality, and Marriage

The issue of gender is perhaps the most socially consequential element of the creation narrative. The dominant—and erroneous—interpretation of the story of Adam and Eve has generated identities, self-images, inequities, and social structures that have affected the human population for centuries. Whether articulated in terms of "original sin" or in more nuanced form, the very idea that Eve is responsible for humanity's alienation from God has justified the subordination of women socially, politically, and religiously in the nations influenced by the monotheistic tradition.

The implications of the monotheistic idea that humans are God's creations and therefore, despite any and all differences, are fundamentally equal, have been on a long road to realization. As this chapter suggests, only in recent times have those implications begun to shape the monotheistic religions. Some variations of Islam, Christianity, and Judaism have implemented changes to achieve gender equity in religious practices. The more traditional versions of the three religions are moving more slowly, but there is evidence of change there as well.

The principle that justifies full inclusion of women in social, economic, and religious life applies equally to LGBT persons.

The important point here is that the values of the monotheistic heritage, particularly its vision of the true nature of human beings, are on a very long fuse. Because humans are creatures of free will, we are naturally slow learners. One hopes that when the lessons of this heritage are learned, they stick.

Study Questions: Gender, Sexuality, and Marriage

Gender and sexuality is a contemporary issue in Judaism, Christianity, and Islam. Discuss

Why are issues of gender and sexuality different today than in historical times?

How do Jews, Christians and Muslims understand marriage?

Does Scripture speak to contemporary issues of gender and sexuality? Explain through examples.

Discuss the traditions and tensions on women as rabbis, priests/ministers and imams.

9

Redemption, Salvation, and Life After Death

The belief that our actions have consequences in not only this life but also after death is a distinctive feature of religions as a whole. Religions share a belief that human existence is not limited by what happens in this concrete, historical life. Within Judaism, Christianity, and Islam, notions of sin and repentance are intimately connected to beliefs in redemption, salvation, and the afterlife. This chapter explores how each religion interprets the ways in which we behave in this life and how they have implications for our lives after death.

Judaism

Sin, Repentance, Forgiveness

Judaism understands what we conventionally call "sin" to be a natural consequence of being human. As beings created in God's image, humans are like God in some respects and unlike God in others. The story of Adam and Eve in the Garden of Eden makes clear that one way human beings resemble God is in having free will. God could have formed humans as programmed automatons, but the Torah understands that humans by nature are free to make choices, and therefore humans are responsible for the choices they make. Humanity's subsequent exile from the Garden of Eden makes humans frail and mortal, and in that respect utterly unlike God. But even after the Flood and the Tower of Babel, God does not deprive humans of free will. Rather, God establishes the structure for living that enables humans to overcome and transcend their failings. At Mount Sinai God gives the Israelites the choice to accept the commandments or not. As Deuteronomy (30.19) states: "I have set before you life and death, blessings and curses. Now choose life so that that you and your children may live."

The fusion of freedom and frailty produces the framework for "sin." Because human beings have free will—which God may foresee but does not control—by their very mortal nature they are likely not to fulfill all the commandments all the time. Thus, as we have seen above, in Judaism, although humans may sin, they are not sinful. There is no need for God to purify them of any innate moral disability or an "original sin." Judaism conceives what we call "sin" in concrete, particular terms rather than as an ontological or generic category or a quality of being.

Some rabbinic teachings frame the matter by suggesting that human beings have two "inclinations": an inclination to do good (yetzer ha-tov) and its opposite, an inclination to do evil (yetzer ha-ra'). Rabbinism's nuanced understanding of human nature suggests that the yetzer ha-ra' is not solely evil and, in fact, can also provoke ambition and productivity in humans. Rabbis regarded the study of Torah as the way the Jewish people can transcend the yetzer ha-ra' while exploiting its energy. Thus, through the study of Torah and acts of repentance (teshuvah, "turning, returning"), the Jewish people can minimize sin and repair their relationships with God and with one another.

Prayers for repentance are part of the daily liturgy throughout the year, but they are central to the Days of Awe: Rosh HaShanah and Yom Kippur (also called the High Holidays). Special prayers for forgiveness (Selichot)—inspired by the description of God's mercy and compassion in Exodus 34.6–7—are recited beginning the month before Yom Kippur in the Sephardic tradition and starting on the Saturday evening before Rosh HaShanah in the Ashkenazi tradition. Although the Tanakh and rabbinic literature have multiple terms for violations of commandments, the High Holiday liturgy highlights the word chet. Often rendered in English as "sin," it actually is a biblical term that denotes falling short, missing the mark, or making a mistake or an error; it is translated that way in the text below.

A popular Sephardic penitential prayer, which invokes God's virtues, is 'Adon HaSelichot ("Lord of Forgiveness"). It reads as follows:

Lord of forgiveness, Who examines the heart,
Revealer of hidden thoughts, Who speaks justice,
We have erred before you. Have mercy on us.

Glorious in wonders, Who is always consoling,
Who remembers the covenant of the ancestors,
Who probes our deepest selves,
We have erred before you. Have mercy on us.

Who is good and benefits all creatures, Who knows all secrets,
Who conquers transgression, Who is clothed in righteousness,
We have erred before you. Have mercy on us.

Who is full of merit, Who is awesome in praise,
Who forgives transgressions, Who responds in times of misfortune,
We have erred before you. Have mercy on us.

Who achieves deliverance, Who sees the future,
Who calls to the generations, Who rides the heavens,

Who hears prayer, Who is perfect in knowledge,
We have erred before you. Have mercy on us.

WILLIAM GREEN and ALAN AVERY-PECK, trans.

The liturgy for the High Holidays asserts that during the Days of Awe, in response to the sincerity of the individual's repentance, God determines her or his fate for the coming year. On *Rosh HaShanah* (also referred to as *Yom HaDin*, or "the Day of Judgment"), God opens the Book of Life to review one's deeds during the past year, and the Book is "sealed" after God's decision on *Yom Kippur*. During those days, people are to reflect on their actions over the past year and seek forgiveness both from God and from those they have offended.

A key component of the *Yom Kippur* liturgy is the communal two-part confession (*Vidui*), which is recited multiple times during the day's services. In the short part of the confession, which is known by its first term, *'Ashamnu* ("We have trespassed"). the congregation rises and worshippers lightly touch the left side of their chests as they recite aloud and collectively and concretely acknowledge each shortcoming of the past year. The text reads as follows:

Our God and God of all generations, may our prayers reach Your presence. And when we turn to you, do not be indifferent.

Adonai, we are arrogant and stubborn, claiming to be blameless and free of sin.

In truth we have stumbled and strayed. We have done wrong.
Of these wrongs we are guilty:
We betray. We steal. We scorn. We act perversely.
We are cruel. We scheme. We are violent. We slander.
We devise evil. We lie. We ridicule. We disobey.
We abuse. We defy. We corrupt. We commit crimes.
We are hostile. We are stubborn. We are immoral. We kill.
We spoil. We go astray. We lead others astray.
. . . You know the secrets of the universe and the secrets of the human heart.
You know and understand us, for You examine our inner lives.
Nothing is concealed from You, nothing hidden from your sight.
Eternal One, our God and God of our ancestors,
We pray that this be Your will: forgive all our wrongs,
Pardon us for every act of injustice, help us atone for all our moral failings.

'Ashamnu is followed by a long confession, called *'Al Chet* ("For the error of our ways . . ."), in which the congregation stands and acknowledges its collective commission of forty-four specific violations or categories of violation. The *Sephardi* version is somewhat shorter. Each specific transgression triggers a recognition or a reflection on a person's conduct during the past year. Contemporary versions of the *Vidui* include

such issues as racism and sexism, and several rabbis have proposed a positive or complementary *Vidui,* in which congregants can acknowledge the good they have done during the past year.

Judaism's understanding of repentance and forgiveness makes the specificity and particularity of "sin" explicit. Judaism does not assume that God's forgiveness of transgressions is automatic or guaranteed. There is no general absolution of sin. Rather, forgiveness requires concrete acts of repentance. Since transgression is the result *of* free will, so also repentance must derive *from* free will. Repentance in Judaism entails four steps: the person's acknowledgment and repair of the transgression; the person's regret for committing the transgression; the person's resolution not to repeat the transgression; and, most important, the person's actual behavioral refusal to repeat the transgression when the possibility arises to do it again.

The concreteness of "sin" includes not only the particular transgression but also the party the transgression affected. Thus, Judaism holds that God does not forgive persons for what they do to other people. Just as one must repent and seek forgiveness from God for transgressions committed against God, so one must repent and seek forgiveness from the particular people against whom a transgression was committed. By the same token, people are obliged to extend forgiveness if the repentance is genuine.

This framework attests to the Judaic dynamic of repentance for sin, which presupposes that humans have the capacity for self-reflection, choice, self-transformation, and growth. It offers a process in which repentance can repair ruptures in the relationship between God and the Jewish people and communal relationships both within and beyond the Jewish people itself.

Respect for the Dead

In Judaism, respect for the dead is an ethical matter. Volunteer members of the community, known as the *Chevra Kadisha* ("holy community"), care for the body of the deceased. They stay with the body until burial, close its eyes, thoroughly cleanse it, and—to make the equality of death concrete—wrap it in a plain linen shroud. Out of respect for the body's integrity, autopsies are discouraged (though organ donation is generally permitted, reflecting the highest Judaic value of saving a life); embalming (except where required by state law) and cremation are prohibited. The funeral and burial occur as soon as possible after death, and the body is not displayed. Ideally, the corpse should come in contact with the earth, from which God fashioned humans. But this too depends on state regulations. If coffins are used, they must be made entirely of wood, which disintegrates in the earth so the body can do so as well.

At the burial, mourners recite the *Kaddish.* The family mourns, usually at home, for seven days (*shiva*)—referred to as "sitting *shiva*"—during which prayers and the *Kaddish* are recited, and friends supply food, nourishment, and company. For the family, grieving extends for 30 days (*sheloshim*) after the funeral, though they return to the world of work after *shiva* concludes. Mourners who have lost a parent recite the *Kaddish* daily for eleven months. It is customary for the family to gather to unveil a stone monument within one year after the death. On the anniversary of the death, called *yahrzeit* in Yiddish, family members light a memorial candle in the home and recite the *Kaddish* in synagogue worship. Memorial services to remember the deceased (*Yizkor*) are part of the liturgies of *Yom Kippur, Shemini 'Atzeret, Pesach*, and *Shavu'ot*.

The Messiah

Judaism teaches that the world in general and the Jewish people in particular are unredeemed. As we have seen, Judaic liturgy prays for an heir of David, an "anointed" leader, a messiah, who will usher in a messianic age, redeem the Jewish people, return them to the land of Israel, and correct the world's injustices. Beyond those general hopes and expectations, however, Judaism offers no comprehensive doctrinal teaching about the messiah's character or appearance, except that the messiah has not yet come. Rabbinic Judaism was cautious about arousing messianic expectations or attempting to provoke by force the messiah's arrival. Indeed, a teaching (*Avot de Rabbi Nathan* 31b) attributed to Rabban Yohanan ben Zakkai says, "If you are planting a sapling and someone tells you that the messiah has come, finish planting the sapling, and then go greet the messiah." Judaism's basic position is that the concerns for this world take precedence over those for the next. What one thinks about the messiah's character has little bearing on Judaism's daily religious practice.

On the other hand, the belief that the messiah *has* come may affect Jewish religious practice on the grounds that the messiah's arrival renders the commandments unnecessary in this world. That was the case in Christianity, which abandoned most of the Torah's ritual commandments, including, for instance, circumcision, dietary conventions, and *Shabbat* (which it replaced with Sunday as "the Lord's Day").

The subversion of *halakhah* also is evident in the episode of Shabbetai Tzvi (1626–1676), a kabbalistic rabbi who proclaimed himself, and was proclaimed by others, to be the messiah. The early seventeenth century was a period of intense Jewish messianic speculation, and Shabbetai Tzvi attracted a considerable following. In 1666 in Constantinople he was arrested and given the choice to convert to Islam or face a trial and death. The self-proclaimed messiah converted. Many of his followers rejected him, but others—drawing on the teachings of Lurianic *kabbalah* described in Chapter 4—understood his conversion to be part of the messianic mission to release the divine sparks that were trapped deeply in the non-Jewish world.

Shabbetai Tzvi engaged in non-halakhic behaviors, and some of his followers believed that willfully violating *halakhah* was a way to hasten the messianic mission. Types of the Sabbatean movement persisted to the twentieth century.

A different expression of Jewish messianism is evident in religious Zionism. As we have seen above, political Zionism was a secular nationalist movement designed to create a secular, democratic, Jewish nation-state. Its aims, programs, and tactics were pragmatic, not pietistic. On the other side, as noted above, segments of the Orthodox community rejected Zionism as an attempt to force God's hand in bringing the messiah.

Between those two positions was a form of Zionism that understood the establishment of the State of Israel as the beginning of redemption, as a harbinger of ultimate redemption that would come in the future. The most influential founding figure of this messianic approach was Rabbi Abraham Isaac Kook (1865–1935), the first *Ashkenazi* Chief Rabbi in the land of Israel under the British Mandatory Palestine, which governed the territory from the end of the First World War to 1948.

Resurrection and the World to Come

As we have seen, Judaism is primarily a this-worldly religion, and its focus is more on this life than on the next. The *Tanakh* does not have an elaborate or explicit teaching about resurrection from the dead, although Ezekiel's vision of the Valley of the Dry Bones and some passages in the Book of Daniel suggest it. In the Second Temple period—perhaps prompted by the experience of Jewish martyrdom, in which Jews opted for death instead of religious transgression—Judaism adopted the idea of resurrection from the dead and appended it to the Torah's religious structure. The Mishnah (*Sanhedrin*, Chapter 11) states that "All Israel has a share in the World to Come" but this teaching also excludes certain categories of the Jewish people, for instance, those who deny that resurrection from the dead is in the Torah, or who deny that Torah is from heaven. Other rabbinic teachings list other exclusions as well. In the rabbis' view, for Jews, living a halakhic life presaged resurrection. As for the fate of non-Jews, a teaching attributed to Rabbi Joshua ben Hananiah says that "the righteous of all nations have a share in the World to Come" (*Tosefta Sanhedrin* 13:2), and this view, also articulated by the Noahide commandments, is Judaism's position.

As with the messiah, Judaic reflection on the nature of resurrection is speculative and diverse. While some teachings emphasize the resurrection of the physical body—which may partly explain Judaism's opposition to cremation—other opinions suggest that the soul alone ultimately survives death. Likewise, some teachings propose that the World to Come will differ from this world only in terms of the end of Israel's oppression; other opinions envision an idealized world free of all physical need and without jealousy or envy; and some imagine a rebuilt Temple in Jerusalem. Judaic flexibility on the relationship between this world and the World to Come is evident in a teaching in the Mishnah (*Avot* 4:7), that avers both that an hour of repentance and acts of lovingkindness in this world is preferable to an entire life in the World to Come and that a single moment of inner peace in the World to Come is better than the whole of a lifetime spent in this world. Some kabbalistic teachings even propose reincarnation, in part to explain the idea that the entire Jewish people was present at Mount Sinai to accept the Torah of Moses.

Reform Judaism's liturgy speaks of God as a "source of all life" and of a worldwide "messianic age" of justice and peace. It downplays resurrection of the dead and the coming of the messiah, although both of these views are now options in recent Reform prayer books. Neither Reform nor Reconstructionist Judaism anticipates the rebuilding of the Jerusalem Temple.

Christianity

Original Sin and the Image of God

Sin and original sin are central categories of Christian understandings of salvation and the afterlife. As discussed in the creation chapter, original sin is essential for explaining Jesus' universal salvation of all of humanity. Because all humans are born in a state of sin, they all require salvation through Jesus Christ. Through his death and resurrection Jesus saves us from the original sin that entered into this world, symbolically depicted in the story of Adam and Eve in the Garden of Eden. Christian understandings of sin and salvation are often discussed in terms of the image of God in humanity and how that image is corrupted by sin.

For many of the Church Fathers (theologians and church leaders in the first five centuries of Christianity), their notion of the image of God was intimately linked to their understanding of the soul and spirituality. The image was most fully realized in the act of contemplation of God. The human being does not truly realize him or herself unless he or she goes beyond their selves and returns to the Being in whose image we are created. While in previous chapters we have discussed the significance of Augustine of Hippo, one cannot underestimate the impact of Irenaeus of Lyons on the history of theology. Born between 140 and 160, Irenaeus has been called the first Christian theologian. A key concern for Irenaeus' theology is the question of God's universal salvific will in light of humanity's creation in the image and likeness of God. Also key is Martin Luther's understanding of the image.

Irenaeus' theology has inconsistencies and he is not a systematic thinker on this topic. He describes humanity as created in the likeness of God, though that likeness was lost in the Fall. Jesus reveals the archetype of humanity's intended likeness to God, which is revealed through his incarnation. Even though we have lost our resemblance, it is reestablished by the incarnation of Jesus in human form. Irenaeus highlights the significance of the incarnation within salvation history and its implications for restoring our creation in the image and likeness of God. Christ's incarnation was necessary, for human beings could not restore the image on their own; they need Christ. The manner in which Christ saves is connected with the importance of obedience in Irenaeus' theology. Jesus' obedience replaces and atones for Adam's disobedience. Similarly, Mary's obedience when she accepts her role as the mother of Jesus undoes the damage inflicted by Eve's disobedience. In Christianity our salvation is the recovery through Christ of what was lost in Adam, namely the image and likeness of God. The Son reflects the image of God and we in turn are the image of the Son. Until the incarnation, the image of God was invisible. Jesus Christ makes visible the invisible God.

Former Roman Catholic monk Martin Luther is known as one of the fathers of the Protestant Reformation. His critique of Church corruption, especially through the selling of indulgences, spurred the greatest historical upheaval in the history of Christianity. Luther argued that Adam's image and likeness (which he saw as one and the same) was destroyed by his sin. This was also the fate of Adam's descendants, who were left with a depraved human nature. Our original righteousness is lost. This creates a bit of an ambiguity in Luther, for he strongly emphasizes the loss of the image while maintaining that a trace of it remains, allowing on certain levels knowledge of God. For Luther, one cannot understand the image and how it exists within us without connecting it to the Fall. We cannot truly understand or know the divine image within us, for it has been seriously damaged in the Fall. It exists within us today in a deficient manner. Before the Fall Adam and Eve had perfect knowledge of God, both in the same degree. Now we only have remnants of this knowledge, and other animals have always completely lacked it. Because of Adam and Eve's sin, the image has been significantly lost and weakened. The image will only be fully renewed in the kingdom of God. The only manner in which we can recover the image in any way is through Christ.

Eschatology

Eschatology is the area of Christianity that centers on the study of the last things (*eschaton*). The *eschaton* is the kingdom of God, which is realized through God's Spirit. Eschatology, however, is not solely future-related. Christians believe that the kingdom of God is here and now, initiated by Jesus' salvific ministry, death, and resurrection, and continually infused by the accompaniment of the Holy Spirit. However, the kingdom will only be realized in its fullness at the end of time. This is the Christian hope. The function of time can become quite complex in Christian teachings of the kingdom. In a sense, Christians teach that humanity has already been redeemed and resurrected in the Spirit. Through participation in the death and resurrection of Jesus Christ, Christians' death has already occurred. Humanity's particular and then final judgment will simply make visible what is already true. Jesus' second coming, the *parousia*, in this sense is a completion of Jesus' first coming.

There was a radical shift in Christianity after Jesus' early followers came to the realization that his second coming was not going to occur in their lifetime. Christian statements on eschatology usually refer to two dimensions: general and individual. This is a heuristic distinction, however, for the Church teaches that there is only one kingdom of God. Individual judgment refers to our place before and then in relationship with God. General judgment refers to the final judgment, the consummation of human history. Throughout Christian history the doctrine of eschatology has struggled to maintain a communal sense of human destiny as a whole while also discussing individual salvation.

Christian teachings on eschatology can be summed up very briefly. Broadly speaking Christianity teaches that human death is a consequence of sin. Implied in this, however, is that because Christ conquered death, to live in Christ is to transcend death. This is seen in the words of Jesus himself in the Gospel of John and the account of his encounter with the Samaritan woman. Jesus has a long theological discussion with a Samaritan woman drawing water from a well. Unlike the earthly water she is gathering, Jesus informs her that if she drinks living water she will never be thirsty. "Everyone who drinks this water will be thirsty again, but whoever drinks the water I give them will never thirst. Indeed, the water I give them will become in them a spring of water welling up to eternal life" (John 4.13–14). This living water will give the drinker eternal life. When she asks where to find this living water, he of course informs her that it comes through his heavenly father. The Samaritan woman then asks for this water and goes on to proclaim Jesus' message to her people.

The story of the Samaritan woman reveals Jesus' promise of eternal life to his followers. At the time of death the body and the soul are temporarily separated, but they will be reunited in the resurrection of the body. Death involves the judgment of your life, for there is always the possibility of final damnation. The fulfillment of life in death is the direct vision and enjoyment of God. This is known as the *beatific vision*, and it represents one's complete union with God. Christ will come again for the final judgment, and the dead will rise with their bodies to be judged.

Four areas in eschatology are of particular interest: purgatory, the resurrection of the body, hell, and limbo. Purgatory, a belief held exclusively by Roman Catholics, is for those who have died in God's grace but have not put everything in their lives in right order. It is best understood not as a place but as a process. Purgatory allows for the possibility of purification, but it is not a second chance; one works things out in purgatory that have begun in one's life (unfinished business). Contained within the doctrine of purgatory is the belief in the value of prayers for the dead (and the efficacy of indulgences). Prior to the fourth century, the Church assumed that the dead were waiting until the last judgment to be judged collectively. Augustine of Hippo's fourth century theology first introduced the idea of immediate individual judgment after death and the possibility of experiencing the beatific vision. This introduced an individual component to the afterlife and also led to a doctrine of purgatory where souls could be purified. The foundation for the resurrection of the body is Jesus' resurrection. This final resurrection will occur communally at the end of time. Christianity's emphasis on the resurrection of the body stems from belief in the redemption of humanity in all its totality—body and soul. This resurrected, glorified body will be in continuity with, yet different from humanity's earthly bodies.

Hell is most easily defined as the rejection of God. Therefore, God does not send individuals to hell; instead, by rejecting God, one chooses the state of hell. While there is great variation on whether Christians affirm that individuals are in hell or not, it is always acknowledged as a *possibility*. The fact that hell only remains a possibility which the individual chooses for his or her own destiny is lost in most popular Christian teachings. Entry into hell takes place immediately after death, though again, Christian churches do not make any official statements about the nature of or presence of individuals in hell. Christianity attempts to hold in balance its belief in the universal salvific will of God embodied in Christ's redemption, while simultaneously maintaining the human freedom to reject and turn from God. For centuries the Roman Catholic Church taught the existence of limbo, the state of being neither in heaven nor hell nor purgatory. Often discussions of limbo center on the question of unbaptized children. For centuries the Augustinian doctrine that unbaptized children went to hell went unchallenged by the hierarchy and theologians. Today limbo has been rejected by the Catholic Church.

A historical overview of the doctrine of eschatology is difficult because Christianity has not produced a systematic body of literature throughout the course of its history clearly defining the topic, and there is also variance among different churches. This hope for the future, Christians believe, must be the ultimate structure of the present, and humans are called to embody the kingdom here on earth, albeit limited by their humanity. It is important to note that while eschatology deals with last things, it should not be treated as divination of the future. One does not find the afterlife predicted, for example, in the book of Revelation. It is already present in the here and how. Through God's grace, the kingdom is already here; it is up to humans to accept the offer of God's grace.

The Kingdom of God

The foundation of human resurrection is Christ's resurrection. The Christian belief in the resurrection of the human body is based on the resurrection of Jesus' body. When our bodies are resurrected, they will be identical to our earthly bodies, yet somehow transformed. The *parousia* is a future, collective event that concludes history. Given that the *parousia* is a future event, there exists an intermediate state after death. During this state, described as the eschatology of souls, the soul serves as the continuity after death until the resurrection. The human person consists of both body and soul. The Christian belief in the immortality of the soul that continues in a transitory state separate from the body until the *parousia*, when it is reunited with the resurrected body, is based on the duality of the human as body and soul. Death is simultaneously good and evil. Death is an evil because it divides and separates us. Death is a good, on the other hand, because it ultimately leads to the resurrection. Without death, the resurrection, our purpose, cannot happen.

Roman Catholics affirm the importance of the invocation of the saints and the need to pray for the dead, cultivating fellowship with the communion of saints. The invocation of saints and intercessory prayers, however, are clearly distinguished from any form of invoking spirits. Also some Christians pray for the dead in order to support the purification of souls. Only souls that are purified will enjoy the beatific vision of God and union with Christ after death. Unlike the rest of creation, humanity reflects God's image and is able to know and love God. Our creation is a result of God's creative love. We only have this lifetime to accept the gratuitous gift of God's friendship and love. Within Christian discussions of last things is a tension between the now and not yet. Jesus' resurrection has initiated a new age, whose presence is here but has not been fulfilled. There will be a judgment at the end of time. Until then the Holy Spirit accompanies us in human history.

Christians with a more liberationist approach to the *eschaton* call their fellow believers to embody the kingdom of God here and now through social justice. Just because this kingdom will be limited by our humanity, we can work towards this ever-present future

FIGURE 28 *Candles with images of saints, © Gregor Schuster, Getty Images.*

in our concrete social action. Language such as new world and new heaven and belief in the resurrection of the body imply a continuity between this world and the eschaton, while simultaneously affirming that "flesh and blood will not inherit the kingdom of God." Christianity has always had an ambiguous relationship with the body, and the role of the body in the afterlife remains a point of contention and debate. Linked to this is the tension between the continuity of the soul and the discontinuity with the world as we know it. The continuity is based on the Christian claim that the kingdom of God is already present among us. The discontinuity is spatially constructed between the world we know now and the new world, or alternatively put the discontinuity of God's presence in this world which is already realized yet not fully manifest.

Islam

Sin is pronounced upon anything that takes one away from God. This is what the Qur'an, generally, teaches Muslims. Islam distinguishes itself from Christianity by declaring strongly that it is acts that are a sin and not the state of being. Muslims speak of a hierarchy of sins and there is much discussion about sins that are committed intentionally and unintentionally and further discussion on sins that are a once-off mistake or are committed over and over again. But what constitutes sin in Islam? The biggest sin that a Muslim can commit is associating anything or anyone with God. This is open to debate too as this could mean believing that animate objects are God or that money and wealth become God. Islamic traditions attempt to offer a moral and ethical framework on "right" conduct. These are the issues that plagued the legal scholars who were trying to make sense of general parameters set in motion in the Qur'an and Hadith.

There are then other categories of sins such as oppression, fraud, injustice, killing—general good ethics, one might say—but this is also complicated by disagreements amongst Muslims. This returns us back to the Qur'anic injunction set upon all Muslims to uphold good and turn away, and advise others, from evil and sin. This instruction has then allowed for a wide variety of statements on what is sinful amongst Muslims. These pronouncements come from learned circles of scholars but in every time, even today, Muslims will often pass judgment on certain practices. What is important to note is that sin in Islam is always set through a rationale that must be connected to submission to only God. Sin is connected to belief so it is a personal matter. The advice and prescriptions from anyone are accepted and acted upon through free will. Islamic traditions, be they stories in the Qur'an or the sayings of the prophet Muhammad, have always tried to make Muslims understand why something is sinful as opposed to just marking it as such. Take for example the drinking of alcohol. It is understood by many as sinful because it takes away from the remembrance of God, but Muslims in the past and present have spent a long time discussing "inebriation" or "intoxication"—at which level does the intoxicated person completely lose sight of God? Could coffee be understood as an intoxicant? Then there are some wayward Sufis, as mentioned earlier, who believe that only in moments of complete intoxication (either alcoholic or hallucinogenic) does one reach the pinnacle of Godly union.

Islamic traditions present a number of consequences of committing sins. For example, when Muslims fail to give their alms tax, it is said that the earth will stop producing crops and fruits. Islamic traditions warn that great calamities will befall human beings who indulge in oppressing others, being rude and mocking them. This highlights that Muslims will suffer consequences on earth before the great day of judgment too.

Redemption from a sin committed against God is rectified through penitence, remorse and resolution. Muslims are reminded time and time again in Islamic traditions that God's mercy overrides God's wrath. That sincerity in belief and a mindful and physical state of remorse will always be looked upon favorably by God and forgiven. This is also highlighted in the story of Adam and Eve. Muslims are taught that God knows exactly what is in their hearts so their sincere intentions are important.

For Muslims, death is not the end but the beginning of a new life—a life after death that is understood to be greater in time and space than what human beings experience on earth. The literal body is understood to be resurrected in this afterlife. Ethics and morality in earthly living is connected to what is yet to come. Reward and punishment are drivers for ethical practice. The earthly world (dunya) is but a grand test of overcoming evil and upholding goodness. The ultimate reward for this comes in the hereafter (akhirah). The potential for such a thought process has been immense. The

Qur'an speaks on numerous occasions about death. These passages make clear that life on earth may seem a long time but in reality is short.

Here are a few select quotations:

They will cry out therein, "Our Lord! Remove us, that we may work righteousness other than that which we used to do." "Did We not give you long life, enough for whosever would reflect to reflect therein? And the warner came unto you, so taste [the punishment]! And the wrongdoers shall have no helpers."

Q35:37

They have taken gods apart from Him, who . . . have no power over death, or life, or resurrection.

Q25:3

O my people! Follow me; I shall guide you unto the way of rectitude, O my people! The life of this world is but fleeting enjoyment, whereas the hereafter is truly the Abode of Permanence. Whosoever commits an evil deed will not be requited, save with the life thereof; but whosoever, whether male or female, performs a righteous deed and is a believer shall enter the garden wherein they will be provided for without reckoning.

Q40:38–40

Every soul shall taste death, and you will indeed be paid your reward in full on the Day of Resurrection. And whosoever is distanced from the Fire and made to enter the garden has certainly triumphed. And the life of this world is naught but the enjoyment of delusion.

Q3:185

Then they were succeeded by a generation who neglected prayer and followed base desires. So they shall meet [the reward of] error, save for those who repent and believe and work righteousness. It is they who shall enter the garden, and they shall not be wronged in the least. Gardens of Eden, those which the Compassionate promised His servants in the Unseen. Verily His Promise shall come to pass.

Q19:59–61

There is an intermediate space between death and resurrection known as *Barzakh*, a time after death and in the grave. Muslims only bury their dead and do not cremate. The dead are said to be in an awakened state during this time, as they are contemplating all that they did during their time on earth. Two angels, *Munkar* and *Nakir*, are said to come to the recently deceased in the grave and ask them questions. These questions are testing the person's belief in God and Muhammad. A believer who answers correctly will see the space in their grave open up and become a sort of garden or heaven with rich green foliage; for those who answer incorrectly, the grave space crushes them, iron hammers are pounded into the person, and they scream. It is said that the constriction is so intense that their ribs burst.

Muslims believe that there will be a final day on which all of creation will be judged. In Islamic traditions there are said to be many signs of that final day. These vary from the building of tall buildings, some sort of smoke, and the arrival of Yajuj and Majuj (biblically known as Gog and Magog). They are said to be unusual individuals who live near the sea and are not obedient to God. They are understood to create much mischief on the earth in a way recalling another end-of-times figure, the *Dajjal*. The Dajjal is the Antichrist who is said to arrive when many good virtues will have faded away—praying will have gone by the wayside and dishonesty, falsehoods, and even Satan worship will be widespread. The Messiah will then arrive in order to correct Yajuj, Majuj, and the Dajjal. As stated earlier, Sunnis and Shi'as differ as to who will be the messiah. A trumpet is blown, which will initiate the resurrection. It is said to be a day of great calamity. "And the agony of death comes with the truth. That is what you were avoiding. And the trumpet is blown. That is the Day of the Threat" (Q50:19). In another passage God states, "O mankind! Reverence your Lord. Truly the quaking of the Hour is a tremendous thing. On the day you see it, every nursing woman will forget what she nurses, and every pregnant woman will deliver her burden, and you will see mankind drunk, though drunk they will not be. Rather, the Punishment of God is severe" (Q22:1–2). These passages are constant reminders for Muslims to uphold good because there are consequences to their actions.

All creation is then assembled for what is known as *al-Hashr* (the Gathering). The righteous believer will not be worried, but those who have done great evils on earth will have great worry on their faces. During this time humanity will go from prophet to prophet, asking whether they will intercede for them. They will all decline except the prophet Muhammad, who will agree and intercede to God. It is then that the good and bad deeds will be presented to God: "So whosoever does a mote's weight of good shall see it. And whosoever does a mote's weight of evil shall see it" (Q99:7–8). Reminder after reminder is found in the Qur'an:

> On the day . . . they shall be arrayed before thy Lord in ranks. "Indeed, you have come unto Us as We created you the first time. Nay, but you claimed that We would never appoint a tryst for you." And the Book will be set down. Then thou wilt see the guilty fearful of what is in it. And they will say, "'Oh, woe unto us! What a book this is! It leaves out nothing, small or great, save that it has taken account thereof." And they find present [therein] whatsoever they did. And thy Lord wrongs no one.
>
> Q18:47–49

The Qur'an speaks of body parts testifying to their actions: "On the day their tongues, their hands, and their feet bear witness against them as to that which they used to do" (Q24:24). Two further passages which connect beliefs with bodily practice state:

On that Day We shall seal their mouths. Their hands will speak to Us, and their feet will bear witness to that which they used to earn.

Q36:65

And they will say to their skins, "Why did you bear witness against us?" They will reply, "God, Who makes all things speak, made us speak. He created you the first time, and unto Him shall you be returned."

Q41:21

It is also during this time that the complete revelation from God is presented to creation. This is understood as the preserved tablet (al-lawh al-mahfuz), of which only snippets were offered to humanity in the form of revealed Scripture. Everyone is given their registry of good and bad deeds. For those who have done good, they will receive them to their right hands and those who have committed evil will receive them to their left and behind their backs. This is where the review will take place. It is here that many will be saved: "Truly those who believe, and those who are Jews, and the Christians, and the Sabaens—whosoever believes in God and the Last Day and works righteousness shall have their reward with their Lord. No fear shall come upon them, nor shall they grieve" (Q2:62). God's attribute of the most just is presented thus: "We shall set the just scales (al-Mizan) for the Day of Resurrection, and no soul shall be wronged in aught. Even if it be the weight of a mustard seed. We shall bring it. And We suffice as Reckoner" (Q21:47).

After judgment is rendered, everyone passes over a bridge. There are numerous stories about how easy or difficult it is to pass over this bridge to heaven or hell. The details about hell all come from the Qur'an, which has a number of descriptions within it:

And as for those who are iniquitous, their refuge is the Fire. Whenever they desire to go forth therefrom, they are returned unto it, and it is said unto them, "Taste the punishment of the Fire that you used to deny." And We make them taste the lesser punishment before the greater punishment, that they might turn back.

Q32:20–21

All those who enter paradise shall remain thirty years of age eternally and shall enjoy everything they desire. There will be rivers flowing of milk, honey and wine. An important understanding of all these traditions is the belief by Muslims that it is the mercy of God, and not their deeds alone, that admits them to paradise.

Afterthought: Sin, Redemption, Afterlife

As we learned in Chapter I, two distinguishing features of religion are its claim to know how to repair the rupture between God and humanity and its comprehensive view of time. The ideas of sin, redemption, salvation, and the afterlife illustrate these traits. These components emerge from the overall pattern of creation, covenant, and commandment. God creates an ideal world and sets terms for human beings to inhabit it; humans violate those terms, and as a consequence face death; God establishes new terms to repair the rupture; and humans then can choose the consequences of choice of fulfilling the terms or not. The monotheistic system thus envisions three realms of time: a time before this world, this world, and a time after this world.

Sin is the category that represents human alienation from God. As we have seen, the monotheistic religions focus on the issue of sin but understand it differently. For Christianity, sin is an indelible immoral bacterium called "original sin," an endemic affliction that infects all humans at birth. Removing the bacterium requires a special moral antibiotic—the resurrection of Jesus Christ—that heals the affliction, creates a condition of moral health, and repairs the relationship with God. Humans then must live in a way that avoids a relapse.

Islam and Judaism understand sin more as the result of human frailty and weakness that humans can repair on their own. Through repentance and self-correction—which entail self-awareness, self-control, discipline, and attention to God's teachings—people can reconcile with God.

Despite their differences, these two approaches generate the same question: What are the consequences of following or not following the religion's program? The idea of life after death—conceived either in terms of an immaterial individual soul or an individual resurrected body—addresses that question and the issue it raises. Put directly, life after death addresses the problems of the monotheistic system's incongruity in this world. It resolves the issues of the wicked who prosper and the righteous who suffer. It allows God's justice to prevail.

However one conceives it, life after death is indelibly speculative because there is no empirical evidence for it. Thus, it is not surprising that the three religions treat life after death somewhat differently and that they each exhibit internal differences as well. Because Judaism's emphasis is this-worldly, its ideas about life after death—which is not limited to Jews—are highly diverse and include differences even about whom it will include and who will be excluded. The teachings of Christianity and Islam tend to be more explicit and detailed.

Study Questions: Redemption, Salvation, and Life after Death

What is the relationship between God, sin, and human creation?
How do the three religions define sin?
How do the three religions understand death?
What are the general principles of 'just war' and how are they understood
    in each of the traditions?
How are heaven and hell understood in Judaism, Christianity, and Islam?
Are there intermediaries to God within Judaism, Christianity, and Islam
    who may help redeem sins?

10

Contemporary Monotheism: Case Studies

Having explored their common heritage, this chapter examines how a localized, geographical study of each tradition can help identify the broader issues, concerns, and growth of these religions in today's world. While today Judaism, Christianity, and Islam are global religions, our emphasis on the local highlights the areas where these religions are growing and being challenged by new cultural, social, and political realities.

Judaism

Judaism in the State of Israel

Background and Context

For nearly two millennia Judaism was a non-sovereign politically dependent minority religion, and Jews in both Christian and Islamic societies were religious, cultural, and political outsiders.

The consequence of that status became evident in events of the late nineteenth century in Europe. Pogroms in Russia (1881–1884 and 1903–1906) and the Dreyfus Affair in France (1894–1906) demonstrated the Jews' precarious status. In the Russian Kishniev pogrom (today's Chișinău, Moldova), street gangs killed 49 people, injured hundreds, and destroyed Jewish homes and businesses. In the Dreyfus Affair, a Jewish captain in the French army, Alfred Dreyfus, was falsely accused of treason and convicted twice. That Dreyfus was a Jew was a primary factor in both the fraudulent accusations and verdicts. The case demonstrated deep strains of anti-Semitism in France—the nation of "liberty, equality, and brotherhood"—and across Europe. These and comparable events were harbingers of worse things to come, and they catalyzed Zionism.

Modern political Zionism is the secular movement of Jewish nationhood, which led to the establishment of the State of Israel. The founder of the movement was a secular

Hungarian Jewish journalist, Theodor Herzl (1860–1904), who judged that the Jews would never be safe or accepted in Europe and needed to found their own national state. The subsequent murder of six million Jews in the Nazi-perpetrated Holocaust (1933–1945) confirmed his judgment. Although all Zionists shared the goal of establishing a national entity that would be a home to the Jews, Zionism was a broad movement that encompassed diverse views about how to achieve that goal and the nature of the eventual Jewish state. Some of these approaches are evident in the range of contemporary Israel's political parties.

The State of Israel was founded on May 14, 1948. Israel's Proclamation of Independence articulates its national narrative and purpose:

> The Land of Israel was the birthplace of the Jewish people. Here their spiritual, religious, and political identity was shaped. Here they first attained to statehood, created cultural values of national and universal significance, and gave to the world the eternal Book of Books.
>
> After being forcibly exiled from their land, the people kept faith with it throughout their Dispersion and never ceased to pray and hope for their return to it and for the restoration in it of their political freedom. . . .
>
> The State of Israel will be open for Jewish immigration and for the Ingathering of the Exiles; it will foster the development of the country for the benefit of all its inhabitants; it will be based on freedom, justice and peace as envisaged by the prophets of Israel; it will ensure complete equality of social and political rights to all its inhabitants irrespective of religion, race or sex; it will guarantee freedom of religion, conscience, language, education and culture; it will safeguard the holy places of all religions; and it will be faithful to the principles of the Charter of the United Nations. . . .

Israel is religiously, ethnically, and politically pluralistic. Between 1882 and 1939 successive waves of immigration brought new populations to the land of Israel, largely motivated by the need to escape the hostility Jews encountered in European and later in Islamic societies. Additionally, In the three years after the state's founding, large numbers of Holocaust survivors and Jews from Arab nations migrated to the state. Additional immigration waves, particularly from the former Soviet Union, followed and continue. By 2018, 75% of Israeli Jewish citizens were native-born.

Israeli Democracy

Although it does not mention God explicitly, the Proclamation of Independence defines the State of Israel as both Jewish and democratic and thereby invokes both sides of the covenant. On the one hand, it establishes the particularistic mission that Israel is the homeland and a place of refuge for all Jews. On the other hand, it affirms that life in the state will exhibit and be shaped by classic universalistic Judaic values of justice, fairness, and equality. Sometimes these two ideas are mutually reinforcing, and sometimes realizing them together creates challenges. Israel is home to a population of Jews who reflect diverse cultural and religious backgrounds and political perspectives—from committed secularity to extremely devout piety—as well as to an Arab population (Muslim and Christian) and a Druze community that descend from those who lived in the land before the state's founding. In addition, since its establishment, Israel has fought eight major wars. The political issues of Palestinian aspirations and refugees and Israel's management of territories it controls as a result of the 1967 Six Day War—which are far too complex to address here—remain contentious both outside and inside Israel. Despite these challenges, Israel has made peace with Egypt and Jordan and exhibits improved relations with other Arab and Muslim states.

Israel has remained open to the kind of vigorous public debate that characterizes modern, secular democracies. Israel's democratic character is evident in its robust and free press, its independent judiciary, and its protracted, intense, and serious national discussions not only about its global and regional political issues but also about Judaism's role in the life of its society. Political parties, for instance, are divided on the issue of whether *Haredi* youth should serve in the Israeli military—which is obligatory on all other Jewish Israelis, male and female, and Druze and Circassian men—and about how extensively *halakhah* should legally shape or even dictate civic and social life. In 2019, for the first time, this issue was central in Israel's re-election campaign.

In July of 2018, the Israeli Knesset narrowly passed the Basic Law, "The Nation Law," of Israel, which defines Israel as the nation-state of the Jewish people. This law has proven controversial. Its adherents argue that it merely affirms the content of Israel's Proclamation of Independence. Its critics—who include *Mizrahi* Jews, secular Israelis, Israeli Arabs, Druze, and the American Reform and Conservative movements—argue that it could compromise Israel's democratic and pluralistic character.

Judaism in Israel

Israel's Zionist founders aimed to create not only a "normal" Jewish society in an independent Jewish polity on the model of European nation-states but also a Jewish nationality, a primarily secular Jewish culture, with its own language and institutions—the antithesis of the two-millennia-long Jewish experience in exile. The State of Israel is the first political structure since the Hasmonean dynasty in which Judaism is the majority religion embedded in a broader polity and culture congruent to it. This integration—and particularly the association of religion and state—creates a context for the practice of Judaism not seen since ancient times.

Following European models, Israel has a parliamentary government that operates on the basis of coalitions formed from a range of numerous political parties. As noted above, Modern Orthodox and *Haredi* political parties have, from the beginnings of the state, been part of the ruling coalitions of various Israeli governments. For most of Israel's history, religious political parties have managed the Ministry of Religious

Services, which oversees government-supported institutions that deal with various aspects of, and services for, Judaism. This means that the predominant official form of Judaism in Israel is controlled by the Orthodox.

Although Israel is not a theocracy, *halakhah* has shaped Israeli government policies in several areas. As we saw in Chapter 5, the Chief Rabbinate, which is led alternately by two Chief Rabbis—one *Ashkenazi* and one *Sephardi*—oversees matters of Jewish personal status, and *halakhah* has influenced Israel's Law of Return and other legislation. Some secular voices in Israel have proposed alternatives to the current model, suggesting that the state should determine who is an Israeli as opposed to determining who is a Jew. In 2018, seven hundred Jewish leaders from Israel and North America issued a "Vision Statement: Israel as a Jewish and Democratic State," which called for "religious freedom" and "equal access to State services and funding for Israel's Jewish and non-Jewish citizens" and citizens' right "to choose their own religious leadership" for purposes of marriage and conversion.

Current research shows how Judaism in Israel is changing. On the basis of the responses of 3,500 Israeli Jews to a detailed questionnaire about their attitudes and behaviors in the areas of Jewish religion and Israeli nationalism, Shmuel Rosner and Camil Fuchs divide Israeli Jews into four groups: "universalists" (13%), "Israelis" (15%), "Jews" (17%), and "Jewsraelis" (55%).

"Universalists" are secular, urban, cosmopolitan, and engage in few, if any, religious or nationalist activities. "Israelis" are secular nationalists, and practice few Jewish religious traditions. "Jews" are primarily *Haredim,* who, as we have seen, are religiously observant but ambivalent about Israeli nationalism. The largest group, "Jewsraelis," represent a new cultural form that merges religion, tradition, and nationalism.

The new research suggests two diverging trends that affect Israeli society's religiosity. On the one hand, the *Haredim* have higher birth rates than the rest of the Israeli Jewish population. They marry early, and nearly half of them are under the age of 16. Estimates are that by 2040 *Haredim* will constitute nearly a quarter of Israel's population.

On the other hand, Israeli Jews are becoming "more secular." Nearly a quarter of those raised as *Haredim* have not remained so. The percentage of Jews who say they observe "part of the Jewish tradition" has declined to 34%, and an additional 26% say they "do not observe even part" of it. That 13% of Israelis identify as Reform or Conservative Jews suggests that, despite the official control exercised by the Chief Rabbinate, Orthodox Judaism in Israel effectively could become a denomination. Moreover, *Haredi* Jews are becoming nationalistic, and modest numbers are volunteering for the Israeli army. These data may signal that Jewish religion in the State of Israel is evolving into a component of national life rather than serving as the sole foundation of collective life and identity, as it did in the communities of the Jewish Diaspora.

Rosner's and Fuchs' research shows how the new Israeli culture, shaped by the context of an independent secular Jewish state, provides a framework for collective and individual identity that includes but transcends religion. Israeli national Jewish culture now resolves some of the issues of collective continuity and persistence that once were addressed by the Jewish religion. *Shabbat, Rosh HaShanah, Yom Kippur, Sukkot, Pesach, Shavu'ot, Hanukkah,* and *Purim* have evolved into national holidays, in the same way that Christmas and Easter are *de facto* American national holidays. In addition to religious holidays, *Yom HaZikaron* (Memorial Day), *Yom Ha'atzmaut* (Israel Independence Day), and *Yom HaShoah* (Holocaust Remembrance Day) are national secular Jewish holidays. Most Israelis participate in a Passover *Seder* and recite some version of the *Haggadah,* and nearly all of them have a holiday dinner on the evening of *Rosh HaShanah.* New national holiday observances are also appearing. For instance, riding bicycles on *Yom Kippur,* when the streets are empty of traffic, is a widespread practice. And nearly half of Israeli Jews celebrate *Mimouna,* a North African Jewish holiday that marks the end of Passover.

"Jewsraelis" represent the new national culture that merges nationalism and religious tradition. On Friday night to mark the onset of *Shabbat,* they are likely to light candles, recite *Kiddush,* and have a family meal, but they will drive and shop on Saturday (which *halakhah* prohibits). They fast for all or part of *Yom Kippur* and raise the Israeli flag on *Yom Ha'atzmaut.* They light candles for the eight days of Hanukkah and believe it is important to serve in the Israeli army. Some traditional activities—*Brit Milah, Bar* and *Bat Mitzvah,* or attaching a *mezuzah* to a household entrance, for instance—have become general cultural actions in Israeli Jewish life. Academic studies of *Tanakh,* along with extensive archaeological excavations, continue to illustrate the nation's historic relationship to the Land of Israel. Whether or not they are religiously observant, Israeli Jews intuitively know they are Jewish and define themselves as such.

To help understand these data, it is useful to remember that nearly all forms of Judaism evolved as strategies of persistence. They are the religious adaptations of a minority—and often migrating—people designed to maintain their relation to the One God, to preserve a collective identity, and practice their way of life in the context of foreign and often hostile cultures. As we have seen, the Torah itself, initially compiled and edited in Babylonia, is an adaptation to the loss of Solomon's Temple. It transformed a religion of cult and sacrifice into a text whose discourse of covenant and commandments connected Jews to one another wherever they were. Likewise, the Oral Torah and halakhic system of rabbinic Judaism—responding to the loss of the Second Temple and the exile from Jerusalem—created the religious, social, and institutional structures that until modern times guided the collective life of most Jewish communities around the world. Reform Judaism, Orthodox Judaism and Conservative Judaism initially are responses to the challenges posed by modern European culture and the Enlightenment, and Reconstructionist Judaism aims to address distinctive aspects of modern American culture. Haredi and Hasidic Judaism acknowledge the pressures of modernity by attempting to restrain them. Against this background, the development of a Jewish national culture—as much as it may evoke the past—is in many ways innovative and unprecedented. It is also dynamic, fluid, and subject to ongoing change. The State of Israel has created a new context for a religion with a long and adaptive history. As such, Judaism as practiced in Israel—as it has been everywhere—is an ever-evolving phenomenon.

FIGURE 29 *A panorama of Jerusalem: the Western Wall of the Temple and the Dome of the Rock,* © *Oren Rosenfeld / Contributor, Getty Images.*

Christianity

Latin American Christianity

While reports in the United States of increasing secularism throughout Europe continue to attract headlines, in the Global South, particularly Latin America, Christianity continues to thrive and grow. The history of Christianity within Latin America is one of conquest, colonialism, and slavery. Christianity in Latin America is marked by a legacy of a colonial Catholicism that was linked to the oppressive regime of the Spanish empire and its conquest of the Americas. The arrival of Christianity is marked by violence and bloodshed, and a Catholic monopoly that dominated the region until the nineteenth century. As a result of this, once Latin American countries gained independence from Spain, the Catholic Church was faced with liberal governments that promoted staunch anti-clericalism just as Protestant missionaries and churches were arriving in the region. Throughout most of Catholicism's history, priests and women religious were predominantly foreign-born. With the arrival of Protestant churches this will slowly change. Even when Catholicism dominated Latin America, the limited number of priests led to a population that was not well instructed in official theological teachings. In this vacuum emerged a mixture of indigenous and African religiosity with Catholic elements that distinctly characterizes Latin American Catholicism. The nature of the Catholic Church's presence as a dominant religious and political force, coupled with the absence of the ecclesial Church in the daily lives of

FIGURE 30 *Cathedral in Antigua, Guatemala, © Byron Maldonado.*

many Latin Americans, left fertile ground for the growth of Protestantism in the twentieth century. As a whole, Latin America is a case study for the diverse forms of Christian expression that mark the contemporary world.

Latin American Liberation Theology

Perhaps no other movement characterizes twentieth-century Roman Catholicism in Latin America more than Latin American liberation theology. Born in the late 1960s, this academic and church-based movement argues that the poor must be the starting point and center of theological reflection. A theology that does not begin with the faith, life, and struggles of the oppressed is not a true Christian theology. Latin American liberation theology functions on three levels: the popular, the pastoral, and the academic. The first two give life to academic reflection: the spirituality and political action of grassroots Christian communities informs theoretical theological reflection. Grounded in the belief that economic and social justice are the center of Christianity's mission, this Latin American theological movement has created a radical new understanding of church that centers on grassroots Christian communities and a transformation of academic theology. The Roman Catholic emphasis on the preferential option for the poor speaks to the global, institutional impact of this movement.

Liberation theology emerged in Latin America in a time when churches were increasingly engaged in social justice issues, particularly surrounding economic and political injustice. In Catholic churches, Catholic Social Teaching was influential in the development of Latin American liberation theology. The see–judge–act method, often attributed exclusively to Latin American thinkers, was in fact designed in the 1940s by Catholic Action. This method is fundamental for understanding the theology of foundational figure Gustavo Gutiérrez, who is considered by many the "father" of Latin American liberation theology. Gutiérrez's volume *A Theology of Liberation* embraced this approach, and its publication is considered the first monograph within Latin American liberation theology. While liberation theology is not the only expression of Catholicism in the region, and in fact includes Protestant churches and theologians, it is the most distinctive expression of Catholicism in the region.

Evangélicos

Turning exclusively to Protestant expressions of Christianity in the region, perhaps no other religious movement within Latin America has received more recent attention by academics than Pentecostalism and *evangélico* (evangelical) movements. In discussing Pentecostalism and Evangelical Christianity, it is important to clarify their distinctiveness among Protestant denominations. In many Spanish-speaking Latin American countries, all Protestants are *evangélicos*, and the term cannot be easily translated as "evangelical." In addition to the distinction in terms of language, Evangelicals in the United States have distanced themselves from Pentecostals in the past, emphasizing Pentecostals' lack of education, their lack of financial support, and what is seen as their excessively effusive style of worship and emphasis on speaking in tongues, healing, and prophecy. Pentecostals emphasize an expressive worship experience (including speaking in tongues) and physical healing. Pentecostalism is thus a particular subtype of Evangelicalism.

Recent figures estimate that at least one in ten Latin Americans are evangelical, with 70–80% Pentecostal. In some countries the figures are even higher. The indigenous nature of Pentecostalism, with its Latin American pastors and leadership, is Pentecostalism's greatest resource. In other words, unlike Catholicism where clergy are often foreign-born, Pentecostalism and other Protestant *evangélico* movements draw their leadership from the local population. Three characteristics of evangelical Protestantism are: authority of Scripture, experience of personal salvation through Jesus Christ, and the importance of the missionary enterprise. The opportunities for native pastoral leadership became one of evangelical Protestantism's greatest appeals. Unlike Catholic clergy, evangelical pastors are not required to pursue higher education. Also, there is more flexibility and greater possibilities for growth at the local level due to the variety and number of evangelical churches.

Pentecostalism has emerged as an unlikely source of empowerment for women. This is in part due to the manner in which Pentecostalism reconfigures the line between public and private life, encouraging men to become more active in the domestic sphere. This is in contrast to liberationist Catholicism that tended to emphasize the public and the structural, at the expense of issues of oppressive paradigms within the domestic sphere. In other words, while Catholicism in Latin America has been characterized from the late twentieth century as having an emphasis on broad social issues, Pentecostalism has focused on everyday life. Evangelical movements within Christianity build on the importance of the personal and domestic for religious life. The importance of testimony in Pentecostalism, bearing witness to one's faith experience, also gives women a space in the public religious sphere that is not available to them within Catholicism.

Often when one thinks of *movimientos evangélicos* in Latin America, the assumption is that these movements are exclusively Protestant. However, the Catholic Charismatic Renewal Movement (CCR) shows an evangelical face of Catholicism. CCR is one of the largest and fastest-growing movements in the Latin American Church, and is also thriving in other parts of the world. It has enormous appeal amongst lay people. One of the factors that distinguish the CCR is its missionary appeal and its use of media. Charismatic Catholicism is similar to Pentecostalism. This is seen in particular in the shared emphasis on the Holy Spirit, which is what distinguishes Charismatics from other Catholic groups. A belief in the gifts of the Spirit, such as faith healing and *glossolalia*, a certain degree of biblical fundamentalism, and asceticism are some of the characteristics Charismatics share with Pentecostals. The birth of CCR was in 1966 at Duquesne University in Pittsburgh. The movement spread to Latin America in the 70s. CCR's first members were predominantly middle class with a large number of women. Though at first there were some suspicions among Catholic leaders about the impact of CCR, in the 1990s it became a welcome and institutionalized expression of Catholicism. While seeing CCR as a way of combating Protestantism, many clergy were concerned that its emphasis on the believer's individual experience of the Spirit would challenge their authority. CCR is characterized by weekly prayer groups (*grupos de oración*) that can be as small as a group of ten or as large as three hundred members. Lay leaders direct them and priests do not often participate. Unlike the clergy-led mass, therefore, charismatic Catholicism empowers lay Catholics to find authority within themselves.

The growth of evangelical Protestant movements in Latin America is often highlighted as an indicator of Catholicism's growing demise within these countries. While this is in part true, movements like CCR coupled with Pentecostalism show us that the face of Christianity in Latin America is changing as a whole. Various factors have contributed to the growth of Pentecostal movements in general. One must also take into consideration the internal dynamics of church communities, the change in the religious environment, and the current socio-political context. A move to a more spiritualized pastoral work is a key factor. In addition, many of the problems the Catholic Church in Latin America faces today are historical. This larger history, both social and intellectual, is fundamental for understanding the Catholicism in Latin America in general and liberation theology in particular.

Pentecostal, Neo-Pentecostal, and charismatic churches all exploded in popularity in the second half of the twentieth century across various denominations. Pentecostal churches trace their genealogy to the spiritual revival in Topeka, Kansas, in 1901, led by Charles Parham, and to the Azusa Street Mission in Los Angeles, California, between 1906 and 1910. Neo-Pentecostal churches, which are often not linked to a Pentecostal denomination and which are independent churches, are very closely connected to politics and economics, and followers are encouraged to be active participants in the public sphere. With the growth of urbanization throughout Latin America, Pentecostal churches provide a much needed sense of family and community when individuals leave the rural settings where their families may have lived for generations. This is also the case for Latin American immigrants in the United States. Although it was introduced to Latin America through missionaries from the United States, Pentecostalism quickly took on the flavor of the local culture, cultivating leadership from within communities versus bringing in foreign church leaders. However, not all Pentecostal churches exist as independent entities; some remain connected to Pentecostal denominations in the United States.

The explosion of Pentecostal movements and those influenced by its spiritual worldview are extremely important for understanding contemporary monotheism within global Christianity. For centuries Christian spirituality has emphasized the first two persons of the Trinity, God the Creator and God the Savior (Jesus Christ). However, beginning in the twentieth century we find a turn to the Holy Spirit. What distinguishes contemporary Christianity from previous eras is this emphasis on the Spirit. Today the Holy Spirit is the privileged person in the Trinity in ways it has not been throughout the history of Christianity. This does not mean that the Father and the Son have in any way been forgotten. In the spiritual and ritual life of the growing sectors of the Christian population, one does find a Spirit-centered Christianity that sees God as active in human history and able to communicate directly with believers.

Mary

In spite of the explosion of Pentecostalism across Latin America, Catholicism continues to be the dominant expression of Christianity. This is clearly seen in the prominence of Marian devotions in these communities, particularly found in popular religious practices and popular culture. Popular religious practices are those religious rituals and devotions that are part of the everyday life of believers. In Latin American Catholic communities many of these rituals center around devotion to Mary or the saints. The sacramental worldview of Catholicism claims that objects participate in what they represent. In other words, a classic ritual often depicted in popular culture is a Catholic in a church lighting a candle and saying a prayer in front of a statue or image of Mary, a saint, or

Jesus. To the outsider, this may appear like idolatry, making an offering to a work of art. However for Catholics, the statue or image participates in the life of the holy person it represents. This does not mean that the statue will in some way come to life. However, it does mean that the believer can communicate with the holy person through the statue or painting. This communication is most often a prayer or petition. Devotion to Mary is the most pervasive example of this in Latin America.

Devotion to Our Lady of Guadalupe is the largest and most widespread Marian devotion in Latin America, and her patronage expands well beyond these communities. In 1999 Pope John Paul II named her patroness of the Americas in his apostolic exhortation *Ecclesia in America*. However, the heart of her story and most of her devotees remain within Mexican communities across the globe. For Mexican and Mexican-American women, Guadalupe is a liberating and empowering feminine symbol. For the Mexican people as a whole, she represents their cultural and religious identity beyond affiliation to the Roman Catholic Church. As a people born of the blood of the conquered and the conqueror, Guadalupe represents the birth of a new people, a *mestizo* Mexican people who are a mixture of both indigenous and Spanish cultures. In the bleakest moment in Mexican history, the conquest, Guadalupe appeared to bring a message of hope and love to the Mexican community.

Our Lady of Guadalupe appeared in 1531 on the mountain of Tepeyac to the indigenous man named Juan Diego. Juan Diego, a convert to Christianity, was walking

FIGURE 31 *Sawdust image of Our Lady of Guadalupe, San Lucas Tolimán, Guatemala,* © *Byron Maldonado.*

to mass early on a Saturday morning when he heard some beautiful music and a voice calling him. He walked up the hillside, drawn to the voice. At the top of the hill, he encountered a beautiful lady, radiant with love and compassion. She identified herself as the Mother of God, mother of creation, who had come in response to the cries of those in the Americas who called to her in their suffering. She then ordered Juan Diego to go to the bishop to request that a shrine be built in her honor on the site of her apparition. Juan Diego protested, claiming he was a nothing, unworthy of the bishop's attention or this important message. Guadalupe assured him that he was the one chosen for this task. The bishop, as Juan Diego predicted, does not believe him, and the next day he returns and reports his failure to her. She sends him back to the bishop, who remains unconvinced and demands a sign as proof.

Juan Diego tries to avoid encountering Guadalupe again but she again appears to him. She instructs Juan Diego to go gather roses on the hillside as proof of her apparition. Since this is winter in the desert, these flowers truly are a miracle. Juan Diego gathers the flowers in his cloak and goes to the bishop. The bishops' servants recognize Juan Diego from his earlier visit and attempt to block his entry. However, the smell of the roses convinces them to allow Juan Diego to enter and see the bishop. In order to present the flowers to him, Juan Diego opens his cloak and as the flowers fall to the floor the image of Guadalupe miraculously appears on his cloak. It is said that this is the very image that hangs in her basilica (shrine) outside of Mexico City.

The narrative of Guadalupe's apparition raises various important themes that are fundamental for understanding Latin American Catholic spirituality. In the narrative, she appears to Juan Diego, a self-proclaimed "lowly" indigenous man who sees little worth in himself and who is also devalued by Spanish ecclesial authorities. We must remember that this apparition occurred during the conquest, the bloodiest moment in Mexican history. In the midst of the bloodshed and trauma of an indigenous community that is having its entire universe overturned, we have a story about Mary reaching out to an indigenous man and empowering him to be her voice. Surely, if Guadalupe wanted her shrine built immediately, the most efficient and appropriate means to communicate this would have been to appear before the bishop. He is, after all, the one who has official authority in transmitting the gospel. However, in this story Guadalupe gave Juan Diego her message. It is he, the indigenous man, who brings Mary's message to the bishop. In a moment when the Catholic Church is imposing the forced conversion of thousands of indigenous men, women, and children, we find an indigenous man converting the bishop to Mary's message. He becomes the bearer of the gospel. Guadalupe's apparition to Juan Diego reminds believers that the gospel message often comes from unlikely sources, and that they must never prejudge based on the messenger.

Guadalupe's feast day is December 12. In Roman Catholic parishes throughout the Americas, but especially in areas with large Mexican populations, celebrations begin at dawn. The celebration traditionally begins with the singing of *Mañanitas* ("early morning tunes") in her honor. They are sung outside of the church and are often accompanied by mariachis. The timing is significant for it is in remembrance of her first appearance to Juan Diego at dawn. After the singing, celebrants enter the church and celebrate mass in her honor. A second significant dimension of the celebration is the reenactment of her apparition. Usually after the homily (if reenacted during mass), this retelling of her apparition reveals its significance for the community. Through reenacting her encounters with Juan Diego and the miracles surrounding it, the community affirms her presence among them and her accompaniment of them in their struggles. The personal encounter of Guadalupe with Juan Diego is highlighted. She is not merely a statue or an image that is venerated; through the retelling of her encounters with Juan Diego, the community reaffirm their encounters, and thus their relationship with her. The story remains alive to the community even today; she continues to appear to them through their faith and devotions. These reenactments are also found for example, among Latino/a communities that reenact the crucifixion of Good Friday. In participating in these reenactments believers transcend their contemporary context and bridge to the historical events in the past, connecting it to the present.

A similar Marian expression is Our Lady of Charity, the patron saint of Cuba, and the manner in which her popularity united Catholic beliefs, Afro-Cuban culture, and Yoruba religion. The late 1800s and early 1900s were pivotal for the elaboration of a Cuban national identity. It was during this time period that Cuba gained independence from Spain and Cubans began the struggle to define themselves. Race and religion functioned significantly in this process. Perhaps the clearest demonstration of this is found in the figure of the patroness of Cuba, La Caridad del Cobre (Our Lady of Charity of Cobre). La Caridad del Cobre is a vital symbol of Cuban religious and national identity. She is, even for those without religious beliefs, a symbol of what it means to be Cuban: La Caridad began as a local devotion within a community of slaves in the seventeenth century and grew over the years to become the national patroness of the island.

The earliest account of La Caridad is a 1687 interview with Juan Moreno, a slave in Cobre. He recounted to church leaders that, while he was searching for salt in the Bay of Nipe with the indigenous brothers Rodrigo and Juan de Hoyo, they came across a statue of Mary with the words *Yo soy la Virgen de la Caridad* ("I am the Virgin of Charity") attached to it. The statue was turned over to Spanish authorities, and a shrine was built in her honor. Devotion spread among the slave community in Cobre. Her popularity and prominence grew as Cuban nationalist sentiments spread across the island. During that independence war, Cuban soldiers began to appeal to La Caridad and to wear images of her on their uniforms. A mass was said at her shrine in Cobre to celebrate Cuba's final victory in 1898. On May 10, 1916, she was named patroness of the island, and a new shrine was constructed for her, expanding and insitutionalizing what was originally a local devotion of a slave community in eastern Cuba. Throughout Cuban history, her significance and her very appearance have shifted to meet the needs of the Cuban community, whose devotion to her has grown from a local to the national level.

La Caridad is also a presence within non-Christian Afro-Cuban religions. This is seen in the growing association of La Caridad del Cobre with the *orisha* Oshun. *Orishas* are spirits that are part of the Yoruba pantheon whose devotions arrived in the Americas through the trans-Atlantic slave trade. The Yoruba population was the dominant population on the island and in the nineteenth century and came to influence Cuban culture, religion, and identity as a whole. Slaves would hide or mask their religious rituals and spirits behind Catholic images, prayer, and rituals. Similar to the story of Juan Diego and Guadalupe, La Caridad is discovered by a slave and two indigenous men. She appears before the marginalized, not those in the centers of power of Spanish colonial Catholicism.

The apparition stories and devotions surrounding Mary not only reveal something about the divine, but also something about the nature of humanity. As the ideal disciple, Mary's preferential option for the marginalized and her accompaniment of marginalized communities, as seen in devotion to both La Caridad del Cobre and Our Lady of Guadalupe, reveal a vital dimension of the human condition and the manner in which our relationships with each other mirror our relationship with the divine. In a similar vein, the strong Marian devotions and devotion to saints that we find within Roman Catholicism throughout the Americas is an example of the manner in which the mediators of one's relationship with God become prominent actors in the spiritual life of devotees. Both Mary and the saints mediate one's relationship with the sacred. Catholics pray to the saints and Mary to pray for them. In addition, the stories surrounding Guadalupe and La Caridad and the devotions that center on them demonstrate the manner in which Catholicism has been transformed in the Americas through its encounter with African and indigenous populations.

Islam

British Muslims

With more than a billion Muslims in the world today, extremely complex, markedly contemporary religious conundrums arise. They are often framed in political terms due to the global prevalence of an attitude that religion should be kept private, distant from what is going on in the civic sphere. The notion of monotheism continues to play a significant role in how Muslims act around the world. Sweeping generalizations no longer hold sway because the diversity and differences that have always existed among Muslims are becoming more vibrant, vocal, and visible. The many strands, however, all do develop from that one central notion of God.

Islamic traditions, through the varied paths of Muslims in history, interacted with other believers, the closest of whom were the Jews and Christians, for after all they were categorized alongside Muslims as people of the Book. As a new layer to monotheism, Islam expanded quite rapidly after the death of the prophet Muhammad— as it is often phrased, from Spain right through to China. In this expansion, Islam could be said to have picked up on the ambitions of the apostle Paul, who wrote of a desire to spread his early Christian gospel to Spain. But of course the more obvious and immediate precursor was the Roman Empire, by that time having receded from the Mediterranean and settled for Byzantium in the east—until Sunni Muslims toppled it in the eleventh century. Long before Rome had become Christian, it had invaded Britain, which hundreds of years later would embark on its own expansion project, colonizing lands whose immigrants in recent decades would bring a new era of Islamic history to the UK—the focus and case study of this section. They make for an interesting case study because of the contemporary challenge to that old dichotomy of "Islam vs the West" which is breaking down due to settled migratory identities today.

The lands where Islam reigned supreme, roughly from the eighth to the fourteenth century, aimed to uphold the highest standards of faith in that One God—great ideals were not always perfect results with moments of peace and war. These were difficult situations as Muslims dealt with Jews, Christians, and other religious traditions and religious systems. There were good times and bad. There were times when some Muslim leaders took a more inclusive approach in dealing with Jews and Christians, and there were times when matters were taken in hand. The concept of jihad that some advocated was a personal struggle of submission to God, but it was also interpreted to mean a physical jihad against not only Jews and Christians but also fellow Muslims who followed a different interpretation of Islam—they were not considered true Muslims.

After the death of Muhammad, Muslims had to administer lands according to their understanding of Islam. There was something that could loosely be called an Islamic empire, but in fact the areas involved were all quite different—albeit with the general unity of Islamic faith and practice. Civil wars ensued between those with different understandings of Islam. Centuries-old religious tensions are still, to some extent, a marker of nation-states today—Iran and Iraq are just one such example. Denominations became more defined. The tensions with Jews and Christians remained forever prevalent. Jerusalem is another example of a religiously torn city. It was and continues to be a central point of contention between Jews, Christians, and Muslims. Each group holds tight to its understanding of God, which has led to many wars and bloodshed in the Holy Land. The Christian Crusaders, of course, waged a holy war against Muslims to place the literal cross in its rightful position. Muslims waged a corporeal jihad against Christian Crusaders. Jews established the State of Israel, which recently passed a governmental bill making clear that it was a Jewish state. The Temple Mount, the al-Aqsa Mosque (contested on the same site), and the Church of the Holy Sepulchre (a few blocks away) are the bricks, mortar, and sacred space to which the monotheistic traditions lay claim, with no clear solution or compromise in sight on how Jews, Christians and Muslims can live at peace in the Holy Land. Their proximity in sacred space is yet another illustration of the monotheistic legacy that builds bridges between Jews, Christians, and Muslims yet burns and bloodies them, too.

Where there has been bloodshed, there has also been scientific and creative advancement in Muslim lands, and wonderful pieces of architecture and art have been inspired by the details and interpretations of that one divine text, the Qur'an. Into the Dome of the Rock's awe-inspiring structure are built various calligraphic delights, each line taken from the Qur'an to bear witness to that one true God. Another great feat of Muslim architecture is the Taj Mahal in India, which the Mughal ruler Shah Jehan built in 1648 for his true love, Mumtaz Mahal. Often removed from iconic photos are the two buildings between which it is sandwiched: one of them is a mosque, the other a guest house. The Taj Mahal remains a monument to human love and to divine love. These two types of devotion have also been central to many poems in various languages that Muslims speak throughout the world.

Scientific and philosophical enterprise have also been key to the culture of Muslim lands. The Qur'an has inspired many Muslims to think not only about the ultimate questions of life but how to find answers to them. These philosophical questions also motivated the legal jurists who needed to find a suitable rationale for legislating on matters. Many Islamic traditions concern gaining knowledge, which has also led to translating many texts and traditions outside of the Islamic world into Arabic. Muslims were pioneers in biology, chemistry, physics, and medicine, during what is often referred to as the golden age, roughly between the eighth and fourteenth centuries. Many early handbooks written by Muslims on the science behind life have been hailed in current times as essential, if not pivotal, to the advances that we now see in areas of philosophy, medicine, and the arts.

Monotheistic connections to the UK date back to as early as the eighth century, when Christians from Britain would travel to the Holy Land and interact with Muslims. Muslim presence in Europe only began to grow rapidly in the twentieth century, with every country and region in Europe having its own history. For quite some time, research on Muslims in Britain has more often than not been about Muslims in England, even though the UK comprises four nations: Scotland, England, Northern Ireland, and Wales. The stories of Muslims in these nations differ. In fact, they differ even from city to city. These complexities are important, once again, to challenge any monolithic understanding that we may have of Muslims globally.

In more modern times, roughly around the 1800s, Judaism, Christianity, and Islam had to deal with a rapidly changing world. The Western God-centric world was changing to a world of commerce, capital, and mercantilism. Western civilization began to organize itself on new Enlightenment theories, distinguishing itself with the idea of secularism. God could be set apart from what is on display, in public. The Enlightenment connected ideas of reason and logic to human life because there was a concern that too much superstition and mysterious tradition had crept into notions of God. These new ideas and practices were the basis on which relationships between the three faiths were to be renewed.

Between the seventeenth and eighteenth centuries, powers from mainly Western, white-dominant lands began to take control of Muslim lands. The world was changing and ideas about God were, too. Western powers had decided that to increase their capital growth they needed to conquer other parts of the world. Colonial rule over Muslim lands brought with it a different understanding of culture which was infused with a different understanding of God: the long-held belief that Islam was a heretical monotheistic movement was mixed into this colonial usurpation. Eventually, colonial rule in Muslim lands did come to an end, but it left a lasting legacy. The world became more polarized, and the emergence of a strengthened dichotomy, which exists even today, pitted Islam against the West.

Once colonial rule receded, how would Islamic nations establish themselves? The answer varies, and this is why each Muslim country is very different. Take, for example, just three: Pakistan, Turkey, and Saudi Arabia. Pakistan emerged as an Islamic republic after the British left and divided India in 1947. Pakistan became its own nation-state, a Muslim state that has to uphold all the traditions associated with that One God. The early founders of the state needed to think hard about how they would institutionalize all that they understood of Islamic traditions in order for the society to be Islamic. The understandings differed amongst the founders. Turkey experienced its own tensions between what would be an ideal Islamic state over and against a secular one. Saudi Arabia is an absolute monarchy led by a king who considers himself the Custodian of the Two Holy Mosques which are central to Muslim piety: the place of pilgrimage at the mosque in Mecca and the place of Muhammad's grave at his mosque in Medina. There are long histories and political commentaries written on the intricate details of these states, but what we can conclude is that they all grapple with how to uphold centuries-old Islamic traditions in the contemporary world. It is the same dilemma that gives rise to extreme fundamentalist groups such as ISIS (or its variation names ISIL, IS or Daesh), which also imagines an ideal way of upholding its understanding of "Islamic."

Muslim movements reacted against the West. Modernist reformists such as Maulana Mawdudi of Pakistan, Syed Qutb of Egypt, and Abd al-Wahhab of Saudi Arabia, to name but a few, all have attempted to make sense of upholding Islamic ideals in a postcolonial world, roughly the eighteenth through the twentieth centuries. The work of these men has in a way become understood as itself sacred. Often we think of the sacred as something "out of this world," or beyond the control of human beings, yet when we begin to understand the Islamic traditions we begin to appreciate how its development is actually quite human—most often resting in the hands of powerful men. This human influence is often not given attention in order to strengthen the tradition. This is why Islamic traditions practiced in any given Arab country will differ from another's—and then to compare that culture with, say, Indonesia or Pakistan would reveal even more differences.

The free movement of people within the British Commonwealth came to an abrupt halt through the Commonwealth Immigrants Act of 1962. This was delivered through Parliament because of growing concerns across political parties that the nation would become "colored." Much has been debated on this issue, and on the reasons for the immigration, which were largely economic: the many "Asians" that arrived came with the intention of earning their "bag of gold" and returning home. The religious and cultural distinctions that we apply to British Asians today were not so distinct back then. Those who arrived in the UK in the 1960s understood themselves as Asians whether they were from East or West Pakistan, India, or Bangladesh. Their common economic objective united them. It is important to think carefully about the mindset that many of these early Muslims in Britain had. They were in an alien country, one that they saw, in the most general of terms, as a Christian land. This mindset worked for a while until it became clearer that the UK would be home not just for the first generation but for their children.

The first immigrants from Muslim lands thought carefully about making Britain their home. Mosques began to grow around the country. Initially Muslims would pray in makeshift mosques: houses and even billiard halls. By 1990 there were 452 registered mosques in the UK, the majority of which were Sunni. Mosques were established upon the understanding of the different postcolonial Islamic movements from "back home." Houses of worship were to be the foundation of Muslim communities in Britain. As the children began to grow up, the first generation needed to make sure that the cultural values and understanding of Islam were taught. Mosques were not just places of worship but places of education. Young Muslims would be sent there to read the Qur'an after their "secular" school days ended. Many mosques in UK cities would also hold weekend schools to teach young Muslims about Islam. Some of these schools would also teach Urdu, one of the main languages of Pakistan. Sunni Muslims continue to be given the most coverage in discussions on British Muslims. Other institutions also began to emerge, such as university Islamic societies and an umbrella group that brought together Islamic societies from across the country—the Federation of Student Islamic Societies (FOSIS). Britain was becoming home to a new generation of Muslims.

The first generation also began participating in British politics, seeing the election of a number of Muslim local councilors and even Members of Parliament. The identity "British Muslim" started to be used more often. While most minority identities were becoming more comfortable in the UK, some were not, leading to the emergence of organizations that harbored suspicion of their host country and wanted to reignite tensions from the colonial past. Certain organizations wanted Muslims in Britain to distance themselves from integrating too much. Extremist groups emerged that not only taught a brand of Islam that burned bridges but advocated for corporeal jihad. These organizations were and continue to be a minority in the UK, but their presence highlights the identity crisis that British Muslims confront while living out their faith.

The internal diversity of Muslim origins in British Muslim identities is often not interrogated. Muslims from other parts of the world began to increase in the UK, but those from Pakistan certainly made up the largest percentage of Muslims in Britain. The Islam of Pakistan was the Islam that the new immigrants brought with them to the UK. The rich did not leave Pakistan, as they had no reason to. Pakistani society then and now is structured by class. Landowners and dishwashers in Pakistan—these occupations did not go away when Pakistanis arrived in the UK. They continue to hold place in conversations between Pakistanis and to some extent are used as identifiers of families in the communities. Class figures in every society—the identifiers and categories—are linked to professions and occupations. The political manifestations of Islam that emerged during the establishment of the Islamic republic were the types of Islamic understandings that Pakistanis brought to the UK. Let us not forget that these emerged in a postcolonial setting, in response to British rule. If the immigration of Muslims to the UK had been temporary, this would have neatly allowed binaries such as "Islam and the West" not only to be strengthened but to be lived out. But such notions have been dramatically complicated by the new immigrants setting up home in the West and subsequently seeing their children identifying as both British and Muslim.

The devastating attack on New York City's Twin Towers and the Pentagon on September 11, 2001, is seen by some as a turning point for Muslims. The tragedy meant that the British Muslim as an identity category was challenged as never before. It has become a defining moment that led to a renewed interest in Islam and Muslims, especially in the Western world. This put added pressure on the majority of British Muslims, who needed to make clear that they were on the side of bridge builders. This was no easy task. The Islam-versus-the-West divide was once again revitalized, even though whole cohorts of Muslims were now born and bred in the UK.

"Islamophobia" is a term often meant to designate the fear and hatred of Islam and Muslims, which has led to stereotypes, prejudices, and hate crimes. Some scholars have also associated Islamophobia with racism and xenophobia. One thing is certain: Islamophobia is on the rise in the Western world. There is a deep fear that is often associated with the idea that "Islam is coming" or that people should be watchful of "creeping Shari'a." The roots of these fears can be traced back to our monotheistic heritage, where Islam added a new layer to understandings of One God. The binary between Islam and the West is now more contested than ever before, with many Muslims in diaspora, such as British Muslims, now identifying as both Muslim and Western. This has led some who wish to preserve the West as solely Judeo-Christian to strengthen the idea that Muslims should be shunned and not welcomed. The issue is highly complex because certain situations have led to Muslims reacting in hateful ways too.

Internal Muslim troubles with freedom of religion or expression and pluralism came into the spotlight with Salman Rushdie's book *The Satanic Verses*. Its publication in 1988 led to mass protests by some Muslims, who deemed it blasphemy. Ayatollah Khomeini, the spiritual leader of Iran, issued a decree against Rushdie, calling for the death penalty. And then in 2010 the US animated television program *South Park* sparked controversy when it appeared to identify an image of Muhammad, which was seen by Muslims as mocking him. Out of respect, Muslims generally do not create images of the prophet, but there are in fact images of him in Islamic societies. It was not so much the likeness of the prophet that led Muslims to anger but the mocking and degrading way that it was being done that sparked a reaction. This was also the case with the Danish newspaper *Jyallands-Posten*, which created a series of cartoons depicting Muhammad in 2005. Whether these images should be read as calls for freedom of speech and expression or as Islamophobic is a complicated question, highlighting some of the tensions that arise in understanding Muslim presence in the world today.

It is not just Christians who have been accused of blasphemy: in Pakistan Muslims themselves have found themselves so charged. In 2011, Salman Taseer, the governor of Punjab province in Pakistan, was assassinated by his bodyguard, who disagreed with his opposition to Pakistan's blasphemy laws. The laws had in certain circumstances been used against Pakistanis who were accused of blasphemy. In 2017, Mashal Khan, a university student, was killed by an angry mob that accused him of posting blasphemous content online. The law has spurred heated debate about what counts as blasphemy, as some argue that merely questioning certain principles is interpreted as blasphemy. In the same year, the US embassy held a pride event that was attended by many LGBT Pakistanis. This led to protests by some factions of the Pakistani community, who described it as "cultural terrorism."

Muslims are having to deal with differences in the contemporary world largely due to the challenge on authority structures that were accepted in the past. The world of social media has seen an outburst of many different Muslim voices. No one voice now speaks for Islam. The world of Twitter, Instagram, and Snapchat has allowed outsiders to see the inner diversity in which Muslims live. The availability of Islamic studies courses being taught in Western universities has strengthened Muslims' own ability to challenge and critique Islam from within. There was a huge increase in Western universities appointing staff to teach Islam after the events of September 11, 2001, as the tragic events sparked renewed interest in questions relating to Islam. In the past, Islam had been largely taught and researched through Arabic and historical studies. Universities are now teaching Islam and Muslim culture through a variety of disciplines, and Muslims are taking these courses. The ethos of teaching religion in Western academic universities is often challenging for those Muslims who are unsure what to make of critical inquiry. Now more than ever before we see Islam being taught by many Muslims who have been born and raised in the West. Studying Islam at what are perceived to be secular Western institutions is often countered by some Western Muslims opting to study at more traditional Islamic seminaries in Muslim countries. Those who graduate from these seminary-type institutions are given authority in local Muslim communities. Whereas men who study at either of the institutions could well be recognized and accepted even as imams of local mosques, the options for Muslim women will be different.

As mentioned earlier, Islam is often credited with being the fastest-growing religion in the world. Those who convert to Islam give many different reasons for their decision. The religious reason would be that they have found Islam to be the truth. For some, it is most convenient to convert to Islam when marrying a Muslim. For others, a visit to a Muslim country may have imparted an appreciation for Muslim life and society. A number of television documentaries have covered the conversion of white Britons to Islam. British Muslim converts can be isolated from religious spaces in the UK, which are often defined by the first generations of Pakistani Muslims. We know that religion does not develop in a vacuum. The rise in Western converts to Islam is often presented as quite alarming for some as it once again blurs the edges of the divide between Islam and the West.

Among the new generation of British Muslims there has been a tendency to organize local and national events where converts to Islam will give public lectures. Listening to these converts, especially if they are white, holds wide appeal. In white Britain, white converts to Islam have helped define a new generation of British Muslims, challenging the racialization of Islam as it connects to Islamophobia. White

Muslim converts also still carry their white privilege and can move between different sections of society in ways that the children of immigrants cannot.

Islam has been appealing to marginalized populations for several reasons. Malcolm X (1925–1965), an American convert to Islam, wrote about the equality and unity that he found when he went to Mecca for the pilgrimage. Islamic traditions of equality among all are attractive to those who have been marginalized within society. It was the prophet Muhammad who said in his final sermon that all Muslims are equal before God. The effect of a role model like Malcolm X has the potential to challenge white privilege in Muslim communities, but race and our valuation of it complicates that possibility. The colonized mindset may be difficult to erase for a new generation of British Muslims who to a certain extent live the legacy of white British colonial rule in the Indian subcontinent. In the past and even present, many community events held up and down the UK invite white converts to Islam: their outsize appeal continues, and it complicates Muslims' connection to race.

The Shari'a is vitally important for British Muslims, indeed for Muslims globally. Shari'a courts have been established in the UK, with some woman leaders too, where they administer issues relating to marriage and divorce. There have been considerable discussions and debate surrounding this, as Muslims in the West try to balance their lives between the secular laws of the land and the divine laws to which they wish to remain faithful. Even though historical Islamic law prohibits certain actions such as drinking, usury, and gambling, many Muslims do participate in them. Muslim countries do not implement the historical Islamic legal codes fully but uphold general ethical principles that resemble European models of law.

Could the new generation of Muslims born in the UK, with their variety of ethnic roots, form a distinct, new identity? The first generation of Muslims that came from diverse lands were clear on their identity. They tried to instill the same understandings of God and living that they had lived "back home." For a very long time, and even to this day to some extent, mosques up and down the country have been run by the first generation. But change is happening. The second generation was stuck between the Islam that their parents were upholding and the Britain that they were living in, which was a Britain presenting itself on the basis of separation of church and state—a secular society, some may say, but with quite a defined Protestant Christian rhythm.

A new British Islam is now emerging. The old cultural divide with roots in that monotheistic tension is now being challenged as Jews, Christians, and Muslims are living side by side. Serious questions about immigration, integration, and assimilation are often presented as issues separate from religion. This is clearly not the case. It is the legacy of historical monotheistic tensions that continue to surface in everyday life in Europe and in what we now understand as the Western world. Identities are constructed through interactions with the other, and so it is not surprising that local customs have impacted second and subsequent generations of Muslim immigrants to Britain. This fusion that cannot be labeled even as "British Islam" is highly localized and complicated. The identity formation of a Scottish Muslim growing up in Inverness will be different from that of one growing up in the East End of London. It is these realities—not just in Britain but throughout Europe—that are bridging the cultural divide between Islam and the West and reconfiguring and highlighting the legacy of monotheism in the twenty-first century.

Islam developed as a final layer to the biblical monotheistic traditions, presenting itself as complementing and bridging Judaism and Christianity, yet it is clearly distinctive. This scriptural and monotheistic tension has played a role in Muslims' interactions with Jews and Christians for centuries. Theological tensions have made for divisions between the three monotheistic faiths. It is the idea of monotheism that brings Muslims closer to Jews and Christians, but the fact that Islam is considered the ultimate truth bears potential for complicated tensions. This should come as no surprise. There has to be an element of conviction in faith. Every Jew, Christian, and Muslim believes that their tradition is the truth—that each has a separate and unique path to the same One God. The differences between the three traditions have also played a role in strengthening each one in relation to the other. If we begin to interrogate certain concepts within Islam, we quite often arrive at quite a simple conclusion: Islam has reacted to what the Jews or Christians were doing. The acts and actions may differ, but that supreme impetus, drive, or jihad toward "truth" comes from the same conviction that Jews and Christians hold true—that there is one true God. And this tension is more intrafaith than interfaith. The one billion or so Muslims are all very different and do react against each other. If those billion or so Muslims are united in their conviction that Islam is the true path to God as opposed to that of Jews and Christians, you can be sure that Islam's internal diversity and reactions are even more intense. It is not uncommon to observe in history or even today one Muslim calling another a non-Muslim because of certain beliefs even though both embrace God.

Whenever we explore contemporary conundrums facing Islam, it is important to bear this foundational tension in mind. We live at a time when the majority of us yearn to strengthen bridges. There is no bigger dilemma than how we can all thrive amid deep pluralism. Although we may think that there is a separation of religion from the secular, the reality is that this is not the case. Even in countries that claim to separate church and state, we still see that there are currents and rhythms of particular religious traditions built into civic culture. Representing a minority faith community in a wider society whose religious commitments are naturalized, British Muslims illustrate modern tensions in identity and politics even where all the major players are monotheistic.

Afterthought: Monotheism Today

The contemporary world has created new contexts for the religions of the monotheistic heritage. Novel and in some ways unprecedented political, social, and cultural circumstances are creating conditions for religious innovation and adaptation.

In the State of Israel, Judaism is being transformed from a religion of exile and preservation into a key part of a modern, national, primarily secular culture. This is an unprecedented shift. For its entire history since 70 CE, Judaism's minority status has kept it and its practitioners separate from the mainstream cultures of the nations in which Jews lived. Diaspora religions tend to be exercises in community maintenance, work to preserve a collective identity, and avoid assimilation. As the State of Israel continues to develop a Jewish national culture, that diaspora dynamic will change. As contemporary studies indicate, Israeli Jews practice a kind of "relaxed" Judaism because Judaism is native to their culture.

The new national culture encounters three basic challenges, all of which have religious dimensions. First, it must integrate the adaptive national cultures—*Ashkenazi* and *Mizrahi*—into a new national culture. Second, it must find ways to enable traditional forms of Judaism to adjust as well to an increasingly diverse global Jewish population and different forms of Judaic religious practice and expression. Third, it will have to strengthen its already established tradition of religious and ethnic diversity and tolerance. The ongoing Israeli-Palestinian conflict both constrains these developments and displays their urgency.

Christianity in Latin America illustrates how native cultures and populations both adapt to colonialism and force colonialist cultures to adapt to them. Roman Catholicism is not native to Latin America or the Caribbean. It was imposed on the region by force. The explosion of Christianity in Latin America shows how native populations adapted a core Christian teaching to native conditions. Liberation Theology and Evangelical and Pentecostal Christianities transformed Christianity into a force for the social and spiritual liberation of the native poor and underprivileged, and of women. They use native figures to symbolize core Christian teachings and emphasize the transformative power of religious experience and energy to ignite social change.

As colonial control of Muslim populations ended, Islam created distinct Islamic national cultures—perhaps somewhat in the same way that Israel is doing now. Saudi Arabia, Turkey, and Pakistan are Islamic nations, but not all in the same way. There are native variations. In Britain, on the other hand, Islam is a religion of exiles, adapting to a native culture that is different from, and in some ways hostile to, it. As was the case with Judaism historically, the first generation of Muslims in Britain worked to preserve the past and preserve the community. The second generation, however, to whom British culture is largely native, is engaging in a new adaptation that may see shifts in religious behavior and identity.

Taken together, these three examples concretely illustrate that the structure of the monotheistic heritage—creation, covenant, commandment, community—contains the components that have allowed and continue to enable its traditions to adapt to new environments and circumstances.

Study Questions: Case Studies

"To understand Judaism, one need only look to Israel." Discuss.

"To understand Christianity, one need only look to Latin America." Discuss.

"To understand Islam, one need only look to the UK." Discuss.

Is it possible to separate the theology of each tradition from the politics of the time?

"In the contemporary world, God is dead—or dying." Discuss.

How have twentieth-century colonialisms affected Judaism, Christianity, and Islam?

Discuss some of the contemporary tensions in understanding the role of religion in secular states.

Epilogue

Is there something exceptional about monotheism that it has persisted for so long? The ancient and challenging idea of One God has played an essential part in civilizations across the globe and continues to influence contemporary nations and societies. Much to the disappointment of atheists and secularists, God is not dead. Monotheism has taken diverse shapes throughout history. The focus of this book has been on the legacy of monotheism in Judaism, Christianity, and Islam.

The chapters in this book have attempted to describe how a shared religious structure undergirds and helps to frame both the interconnections and disconnections among the three faiths. The disagreements among these monotheistic traditions are not random. Rather, they focus in large measure on what we might think of as a shared family heritage of Scripture, creation, covenant, cult, commandment, peoplehood, and redemption. The arguments among the three were and are often intense because—as is frequently the case in families—the stakes are high. Since each religion offers a competing claim to and about God, tensions among them are inevitable. At the same time, the shared biblical legacy created and creates possibilities of mutual understanding. Judaism, Christianity, and Islam have worked with and against each other. They have both built and destroyed bridges to each other. But their differences presuppose an underlying similarity that is not always obvious to believers.

A primary component of the shared monotheistic legacy is the primary of Scripture. At the heart of the sacred Scriptures of Judaism, Christianity, and Islam is the One God. The Scriptures recount each community's foundational experience of the One God—at Sinai, in Jesus' resurrection, in the revelation of the Qur'an—that has grounded and guided their discrete developments. But however these traditions may differ in their understanding of God's nature, God remains at the center.

The Scriptures also provide the religions' initial answers to three fundamental human questions: Where did I come from? What am I doing here? Where will I end up? The answer in part is in the story of creation. The story of Adam and Eve may seem preposterous in an age of science and evolution, but it frames the three religions' understandings of human nature. It is not a simple story, and its interpretation highlights issues of gender and sexuality in our own day. The narratives in the Hebrew Bible, the New Testament and the Qur'an are not dissimilar to one another. They are stories of value. They attempt to show how good overcomes evil and how God plays a role in that conflict. They relate the way individuals fought against social injustice to create a better society. Through these varied sacred Scriptures right and wrong actions become clearer for believers. Where did we learn that telling a lie is a bad thing? Or that killing someone is bad? Why do we give charity to the poor? For Jews, Christians, and Muslims, the continual reading and interpreting of Scriptures keeps God at the center of understanding and dealing with social issues. This reading of Scripture throughout the centuries becomes framed by authority, tradition, culture, and geography.

As communities of the One God, Judaism, Christianity and Islam have engaged with and disengaged from each other over time in history. The edges were blurred among the three faiths. These differences led to what we understand in general terms as Judaism, Christianity, and Islam.

As much as these three traditions share an opposition to polytheism and idolatry and cannot accept atheism, the chapters above show that the legacy of monotheism is not neat. God's oneness has yielded not uniformity but diversity and difference. Among the traditions, difference becomes intense particularly—as we learn from the Crusades and the contemporary Middle East—when politics and territory are involved. As Madeleine Albright said at a plenary panel of the American Academy for Religion a few years back, "If the issue were about real estate, it would have been resolved years ago." What we might call monotheism's "messiness" appears not only between but also within the religions. From Orthodox to Reform, from Shi'a to Sunni, from Catholic to Protestant, variants of the monotheistic structure have emerged, and the religions have to work to understand themselves as well as one another.

The diversity within each religion is geographical as well as theological. Judaism, for instance, is in some ways lived differently in the United States, Scotland, and Israel. Islam in Britain is not quite the same as Islam in Pakistan. While Christianity continues to grow and thrive in Latin American and Africa, in Europe and in the United States we are seeing increasing departures from churches. For younger generations, issues with Christianity's stance on gay marriage, abortion, and women are often cited, as well as an overall distrust of religious institutions. As this book has argued, however, there is not one Christian view on these topics and one finds substantial diversity within all three religions on social issues.

Globalization challenges conventional understandings of the three religions. Social media now offers broad platforms for people to speak for and about their faith. Who speaks for each religion is less clear than it once was, as a multitude of voices and viewpoints are accessible globally. Social media also reveals the comprehensiveness of how monotheism impacts popular culture as a whole, impacting food, fashion, art, and music. These new conditions should warn us not to generalize about all Jews, all Christians, or all Muslims.

Because the agreements and disagreements among Judaism, Christianity and Islam are about truths rather than facts, they are likely to endure. Interfaith initiatives that aim to counter misunderstanding, violence, and bloodshed continue to emerge, locally, regionally, and globally. The religions themselves will have to decide how they will honor God's highest expectations for each of them and live at peace with each other. Perhaps the monotheistic religious structure outlined in this book can contribute to that effort.

Timeline

1521	*Diet of Worms* condemns Luther
1545–1563	Council of Trent – Roman Catholic Reformation
1567	*Shulkhan Arukh* (code of *halakhah*)
1689–1740	*Baal Shem Tov*, Founder of Hasidism
1730–1760	"Great Awakening" revival movement among Protestants in the United States
1818	First Reform Jewish congregation (Hamburg, Germany)
1870–1871	Vatican I Council (Roman Catholic Church)
1876	Orthodox Judaism formally established in Frankfurt am Main (Germany)
1887	William Henry Quilliam (known as Abdullah Quilliam) established the first UK mosque in Liverpool
	Muhammad Abdul Kareem (CIE & CVO) of India appointed as "Munshi" (Clerk) to Queen Victoria
1894–1899	Dreyfus Affair
1906	Azusa Street Revival, birth of Pentecostalism
1923	Republic of Turkey established
1932	Kingdom of Saudi Arabia established
1933–1945	Nazi Holocaust
1947	State of Pakistan established
	Dead Sea Scrolls discovered; official excavations of Qumran site begin in the 1950s
1948	State of Israel established
	World Council of Churches founded
1962–1965	Vatican II Council (Roman Catholic Church)
1967	Six Day war between Arabs and Israelis; Israel captures Jerusalem
1972	Sally Priesand ordained by Reform Judaism as first US female rabbi
1973	Yom Kippur War
1979	Egypt–Israel peace treaty
1988	Benazir Bhutto first elected Prime Minister of Bangladesh
1991	Khaleda Zia first elected as Prime Minister of Bangladesh
1993	Tansu Ciller elected as Prime Minister of Turkey
1998	The Right Hon. Baron Waheed Alli, the first openly gay Muslim, is elected to the UK House of Lords
1999	Signing of the Joint Declaration on Justification by the Lutheran and Roman Catholic Churches
	The national organization Imaan UK is established to offer LGBT Muslim support
2001	Attacks on Twin Towers in New York and in Washington, DC
	Megawati Sukarnoputri elected President of Indonesia
2005	Amina Wadud leads mixed-gender Muslim prayer
2012	Inclusive Mosque Initiative (IMI) funded for gender, sexuality, and sectarian inclusive worship

	The Scottish Islamic tartan is lodged at the Scottish Register of Tartans
2013	Election of Pope Francis, the first Latin American Pope
2016	Sadiq Aman Khan is elected Mayor of London

References and Suggested Readings

Introduction

Bellah, Robert N., *Religion in Human Evolution: From the Paleolithic to the Axial Age* (The Belknap Press of Harvard University Press, 2011)

Rappaport, Roy A., *Ritual and Religion in the Making of Humanity* (Cambridge University Press, 1999)

Sosis, Richard, "Religions as complex adaptive systems," in N. Clements, ed., *Mental Religion: The Brain, Cognition, and Culture,* Macmillan Interdisciplinary Handbooks on Religion (Macmillan, 2016), pp. 219–236

Judaism

American Jewish Yearbook (Springer, 2020)

Antler, Joyce, *Jewish Radical Feminism: Voices from the Women's Liberation Movement* (NYU Press, 2018)

Aran, Gideon and Hassner, Ron E., "Religious Violence in Judaism: Past and Present," *Terrorism and Political Violence* (2013) 25:3, 355–405. DOI: 10.1080/09546553.2012.667738

Baskin, Judith, ed., *The Cambridge Dictionary of Judaism and Jewish Culture* (Cambridge University Press, 2012)

Baskin, Judith, and Kenneth R. Seeskin, eds., *The Cambridge Guide to Jewish History, Religion, and Culture* (Cambridge University Press, 2010)

Batnitzky, Leora, *How Judaism Became a Religion: An Introduction to Modern Jewish Thought* (Princeton University Press, 2013)

Bellah, Robert N., *Religion in Human Evolution: From the Paleolithic to the Axial Age* (The Belknap Press of Harvard University Press, 2011)

Berman, Saul, *Jewish Environmental Values: The Dynamic Tension Between Nature and Human Needs.* https://www.schechter. edu/a-responsum-regarding-the-environment-and-air-pollution/

Biale, David, *Cultures of the Jews: A New History* (Penguin Random House, 2002)

———, David Assaf, Benjamin Brown, Uriel Gellman, Samuel Heilman, Moshe Rosman, Gadi Sagiv, and Marcin Wodziński. *Hasidism: A New History* (Princeton University Press, 2017)

Brenner, Michael, *A Short History of the Jews* (Princeton University Press, 2010)

———, *In Search of Israel: The History of an Idea* (Princeton University Press, 2019)

Carr, David M., "The Rise of Torah," in Knoppers, Gary N. and Levinson, Bernard M., eds. *The Pentateuch as Torah: New Models for Understanding its Promulgation and Acceptance* (Eisenbraus, 2007), pp. 39–56

Collins, John, *The Invention of Judaism: Torah and Jewish Identity from Deuteronomy to Paul* (University of California Press, 2017)

Cohen, Shaye J. D., *Why Aren't Jewish Women Circumcised? Gender & Covenant in Judaism* (University of California Press, 2005)

Dan, Joseph, *Kabbalah: A Very Short Introduction* (Oxford University Press, 2005)

Dershowitz, Idan, "Revealing Nakedness and Concealing Homosexual Intercourse: Legal and Lexical Evolution in Leviticus 18," *Hebrew Bible and Ancient Israel* (HeBAI), (2017) 6, 4, pp. 510–526

Dorff, Eliot and Jonathan K. Crane, eds., *The Oxford Handbook of Jewish Ethics and Morality* (Oxford University Press, 2013)

Eisen, Robert, *The Peace and Violence of Judaism: From the Bible to Modern Judaism* (Oxford University Press, 2011)

Fonrobert, Elisheva, and Martin S. Jaffee, eds., *The Cambridge Companion to the Talmud and Rabbinic Literature* (Cambridge University Press, 2007)

Fonrobert, Charlotte Elisheva, "Gender Identity in Halakhic Discourse," *Jewish Women: A Comprehensive Historical Encyclopedia.* 1 March 2009. Jewish Women's Archive.

Geller, Stephen, *Sacred Enigmas: Literary Religion in the Hebrew Bible* (Routledge, 1996)

Glinert, Lewis, *The Story of Hebrew* (Princeton University Press, 2017)

Goldscheider, Calvin, *Israeli Society in the Twenty-First Century: Immigration, Inequality, and Religious Conflict* (University Press of New England, 2015)

Goldstein, Elyse, ed., *New Jewish Feminism Probing the Past, Forging the Future* (Jewish Lights Publishing, 2008)

Golinkin, David, "The Basic Principles of Jewish Business Ethics," https://www.schechter.edu/the-basic-principles-of-jewish-business-ethics/

Goodblatt, David, "Ancient Jewish Identity," https://www.ancientjewreview.com/articles/2018/10/240ancient-jewish-identity

Goodman, Martin, *A History of Judaism* (Princeton University Press, 2018)

Green, William Scott, "A 'Humanly Relevant' Cosmos: What We Study When We Study Religion," in Jacob Neusner, ed., *Introduction to World Religions* (Abingdon Press, 2010), pp. vii-xxiii

———, "Romancing the Tome: Rabbinic Hermeneutics and the Theory of Literature," *Semeia* 40 (1987): 147–68

———, "Levitical Religion," in J. Neusner, W.S. Green, A.J Avery-Peck, eds., *Judaism from Moses to Muhammad: Turning Points and Focal Points* (E.J. Brill, 2005), pp. 3–18

———, "Judaism Evolving: An Experimental Preliminary Translation," in A. J. Avery-Peck. B. Chilton, W. S. Green, G. G. Porton, eds., *A Legacy of Learning: Essays in Honor of Jacob Neusner* (Brill, 2014), pp. 110–131

Gross, Aaron S., Meyers, Jody, Rosenblum, Jordan D., eds., *Feasting and Fasting: The History and Ethics of Jewish Food* (New York University Press, 2019)

Hahn Tapper, Aaron J., *Judaisms: A Twenty-First-Century Introduction to Jews and Jewish Identities* (University of California Press, 2016)

Hazony, David, "The Man Who Saved God from the Holocaust," *Shofar*, 31:4 (Summer 2013), pp. 54–73

Hodge, Caroline Johnson, *If Sons Then Heirs: A Study of Kinship and Ethnicity in the Letters of Paul* (Oxford University Press, 2007)

Horwitz, Daniel M., *A Kabbalah and Jewish Mysticism Reader* (Jewish Publication Society, University of Nebraska Press, 2016)

Kadari, Tamar, "Eve: Midrash and Aggadah," *Jewish Women: A Comprehensive Historical Encyclopedia.* 20 March 2009. Jewish Women's Archive.

Kaplan, Nathan Lee, *Management Ethics and Talmudic Dialectics: Navigating Corporate Dilemmas with the Indivisible Hand* (Springer VS, 2013)

Katz, Steven T., Shlomo Biderman, Gershon Greenberg, eds., *Wrestling with God: Jewish Theological Responses During and After the Holocaust* (Oxford University Press, 2007)

Kraemer, David C., *Jewish Eating and Identity Through the Ages* (Routledge, 2007)

———, *A History of the Talmud* (Cambridge University Press, 2019)

Kugel, James, *The Great Shift: Encountering God in Biblical Times* (Houghton Mifflin Harcourt, 2017)

Levine, Lee I., *The Ancient Synagogue* (Yale University Press, 2005)

Lim, Timothy H., *The Formation of the Jewish Canon* (Yale Reference Library, 2013)

Lipstadt, Deborah, *Antisemitism: Here and Now* (Schocken Books, 2019)

Magid, Shaul, *American Post-Judaism: Identity and Renewal in a Postethnic Society* (Indiana University Press, 2013)

Matt, Daniel C., *The Essential Kabbalah* (HarperCollins, 1996)

Meyers, Carol, *Rediscovering Eve: Ancient Israelite Women in Context* (Oxford University Press, 2013)

Mnookin, Robert H., *The Jewish American Paradox: Embracing Choice in a Changing World* (Public Affairs, 2018)

Morin, Richard, et al., eds., *The Religious Typology: A new way to categorize Americans by religion* (Pew Research Center, 2018)

Neusner, Jacob, *Invitation to the Talmud: A Teaching Book* (HarperCollins, 1984)

———, *Judaism: The Evidence of the Mishnah* (University of Chicago Press, 1981)

——— and Alan Avery-Peck, eds., *The Routledge Dictionary of Judaism* (Routledge, 2004)

———, Bruce D. Chilton and R. E. Tully, eds., *Just War in Religion and Politics* (University Press of America, 2013)

Nishma Research, *The Nishma Research Profile of American Modern Orthodox Jews* (Nishma Research, September 28, 2017), available at nishmaresearch.com

Parfitt, Tudor and Natanel Fisher, eds., *Becoming Jewish: New Jews and Emerging Communities in a Globalized World* (Cambridge Scholars Publishing, 2016)

Pew Research Center, "A Portrait of Jewish Americans" (October 1, 2013), http://pewrsr.ch/16IN5U4

———, "The Future of World Religions: Population Growth Projections, 2010–2050#x201D; (April 2, 2015)

———, "Israel's Religiously Divided Society" (March 8, 2016)

———, "The Changing Global Religious Landscape" (April 5, 2017)

Plaskow, Judith, *Standing Again at Sinai* (HarperCollins, 1990)

Raphael, Melissa, *The Female Face of God: A Jewish Feminist Theology of the Holocaust* (Routledge, 2003)

Rosner, Shmuel, "Jewsraelis: A Cultural Revolution," *Jewish Journal*, December 19, 2018

——— and Fuchs, Camil, *Israeli Judaism: Portrait of a Cultural Revolution* (The Jewish People Policy Institute, 2019)

Rubinstein, Richard, *After Auschwitz: Radical Theology and Contemporary Judaism* (Bobbs-Merrill, 1966)

Schmid, Konrad, "Who Wrote the Torah? Textual, Historical, Sociological, and Ideological Cornerstones of the Formation of the Pentateuch," https://www.ias.edu/ideas/2018/schmid-torah

Silverstein, Adam J. and Guy. G. Stroumsa, *The Oxford Handbook of the Abrahamic Religions* (Oxford University Press, 2015)

Sommer, Benjamin D., *Revelation and Authority: Sinai in Jewish Scripture and Tradition* (Yale University Press, 2015)

———, ed., *Jewish Concepts of Scripture: A Comparative Introduction* (NYU Press, 2012)

Stern, David, *The Jewish Bible: A Material History* (University of Washington Press, 2017)

Tirosh-Samuelson, H., "Nature in the Sources of Judaism," *Daedalus*, 130(4), 99–124 (2001)

———, ed., *Judaism and Ecology* (Harvard University Press, 2002)

Walzer, Michael, "The Ethics of Warfare in the Jewish Tradition," *Philosophia* (2012) 40:633–641

Watts, James, *Understanding the Pentateuch as Scripture* (Wiley Blackwell, 2017)

Weitzman, Steven, *The Origin of the Jews: The Quest for Roots in a Rootless Age* (Princeton University Press, 2017)

Wertheimer, Jack, *The New American Judaism: How Jews Practice Their Religion Today* (Princeton University Press, 2018)

Zohar, Zion, ed., *Sephardic and Mizrahi Jewry: From the Golden Age of Spain to Modern Times* (New York University Press, 2005)

Websites

https://aish.com/
https://bcc-la.org
https://www.chabad.org
https://cbst.org
http://www.chai-online.org/en/home/e_index.htm
http://www.eshelonline.org
http://www.exteriores.gob.es/Consulados/LOSANGELES/en/ServiciosConsulares/CSLA/Paginas/CSLA%20(English)/Nationality-for-Sephardic-Jews.aspx
https://www.facebook.com/jewcology/
https://www.greenfaith.org
https://hazon.org
http://hiddush.org/subchannel-18-0-Same_Sex_Marriage.aspx
http://ippi.org.il/new/en/#.XsucFC2ZOu4
http://kenissa.org
https://jewcology.org/
https://www.jewishinitiativeforanimals.org/
https://www.jewishfarmschool.org/
https://www.jewishvirtuallibrary.org/
https://jewishweek.timesofisrael.com/marking-the-fourth-decade-of -womens-tefilla-at-the-kotel/
http://jppi.org.il/new/en/article/aa2016/part3/orthodox-jews-in-the-united-states
https://jwa.org/encyclopedia/article/eve-midrash-and-aggadah
https://jwa.org/encyclopedia/article/gender-identity-in-halakhic-discourse
https://masorti.org/vision-statement-israel-jewish-democratic/
https://www.mayimhayim.org
https://www.myjewishlearning.com/
https://onetable.org
https://ots.org.il/program/susi-bradfield-wihl/
https://www.sefaria.org/
https://svara.org
http://www.shamayimvaretz.org/
https://urbanadamah.org/
https://urj.org/what-we-believe/resolutions/civil-marriage-gay-and-lesbian-jewish-couples
www.womenofthewall.org.il
http://www.yeshivatmaharat.org
http://www.yoatzot.org/yoatzot-halacha-intro

Christianity

Allen, P., *The Concept of Woman*, Vol. 1, *The Aristotelian Revolution, 750 B.C. – A.D. 1250* (William B. Eerdmans, 1985)

———, *The Concept of Woman*, Vol. 2, *The Early Humanist Reformation, 1250–1500* (William B. Eerdmans, 2002)

Anderson, Allan, *An Introduction to Pentecostalism: Global Charismatic Christianity* (Cambridge University Press, 2014)

Armstrong, K., *A History of God: The 4,000 Year Quest of Christianity, Judaism, and Islam* (Ballantine Books, 2011)

Boff, L., *Trinity and Society* (Orbis Books, 1998)

——— and C. Boff, *Introducing Liberation Theology* (Orbis Books, 1987)

Bowker, J., *God: A Very Short Introduction* (Oxford University Press, 2014)

Brown, P., *The Body and Society: Men, Women, and Sexual Renunciation in Early Christianity* (Columbia University Press, 1988)

Copeland, M., *Enfleshing Freedom: Body, Race, and Being* (Fortress Press, 2009)

Fiorenza, F., and J. Galvin, eds., *Systematic Theology: Roman Catholic Perspectives* (Fortress Press, 1991)

Korte, H., et al., *The Boundaries of Monotheism: Interdisciplinary Explorations into the Foundations of Western Monotheism* (Brill, 2009)

Jacobsen, D., *Global Gospel: An Introduction to Christianity on Five Continents* (Baker Academic, 2015)

Johnson, Elizabeth A., *Quest for the Living God: Mapping Frontiers in the Theology of God* (Continuum, 2007)

Johnson, P., *A History of Christianity* (Atheneum, 1976)

Jonas, B., ed., *The Image of God in an Image Driven Age: Explorations in Theological Anthropology* (InterVarsity Press, 2016)

Jones, S., and P. Lakeland, eds., *Constructive Theology: A Contemporary Approach to Classical Themes* (Fortress Press, 2005)

Kvam, K., L. Schearing, and V. Ziegler, *Eve and Adam: Jewish, Christian, and Muslim Readings on Genesis and Gender* (Indiana University Press, 1999)

LaCugna, C., *God For Us: The Trinity and Christian Life* (HarperSanFrancisco, 1993)

Levenson, J., *Inheriting Abraham: The Legacy of the Patriarchy in Judaism, Christianity, and Islam* (Princeton University Press, 2012)

McFague, S., *The Body of God: An Ecological Theology* (Fortress Press, 1993)

McGrath, A., *Christianity: An Introduction* (Wiley-Blackwell, 2015)

McGrath, J., *The Only True God* (University of Illinois Press, 2009)

McManner, J., ed., *Oxford History of Christianity* (Oxford University Press, 2002)

Orsi, R., *History and Presence* (Harvard University Press, 2016)

Pinn, A., and S. Floyd-Thomas, *Liberation Theologies in the United States: An Introduction* (New York University Press, 2010)

Saracino, M., *Christian Anthropology: An Introduction to the Human Person* (Paulist Press, 2015)

Schneider, L., *Beyond Monotheism: A Theology of Multiplicity* (Routledge, 2008)

Silverstein, A., et al., *The Oxford Handbook of the Abrahamic Religions* (Oxford University Press, 2015)

Vatican, *The Documents of Vatican II: Vatican Translation* (Alba House, 2009)

Voss Roberts, M., *Body Parts: A Theological Anthropology* (Fortress Press, 2017)

Weaver, M., and D. Brakke, *Introduction to Christianity* (Cengage Learning, 2008)

Wiley, T., *Original Sin: Origins, Developments, Contemporary Meaning* (Paulist Press, 2002)

Woodhead, L., *Christianity: A Very Short Introduction* (Oxford University Press, 2004)

Islam

Abu-Lughod, L., *Do Muslim Women Need Saving?* (Harvard University Press, 2015)
Ahmed, L., *Women and Gender in Islam* (Yale University Press, 1993)
Ahmed, R., *Sharia Compliant: A User's Guide to Hacking Islamic Law* (Stanford University Press, 2018)
Al-Rouayheb, K., *Before Homosexuality in the Arab-Islamic World 1500–1800* (Chicago University Press, 2005)
Ali, K. and Leaman, O., *Islam: The Key Concepts* (Routledge, 2007)
Ali, K., *Marriage and Slavery in Early Islam* (Harvard University Press, 2010)
Ali, K., *Sexual Ethics and Islam: Feminist Reflections on the Qur'an, Hadith and Jurisprudence* (Oneworld Publications, 2006)
Ali, K., *The Lives of Muhammad* (Harvard University Press, 2016)
Arjana, S. R., *Muslims in the Western Imagination* (Oxford University Press, 2015)
———— , *Pilgrimage in Islam: Traditional and Modern Practices* (Oneworld, 2017)
———— with Fox, K., *Veiled Superheroes: Islam, Feminism, and Popular Culture* (Lexington Books, 2017)
Armstrong, K., *A History of God: The 4,000 Year Quest of Judaism, Christianity and Islam* (Ballantine Books, 1993)
Asali, K. ed., *Jerusalem in History* (Interlink Publishing Group, 1989)
Aydin, C., *The Idea of the Muslim World: A Global Intellectual History* (Harvard University Press, 2017)
Azam, H., *Sexual Violation in Islamic Law* (Cambridge University Press, 2015)
Barlas, A., *Believing Women in Islam: Unreading Patriarchal Interpretations of the Qur'an* (University of Texas Press, 2004)
Beydoun, K. A., *American Islamophobia: Understanding the Roots and Rise of Fear* (University of California Press, 2018)
Bonino, S., *Muslims in Scotland: The Making of Community in a Post-9/11 World* (Edinburgh University Press, 2017)
Bucar, E., *Pious Fashion: How Muslim Women Dress* (Harvard University Press, 2017)
Chaudhry, A., *Domestic Violence and the Islamic Tradition* (Oxford University Press, 2013)
Corrigan, J., Denny, F. M., Eire, C. M. N. and Jafee, M. S., *Jews, Christians and Muslims: A Comparative Introduction to Monotheistic Religions* (Prentice Hall, 1998)
Cragg, K., *Jesus and the Muslim: An Exploration* (Oneworld, 1999)
De Sondy, A., *The Crisis of Islamic Masculinities* (Bloomsbury, 2014)
Donner, F. M., *Muhammad and the Believers: At the Origins of Islam* (Belknap Press, 2012)
El-Saadawi, N., *The Hidden Face of Eve: Women in the Arab World* (Zed Press, 1980)
Elisa, J., *Aisha's Cushion: Religious Art, Practice, and Perception in Islam* (Harvard University Press, 2012)
Eltantawi, S., *Shari'ah on Trial: Northern Nigeria's Islamic Revolution* (University of California Press, 2017)
Ernst, K., *How to Read the Qur'an: A New Guide, with Select Translations* (Edinburgh University Press, 2011)
Esack, F., *The Qur'an: A Short Introduction* (Oneworld, 2002)
Esposito, J. L., *Islam: The Straight Path* (Oxford University Press, 2011)
Geissinger, A., *Gender and the Construction of Exegetical Authority* (Brill, 2015)
Gottschalk, P., *Religion, Science, and Empire: Classifying Hinduism and Islam in British India* (Oxford University Press, 2012)

Grewal, Z., *Islam is a Foreign Country: American Muslims and the Global Crisis of Authority* (NYU Press, 2013)

Habib, S., *Female Homosexuality in the Middle East* (Routledge, 2007)

Haider, N., *The Origins of Shia: Identity, Ritual, and Sacred Space in Eighth-Century Kufa* (Cambridge University Press, 2011)

Hamdy, S., *Our Bodies Belong to God: Organ Transplants, Islam and the Struggle for Human Dignity in Egypt* (University of California Press, 2012)

Hammer, J., *American Muslim Women, Religious Authority and Activism: More Than a Prayer* (University of Texas Press, 2013)

Hammer, J., Safi, O., *The Cambridge Companion to American Islam* (Cambridge University Press, 2013)

Harvey, R., *The Qur'an and the Just Society* (Edinburgh University Press, 2017)

Hazleton, L., *After the Prophet: The Epic Story of the Shia-Sunni Split* (Anchor Books, 2010)

Hidayatullah, A. A., *Feminist Edges of the Qur'an* (Oxford University Press, 2014)

Hillenbrand, C., *Islam: A New Historical Introduction* (Thames and Hudson, 2015)

Hussain, A., *Muslims and the Making of America* (Baylor University Press, 2016)

Jurgensmeyer, M., ed., *The Oxford Handbook of Global Religions* (Oxford University Press, 2006)

Karamustafa, A. T., *God's Unruly Friends: Dervish Groups in the Middle Period 1200–1500* (Oneworld, 2006)

Kealhofer-Kemp, L., *Muslim Women in French Cinema* (Liverpool University Press, 2016)

Khabeer, S. A., *Muslim Cool: Race, Religion, and Hip Hop in the United States* (NYU Press, 2016)

Khan, S., *The Battle for British Islam* (Saqi Books, 2016)

Khoja-Moolji, S., *Forging the Ideal Educated Girl: The Production of Desirable Subjects in Muslim South Asia* (University of California Press, 2018)

Knight, M. M., *Muhammad: Forty Introductions* (Soft Skull Press, 2019)

Knysh, A., *Islam in Historical Perspective* (Prentice Hall, 2011)

Kugle, S., *Homosexuality in Islam: Critical Reflection on Gay, Lesbian, and Transgender Muslims* (Oneworld, 2010)

Kugle, S., *Living Out Islam: Voices of Gay, Lesbian, and Transgender Muslims* (NYU Press, 2013)

Kung, H., *Islam: Past, Present and Future* (Oneworld, 2008)

Lange, C., *Paradise and Hell in Islamic Traditions* (Cambridge University Press, 2015)

Lawrence, B. B., *The Koran in English: A Biography* (Princeton University Press, 2017)

Lewis, P., Hamid, S., *British Muslims: New Directions in Islamic Thought, Creativity and Action* (Edinburgh University Press, 2018)

Lewis, R., *Muslim Fashion: Contemporary Style Cultures* (Duke University Press, 2015)

Love, E., *Islamophobia and Racism in America* (NYU Press, 2017)

Mahmood, S., *Politics of Piety: The Islamic Revival and the Feminist Subject* (Princeton University Press, 2011)

Menacol, M. R., *The Ornament of the World: How Muslims, Jews and Christians Created a Culture of Tolerance in Medieval Spain* (Back Bay Books, 2003)

Mernissi, F., *The Veil and the Muslim Elite: A Feminist Interpretation of Women's Rights in Islam* (Addison Wesley, 1991)

Mir-Hoseini, Z., *Islam and Gender: The Religious Debate in Contemporary Iran* (Princeton University Press, 1999)

Mir, S., *Muslim American Women on Campus: Undergraduate Social Life and Identity* (UNC Chapel Hill, 2016)

Moosa, E., *What is a Madrasa?* (UNC Chapel Hill, 2015)

Morales, H., *Latino and Muslim in America: Race, Religion, and the Making of a New Minority* (Oxford University Press, 2018)

Nasr, S. H., ed., *The Study Qur'an* (HarperOne, 2015)

Nielsen, J., *Muslims in Western Europe* (Edinburgh University Press, 2004)

Nyugen, M., *Modern Muslim Theology: Engaging God and the World with Faith and Imagination* (Rowman and Littlefield, 2019)

O'Brien, J., *Keeping it Halal: The Everyday Lives of Muslim American Teenage Boys* (Princeton University Press, 2017)

Oxtaby, W. G., Hussain, A., Amore, R. C., *World Religions: Western Traditions* (Oxford University Press, 2014)

Petersen, K., *Interpreting Islam in China: Pilgrimage, Language, and Scripture* (Oxford University Press, 2017)

Pierce, M., *Twelve Infallible Men: The Imams and the Making of Shiism* (Harvard University Press, 2016)

Purohit, T., *The Aga Khan Case: Religion and Identity in Colonial India* (Harvard University Press, 2012)

Ragab, A., *The Medieval Islamic Hospital* (Cambridge University Press, 2015)

Ridgeon, L., ed., *The Cambridge Companion to Sufism* (Cambridge University Press, 2015)

Rippon, A., *Muslims: Their Religious Beliefs and Practices* (Routledge, 2001)

Ruthven, M., *Islam: A Very Short Introduction* (Oxford University Press, 2000)

Safi, O., ed., *Progressive Muslims: On Justice, Gender and Pluralism* (Oneworld, 2003)

———, *Radical Love: Teachings from the Islamic Mystical Traditions* (Yale University Press, 2018)

Said, E., *Orientalism* (Penguin Books, 2003)

Schimmel, A., *My Soul is a Woman: The Feminine in Islam* (Continuum, 2003)

———, *Mystical Dimensions of Islam* (UNC Chapel Hill, 1975)

Shaikh, S., *Sufi Narratives of Intimacy: Ibn Arabi, Gender and Sexuality* (UNC Chapel Hill, 2012)

Shepherd, W. S., *Introducing Islam* (Routledge, 2014)

Siddiqui, M., ed., *The Routledge Reader in Christian–Muslim Relations* (Routledge, 2013)

———, *How to Read the Qur'an* (Granta Books, 2008)

———, *The Good Muslim: Reflections on Classical Islamic Law and Theology* (Cambridge University Press, 2012)

Sloane-White, Patricia, *Corporate Islam: Sharia and the Modern Workplace* (Cambridge University Press, 2017)

Sosis, Richard, "Religions as complex adaptive systems," in N. Clements, ed., *Mental Religion: The Brain, Cognition, and Culture,* Macmillan Interdisciplinary Handbooks on Religion (Macmillan, 2016), pp. 219–236

Spellberg, D., *Politics, Gender and the Islamic Past: The Legacy of Aisha Bint Abi Bakr* (Columbia University Press, 1996)

———, *Thomas Jefferson's Qur'an: Islam and the Founders* (First Vintage Books, 2014)

Stowasser, B., *Women in the Qur'an: Traditions and Interpretation* (Oxford University Press, 1994)

Wadud, A., *Inside the Gender Jihad: Women's Reform in Islam* (Oneworld, 2006)

———, *Qur'an and Women: Rereading the Sacred Text from a Women's Perspective* (Oxford University Press, 2008)

Waines, D., *An Introduction to Islam* (Cambridge University Press, 2009)

Warsi, S., *The Enemy Within: A Tale of Muslim Britain* (Penguin Books, 2018)

Weddle, D. W., *Sacrifice in Judaism, Christianity, and Islam* (NYU Press, 2017)

Wheeler, B. M., *Prophets in the Qur'an* (Continuum, 2002)

Zakaria, R., *Veil* (Bloomsbury Academic, 2017)

Index

Page numbers in **bold** refer to figures.